The Assault on Labor

The Assault on Labor

The 1986 TWA Strike and the Decline of Workers' Rights in America

Sandra L. Albrecht

LEXINGTON BOOKS
Lanham • Boulder • New York • London

Published by Lexington Books
An imprint of The Rowman & Littlefield Publishing Group, Inc.
4501 Forbes Boulevard, Suite 200, Lanham, Maryland 20706
www.rowman.com

Unit A, Whitacre Mews, 26-34 Stannary Street, London SE11 4AB

British Library Cataloguing in Publication Information Available
The hardback edition of this book was previously catalogued by the Library of Congress as follows:

Library of Congress Cataloging-in-Publication Data Available
ISBN 9781498537704 (cloth: alk. paper)
ISBN 9781498537728 (pbk. : alk. paper)
ISBN 9781498537711 (electronic)

∞™ The paper used in this publication meets the minimum requirements of American National Standard for Information Sciences—Permanence of Paper for Printed Library Materials, ANSI/NISO Z39.48-1992.

Printed in the United States of America

To my daughter, Molly

Contents

Acknowledgments		ix
Preliminary Notes		xi
	Introduction	1
1	Setting the Stage: Prestrike Events	17
2	Lost Chances: Unintended Consequences of Improved Conditions	39
3	Things Worsen: Carl Icahn Enters the Picture	51
4	Labor Deals with Icahn: White Knight or Predator?	63
5	Off the Line: Strike!	79
6	Strike Solidarity and Labor Discord	99
7	Permanently Replaced and the Long Struggle Back	127
8	Legal Challenges and the Development of Labor Law	153
Conclusions		175
Bibliography		201
Index		211
About the Author		219

Acknowledgments

I want to thank the Independent Federation of Flight Attendants for giving me the opportunity to share their story. This book is for the full-term strikers who stood up against unjust treatment and waged a fierce battle against permanent replacement to regain their jobs. I want to sincerely thank all the flight attendants who spoke with me and relayed their experiences. I could not have written this book without the help of Mary Ellen Miller, Director of Safety, Legislation and Communication. She was generous with her time, supplied me with mountains of documents and publications, helped me gain access to meetings and interviews, and is responsible for the vast majority of archival photos that appear in the book. I also want to thank Vicki Frankovich-Gray, president during the strike and its aftermath, for meeting with me despite multiple demands and a schedule already too busy. I spent time in the law office of Jolley, Walsh, Hager and Gordon, now Jolley, Walsh, Hurley and Raisher, reading transcripts and court documents. I thank everyone for being so nice and accommodating, and, in particular, Bill Jolley. He was extremely helpful to me in understanding the large number of court cases and was open to my many questions.

Thank you to Elinor Schroeder in the KU School of Law for allowing me to immerse myself in the study of labor law. Attending her classes and meeting with her gave me a better understanding of the legal dimensions of my study. Through a Keeler Family Intra-university Professorship, I spent an invaluable semester guided by her expertise. I also want to acknowledge Joane Nagel for reading my book prospectus and the anonymous reviewers of my manuscript whose thoughtful comments greatly improved my final book. I want to thank the editorial staff that I have had the pleasure of working with from assistant editor, Brighid Stone, to associate acquisitions editor, Sarah Craig, and assistant editor, Bethany Davis.

I want to give recognition to my mentors, Judy Corder and Steven Deutsch, who graciously became lifelong friends. Many thanks to Bonnie Buchele and Sara Gutierres who have sustained me in more ways than I can count or ever repay. I am grateful for my goddaughter, Isabel, whose exuberant joy reminds me on a weekly basis of everything that is important. I am also grateful for Maddie, the canine diva of our household, who unexpectedly and cheerfully turned into my loyal sidekick in the final stages of writing. Most importantly, I want to thank my daughter, Molly, for always being my biggest supporter and my greatest inspiration.

Preliminary Notes

One of the challenges in working with a variety of different primary sources, e.g., union and company publications, multiple forms of court documentation, taped phone messages, audiocassettes and videos, was that there was no uniformity in how words were spelled and how they were used. I did not alter any quoted material, but in my own writing, I made some judgment calls to create as much consistency as possible.

There were three major unions at TWA which I wrote about, in order of frequency: Independent Federation of Flight Attendants (IFFA), International Association of Machinists and Aerospace Workers (IAM), and Airline Pilots' Association (ALPA). The Independent Federation of Flight Attendants always referred to themselves as IFFA, not *the* IFFA, and I adopted that style for all three unions. This style was typically not a problem for ALPA, but in many of the primary sources, IAM is referred to as *the* IAM.

The spelling of words, primarily dealing with negotiations and contracts, also varied among the primary documents. For my own writing, I chose the spelling that seemed to represent the majority way: two-tier; self-help; buyout; and snap-back.

With a few exceptions, when I first introduced someone, I would use his/her whole name and position. After that, I would use only their last name.

Introduction

For organized labor, the decade of the 1980s was one of heightened conflict between labor and management. These struggles pierced the very core of the American Labor Movement and resulted in declines in both the overall membership and the political-economic strength of labor. The social contract between labor and management that had brought fairly cooperative labor relations in the post–World War II era broke down and was replaced by highly conflictual relations much more reminiscent of the 1930s' labor struggles. Early in the 1980s, the Professional Air Traffic Controllers Organization (PATCO) air controllers' strike was defeated by President Reagan's swift firing of 12,000 strikers.[1] Although Reagan directed his action against a public sector union, the message of hard times for labor was not lost on the private industrial and service sectors.

Reagan's action against PATCO was part of the rapidly changing airline industry landscape. In the competitive environment of post-1978 deregulation, the airline industry was characterized by a proliferation of new entrants into the market, successive waves of fare wars, corporate raiding and takeovers, and multiple stages of realignment of the industry. These changes in the airline industry had a dramatic impact on labor. Known for their high level of union organization, airline industry workers faced declining wages, job loss, union decertifications, and elimination through the use of bankruptcy laws. Workers responded by concessionary bargaining, legal suits, and strikes in attempts to both secure their jobs and preserve their unions.

In the airline industry, and industries throughout the United States, employers increasingly utilized permanent replacement of strikers, giving the 1980s the reputation as "arguably the bleakest decade in the entire history of the U.S. labor movement."[2] A strike where employers utilize permanent replacements transforms what can be a fairly normal work action in the course of contract negotiations into a work action that can result in the workforce being permanently replaced and ultimately the destruction of the union itself.[3] Even though the right of employers to permanently replace strikers dates back to the 1938 Mackay Doctrine, it was only in the latter 1970s and in the 1980s that it became common for employers to either threaten, or carry out, permanent replacement. The line between permanent replacement and unemployment is so thin as to question whether labor's fundamental right to strike remains viable.

The 1986 strike by The Independent Federation of Flight Attendants against Trans World Airlines (TWA) provides one of the most dramatic cases of the heightened labor conflict of the 1980s. Under TWA's new owner, Carl Içahn, and faced with a concessionary package that they saw as unfair and unnecessarily harsh, 6,500 flight attendants went out on strike at midnight on March 7, 1986. Throughout the strike, IFFA membership support remained exceptionally strong, both contrary to the expectations of TWA and in a climate of increasingly worsened conditions. TWA had started making preparations to hire permanent replacements prior to the strike, and as Icahn reportedly said on the eve of the strike, "if you leave, you are never coming back."[4] Because of the mounting threat that there would be no jobs to return to, IFFA made an unconditional offer to return to work on May 17, 1986. By that time, TWA had replaced virtually the entire labor force of predominantly female, senior flight attendants. Fewer than 200 positions were made available to the full-term strikers. It would take IFFA over three years, July 1989, to successfully return over 5,000 strikers back to work.

With advanced domestic tickets purchased and international flights chartered, they walked off their planes and into one of the most intense, sustained struggles in labor history. Through it, they remained in solidarity with one another, maintained their focus on their goal of returning everyone to the line, and developed strategies of labor survival that gained them the reputation of the "pit bulls" of the labor movement. A labor force that had been imprisoned in the public's mind by the sex stereotypical image of "coffee, tea, or me," emerged as seasoned unionists who understood that their strike was being played out in a new era of labor politics and the stakes were both their jobs and their union.

FLIGHT ATTENDANT UNION IDENTITY

IFFA members maintained an exceptionally high degree of commitment to the very end of the ten-week strike. Their solidarity and labor militancy had been forged over the years in their dual challenges: confronting the gendered restrictions imbedded in their occupation and developing their own union identity. In a heavily female-dominated occupation, TWA flight attendants were typical of the industry as a whole, with 85 percent female and 15 percent male. Similar to the historical development of the clerical occupation, the occupation was originally male. The first commercial flight was the 1926 Western Air Express flight from Los Angeles to Salt Lake City.[5] The earliest attendants were the sons of the rail, steam, and industrial owners who financed the fledgling industry. With the stock market crash and the need to cut costs, this position was eliminated, but quickly replaced in the 1930s with "mates." Again, the position was male, and the mates in this young industry were a combination of flight attendant and co-pilot.

The position of mates is fairly short lived and is overlapped and taken over by the hiring of females for this position. United Airlines already introduced female attendants in 1930, with American doing so in 1933. The President of TWA at this time, Jack Frye, delayed the introduction of female "hostesses" until 1935. According to Robert Serling in *Howard Hughes' Airline*, Frye was influenced by the customer surveys that showed an overwhelming preference (80%) for male attendants. However, he changed his mind in 1935 because he believed that the very same passengers who said they preferred male service "were going to United and American because they had pretty girls."[6] From its very beginning, then, as a female occupation, concepts of physical attractiveness as a requirement for the job were established and became institutionalized in a variety of regulations over time.

The idea of attendants as young, pretty, and unmarried paralleled the vision that they were to be short-term participants in the labor force—concepts that became progressively challenged. Beginning in the late 1950s but accelerated by the 1964 Civil Rights Act and the establishment of the Equal Employment Opportunity Commission (EEOC), requirements regarding such things as age, marital status, and maternity were liberalized and practices of occupational exclusion by sex were abolished.[7] Coupled with work rule changes that created some forms of stability and predictability for a labor force that does not operate on a regular work schedule of 9 to 5, flight attendant seniority greatly increased. Whereas eighteen months was the average term of employment for a flight attendant in 1967, TWA flight attendants had an average seniority of fourteen years when they went out on strike in 1986 and 69 percent were thirty-five years old or over.[8]

Many of these occupational changes would be implemented within collective bargaining agreements in an industry that organized early and in which all major employees have been historically represented by unions.[9] As a whole, the airline industry underwent unionization in the forties. Although the flight attendants had been organized under the TWA Hostess Association since the mid-thirties, it was not until 1947 that they became organized as a labor union. In 1947, the TWA flight attendants organized under the Airline Stewards/Stewardess Association (ALSSA) which was affiliated and under the Air Line Pilots Association (ALPA). In fact, most of the flight attendant groups at the various airlines organized as ALSSA, under ALPA.[10] Fairly early on the flight attendants started to feel constrained by the male authority exercised by the pilots union and began to struggle for self-determination.[11] In 1961–62, there was a big rift where about half of all the ALSSA unions split away from ALPA and affiliated under the Transport Workers Union (TWU). Initially, all the flight attendants from different airlines were organized under TWU Local 550, but in 1974, they were split up into airline-specific locals. For TWA flight attendants, they became Local 551 with an Executive Board headed by flight attendant, Arthur Teolis.[12]

Similar to the mass move away from the pilots' union in the 1960s, however, over sixteen thousand flight attendants disaffiliated from TWU in the late 1970s over issues of male domination and the desire for greater self-determination. In one year alone, TWA, American, and Pan American (Pan Am) flight attendants broke away to form their own independent unions. In April 1977, The Independent Federation of Flight Attendants, representing 6,000 members, became the officially recognized bargaining unit for TWA flight attendants.

IFFA rose out of a conflict that involved both TWU and TWA that began in 1975. In April of that year, TWA issued a section 6 notice to TWU and Local 551 to begin contract negotiations. By August 1975, they were in the fifth month of negotiations and unable to reach agreement. TWA requested a mediator from the National Mediation Board (NMB), which oversees negotiations in the airline industry. By May 1976, the NMB announced that mediation had failed though the parties continued to meet in its presence. Finally on June 5, 1976 the three parties—TWA, TWU and Local 551—came to an oral agreement. The next day, TWA and TWU, authorized by Local 551, completed a written agreement. But when it came time for the Local 551 to sign the agreement, they refused. The negotiating committee, in a letter to all flight attendants, explained that "the contractual language contained in the tentative (June 6, 1976) agreement does not accurately reflect what the Local 551 negotiating committee believed to have been the understanding reached during the negotiations." TWU in a letter to all flight attendants urged them to "overwhelmingly ratify" the agreement and disparaged their local president Teolis whose "only ambition is to fulfill a vendetta against TWA and cause a crippling strike." When the tentative agreement went out to the flight attendants, their support was with their local leadership and the membership rejected the agreement in a vote of 2,325 to 1,461. Local 551 threatened a strike to begin on July 2, 1976, potentially disrupting major travel revenues in the United States just as the country was starting its 200-year celebration.

TWA filed suit against both TWU and Local 551 on June 30, 1976.[13] In the end, TWU overrode the flight attendant membership vote and removed the local leadership. Finally, the local leadership accepted the agreement, but the collective feeling that they had been sold out by TWU became the impetus for a representation election. On April 1, 1977, TWA flight attendants handed The Independent Federation of Flight Attendants a decisive victory.[14] Teolis became the first president of IFFA while another member of this "rebellious leadership," Victoria (Vicki) Frankovich, would lead IFFA during its most difficult period, the 1986 strike and its aftermath.[15]

Even before the events that propelled the final split, there had been a growing sense on the part of the flight attendants that they needed to represent themselves and that TWU was not in touch with their needs. It was both a reflection of the fact that flight attendants were redefining their identities as workers and their sense that a union run by and representing male workers was not in their best interests.[16]

The newly emergent IFFA would be joined in that year by other flight attendants who also became disaffected from male labor unions. This independent status would give the flight attendants a distinct, and often more militant, character.[17] It would be this independent union that would go up against what was then the fourth largest airline in the United States and one of America's leading corporate raiders.

THE ERA THAT RECAST LABOR-MANAGEMENT RELATIONS

An examination of the IFFA/TWA strike within the broader context of the political and economic changes of the 1980s provides a more detailed understanding of the impact of those changes for American workers. Up until the latter 1970s, the postwar economic growth had translated into a raised standard of living for workers. Post–World War II economics had been an extension of the Keynesian policies of the New Deal, based on full employment and public sector growth in social programs. The unparalleled U.S. economic growth in the three decades after World War II meant that productivity gains were shared with more American families than ever before. In the period of the strongest economic growth, 1950 to 1965, hourly wages rose 81 percent for production workers, service workers standard of living grew, and the percent of workers with wages below the poverty line declined. "Not only was the pie growing, but especially during the 1960s, the shares were becoming more equally distributed among working people and their families."[18] With a policy of full employment, as the economy grew, labor particularly in the manufacturing sector, was in a strong enough position to bargain with employers to translate increasing profits into higher wages and benefits.[19] A form of business unionism developed in these decades that brought fairly stable labor-management relations. It was a social contract where labor participated in the benefits of a growing economy and employers maintained decision making over production.

This truce between labor and management began to unravel in the 1970s when profits started to decline. For the first time in almost thirty years, corporations faced a "profit squeeze." Declining profits were primarily from rapidly expanding global competition, but deepened by rising oil prices, and growing pressures on the expansion of the public sector as more Americans wanted to share in the postwar prosperity.[20] The social contract developed during good economic times quickly flipped as the nation faced rising inflation and rising high unemployment. The response to what came to be known as stagflation in the late 1970s was to tighten monetary policy to reduce inflation and permit unemployment to rise.[21]

The tight monetary policy enacted by the Federal Reserve in the late 1970s was fully embraced by President Ronald Reagan when he took office in 1981 and became an important component of his overall supply-side policies designed to return the United States to a free market economy. So closely allied is his presidency to the "great u-turn" away from the Keynesian welfare state to a free market stance that his return to laissez-faire came to be known by the shorthand, Reaganomics. His supply-side budget agenda focused on marginal tax rate cuts, corporate tax cuts, deregulation, privatization, and decreased government spending on social programs.[22] Resolving high inflation through a tight monetary policy raised interest rates and threw the United States in 1981–1982 into the worst recession since the Great Depression.[23] The cost was devastating for workers and exposed a primary avenue through which Reagan would engineer his transformation of the U.S. economy, driving down the strength of labor. Unemployment steadily rose and reached 10.8 percent by the end of 1982.[24] Because Reagan had already made good on his agenda to reduce government spending on social programs, workers faced the loss of jobs with a perishing social safety net to help them ride out the economic crisis. The federal government had substantially decreased workers' rights to unemployment insurance by establishing more restrictive eligibility requirements. At the height of the recession, 1982, only 45 percent of the unemployed received benefits compared to 76 percent who qualified for unemployment insurance in the recession year of 1975. Programs to aid the poor—Medicaid, Aid to Families with Dependent Children, food stamps—were cut and cut again. As one staunch Republican commented about Reagan's 1982 budget, "somebody else is going to have to start taking a hit besides welfare recipients."[25]

The high unemployment and dwindling social programs increased the vulnerability of labor and spurred employers to not only abandon the social contract but to aggressively pursue antiunion strategies. They fully appreciated that Reagan's agenda to "let the market do its thing," not only meant the primacy of business interests but the diminution of labor.[26] "A frontal assault on the power of organized labor is definitely a part of his economic program."[27]

Employers retreated from collectively bargained agreements that had been constructed over years of negotiations and replaced them with a one-sided, take it or leave it approach. Workers faced new owners and CEO's more removed than ever from the workplace and the community, demanding major concessions in wages, benefits, and work rules. The traditional negotiating process was disrupted from beginning to end: employers pressed for earlier than normal openers and agreements that had historically been achieved in the last hours, even the last minutes of negotiating, became difficult to predict and risky to consider with a new union-avoidance management. Employers set the stage with a forewarning that they were looking for *change*. In reality, it turned out not to be change so much as a "whole new contract."[28] Wages were to be cut, frozen, and two-tiered; benefits were to be retracted, reduced and increasingly paid by worker contributions; and, work rules were to be eliminated or rewritten to increase employers' flexibility.

With management increasingly unwilling to move from their opening positions, labor often found themselves between the difficult choices of agreeing to significant concessions or exercising their right to strike. Employers strengthened their hand by a resurgence in the use of permanent replacements, or strikebreakers. The *threat* of permanent replacement permeated concessionary negotiations, and workers who went out on strike faced the real possibility that strikebreakers would be hired to permanently replace them.

REVIVAL OF STRIKEBREAKING

Workers in industries throughout the United States fought against employers' use of permanent replacements. Collectively, these strikes illustrated the severity of the assault and workers' struggles to retain their livelihoods. The decade opened with the PATCO strike and Reagan's firing and replacement of 12,000 public sector workers, and quickly turned to the private sector as the major battleground.[29] After PATCO, one of the first indications of management's offensive against labor in the private sector came in the mining industry. In response to a heavy concessionary demand, 2,400 Arizona copper miners, mill and smelter workers of the United Steelworkers of America struck Phelps Dodge in June 1983.[30] In addition to wage and benefit cuts and the termination of cost-of-living adjustments, the company package included the elimination of all side agreements which had been made over the years. Phelps Dodge called for a return to the "notorious" twenty-six and two work schedule: 26 consecutive work days and then two days off. The company negotiator emphasized, "We're not going to back down."[31] In August, shortly after the strike began, Phelps Dodge announced that they would bring in permanent replacements, and the governor activated the National Guard. By September, the company had notified the workers that they had all been replaced. "When the dust (and the last court challenges) had settled more than 2 years later, Phelps Dodge had wiped out thirty union locals made up of more than two thousand workers. Its antiunion stand destroyed the entire bargaining structure in the copper industry."[32] In the years to come, Phelps Dodge would become "an emerging 'superstar,' in the words of an admiring business press, churning out record profits."[33]

In August 1985, 1,700 workers from Local P-9 of the United Food and Commercial Workers (UFCW) went on strike against George A. Hormel and Co., in Austin, Minnesota.[34] Despite productivity up, profits up, CEO pay up, Hormel never budged from a concessionary package of wage cuts. "More than anything else, it was the unfairness of Hormel's demand that united the rank and file."[35] Workers at the meatpacking plant had already taken concessions in 1978. The demand for a further wage cut, promises broken, and the increased injury rate in the newly designed plant, resulted in a 93 percent strike authorization vote by the workers on August 14, 1985, and the strike commenced shortly thereafter. In January 1986, Hormel reopened the plant and hired permanent replacements, protected by the National Guard. Put into trusteeship by the UFCW, P-9 was forced to call off the strike in May 1986. The first P-9ers would not be recalled until the Summer of 1989 and only after an agreement which resulted in the loss of seniority by all workers on the recall list. In the decade of the 1980s, "Average real take-home wages in the U.S. meatpacking industry fell by 44 percent. Meanwhile, Hormel Chief Executive Officer Richard Knowlton's annual salary, plus stock options, rose from $238,000 to more than $3,000,000."[36]

In the same year that P-9 struck Hormel, workers at the Diamond Walnut Growers processing plant in Stockton, California agreed to a 30–40 percent wage cut to help Diamond weather the bad economy and avoid bankruptcy.[37] When Diamond regained profitability, 1990 and 1991, the company continued downward pressure on worker wages and benefits. The company offer was an increase in 10 cents an hour coupled with a $30 a month worker contribution to health insurance, leaving workers making less than they did prior to the 1985 wage cut. Rather than reward workers for their sacrifices in the bad economy, they "slapped us in the face."[38] In September 1991, 500 regular and seasonal workers from Teamsters Union Local 601 went on strike. During negotiations, Diamond had hired new workers and made the employees train them for what turned out to be a seamless transition of permanent replacements into their jobs. Despite tremendous hardship from a primarily female workforce with 40 percent single mothers, only thirty-three of the 300 full-time workers crossed. Disregarding the years of work and past willingness to give significant concessions by the strikers, Diamond announced, "Our commitment is to the replacement workers." As one twenty-six year veteran worker said, "We thought when we walked out we would negotiate and in two weeks we would go in and have our jobs back. Then they bring people in for us to train and tell us we're not getting nothing. All we wanted was a dollar."[39] It would be thirteen years, 2005, before the strike would end with the ratification of a new contract and little expectation that any of the original strikers would be in a position to return.[40]

From June 1987 to October 1988, 1,200 workers of Local 14 of the United Paperworkers International Union struck International Paper Company's (IP) Androscoggin mill in Jay, Maine.[41] The concessionary package was steep, involving subcontracting and speedup, and the union estimated a loss of 500 jobs if the agreement was put in place. IP was unwilling to bargain on the proposals that the union brought to the bargaining table and presented an essentially all or nothing package. Some items carried particular meaning to the workers—IP called for the termination of premium pay for Sunday work and an end to the tradition that the mill shut down completely one day a year (Christmas). "They were asking for stuff that we've had for 25 years in our contract. And it was at a time when the profits with the company were setting records. And at the same time now, they gave executives an average of a 38% increase in salary. It boggles the mind."[42] With a 92 percent strike vote, Local 14 went out on June 15, 1987. It was clear during negotiations that IP planned to hire permanent replacements and they quickly replaced 500 workers in the first three weeks, and the total labor force by the end of the summer.[43] Without the support of the international union, Local 14 reluctantly called off the strike after seventeen months. Only 100 workers had been recalled one year after the strike, and the union was decertified in 1992.

These strikes involving permanent replacements are representative of the onslaught of strikebreaking in this period. The collective solidarity of workers who were confronted by this assault on their jobs demonstrated that rank and file workers possessed untapped reserves of activism. They challenged the prevailing view, and often reality, of workers under business unionism. This postwar development had widened the distance between the rank and file and the union bureaucracy and workers became less identified and less involved in union activities.[44] It was not uncommon in many of the strike situations to hear workers say that, before the strike, they rarely attended a meeting, took notice, etc. That was before. In strikes across industries, workers mobilized with other workers in their union, across unions, in corporate campaigns, in community activities, with groups outside the union movement, and with international movements. They created a solidarity that went beyond the strike and reenergized rank and file unionism. As Fantasia and Voss related:

> Communities were forced to defend unionism because their jobs and livelihoods depended on it. The irony is that in their defense of unionism they often created a union that was worth defending! In strike after strike (by copper miners in Arizona, coal miners in Virginia, paper workers in Maine and Wisconsin, food-processing workers in California, Iowa, and Minnesota, newspaper workers in New York and Detroit, and bus drivers and airline workers across the nation, strikes for which systematic analyses are available) solidarity and militancy were the absolute defining characteristics particularly once replacement workers were hired and any possibility of collective retreat was foreclosed.[45]

AIRLINE INDUSTRY

The airline industry, and its employees, were very much affected by the economic turmoil of the 1980s. Similar to other industries, airlines suffered from the economic downturn in the U.S. economy and the corresponding attacks on labor. Further, all of this was played out in a newly deregulated climate which intensified the economic upheaval and set the parameters and outcomes of labor-management relations. These outcomes became increasingly dominated by management's desire for both wage and work rule concessions and the threat of permanent replacement.

Having just undergone deregulation in 1978, the airline industry would have major setbacks. The early 1980s would see a tripling of fuel prices, high inflation, and the recession impact on travel.[46] It would be in this period that the industry would see the first of the new brand of low-cost airlines which would put further pressure on the major airlines and their labor forces. In the mid-1980's, the airline industry was completely and rapidly transformed by mergers and acquisitions. For example, between June 1985 and October 1987, there were fourteen airliner mergers. When the dust settled there were fewer carriers than before deregulation.[47] When questioned, union leaders ranked mergers and acquisitions as their number one concern.[48]

The Reagan administration pulled back from antitrust laws and actively encouraged large mergers and embraced takeovers.[49] One of the primary reasons that takeovers of large corporations multiplied in the 1980s was because of the increased use of junk bonds. Also known as high yield bonds, they are considered as high risk debt because they are not attached to collateral. It was in the late 1970s and early 1980s that junk bonds became a significant player in the stock market. It was the former Wall Street investment bank of Drexel Burnham Lambert, and in particular the man who would be the "king" of junk bonds, Mike Milken and his junk bonds department, that was in the forefront of what seemed to become the craze on Wall Street. "Merger and acquisition consulting has become the most profitable line of business for almost all of the major investment banks. Some Wall Street bankers have even suggested specific takeover targets to raiders."[50]

The use of junk bonds made it possible for corporate raiders, with little money themselves, to seize—if only long enough to extract greenmail—one company after another.[51] All of this had an even greater impact on workers and their unions, as represented by the hostile takeover of TWA by raider Carl Icahn in 1985–1986 with the help of Drexel Burnham Lambert and the junk bond market.

The events that took place at TWA in the mid-1980s are representative of situations that faced unionized labor throughout industries in the United States. Backed by the full support of their membership, IFFA faced this threatening climate and mobilized in an attempt to survive an economic situation not of their making, but clearly one that would dominant their members' energies and define their livelihoods in the years to come.[52]

PLAN FOR THE BOOK

This book chronicles the events that led up to the 1986 strike of The Independent Federation of Flight Attendants against TWA, detailing the strike and its aftermath. Chapter 1 develops the history of negotiations between TWA and IFFA from the first set of negotiations of the newly formed independent union in 1978 to the first stage of negotiations in 1984 that will ultimately end in a strike two years later. It underscores the lengthy nature of negotiations under the Railway Labor Act (RLA) and the added complexity of compensation packages and work rules in the airline industry. Negotiations in this first stage center on concessionary bargaining in the newly deregulated environment. Negotiations were adversarial from the very beginning, but as Chapter 2 shows, the relationship between TWA and IFFA improved with the entry of new management and a better economic picture in the airline industry. With profits up and TWA's proposals down, there was no period where agreement was closer than in the first half of 1985.

Chapter 3 explains why the earlier optimism for a negotiated agreement did not materialize. The normal process of negotiations was disrupted as havoc was wreaked on TWA with the hijacking of the Athens/Rome Flight 847. For seventeen days, TWA and the nation, were focused on crisis resolution and the safe return of the hostages. This international crisis was further complicated on the domestic side by Carl Icahn's takeover pursuit of TWA. In an effort to thwart his intentions, TWA management sought out Frank Lorenzo of Texas Air Corporation as a buyer. Lorenzo was already infamous for having used Chapter 11 bankruptcy law to eliminate union contracts and reorganize Continental as a nonunion carrier. In the first ever collaboration between a corporate raider and labor, the pilots and machinists formed an alliance with Icahn that made possible his ownership bid for TWA. The flight attendants, original members of the labor coalition, were left isolated and faced difficult negotiations with Icahn. Chapter 4 highlights the confrontational buildup between IFFA and Icahn. IFFA charged that Icahn's demands from a predominately female labor force far exceeded his demands from the comparable male labor force, and, when Icahn explained that women were not breadwinners like men, he incensed a senior labor force with a history of having to fight sex discrimination in order to keep their jobs.

In chapter 5, the impact of Icahn's new ownership of TWA is examined. In collaboration with TWA management, Icahn doubled the demands placed on the flight attendants and TWA announced their intentions to hire permanent replacements in the event of a strike. The new package, which would be the basis of the strike, represented a 44 percent reduction in their contract, 22 percent from wage reductions and 22 percent in increased productivity from work rule changes. This chapter covers the events during the final thirty-day countdown to release mandated by the RLA, concluding with the final evening when negotiations failed.

Chapter 6 focuses on the events within the ten-week strike period, March 7–May 17, 1986. Virtually the entire labor force of over 6,000 flight attendants went on strike. Despite the fact that TWA had believed that 20 percent of the flight attendants would cross the picket line on the first day, with even greater numbers of crossovers in the days following, this did not happen. Two weeks into the strike, over 96 percent of the flight attendants were still engaged strikers. IFFA utilized a widely representative union structure to keep workers informed, picket lines running, and informational meetings going. This chapter covers the direct confrontations and efforts at resolution that occurred during the strike. Central to this conflict was the decision of TWA to utilize permanent replacements.

Chapter 7 focuses on the impact of permanent replacement on workers. When the strike was called off, TWA announced that only 200 flight attendant positions remained unfilled, all other positions had been filled with quickly trained new hires and crossovers. IFFA faced an uphill battle to insure over 5,000 of their workers would eventfully be called back to work. Barred from the property, facing the possibility of decertification, with so few of its members recalled, IFFA set about the task of reasserting its place as the union of record and its members as the occupants of the positions. Return would come exceedingly slow at the beginning, but in increments, all full-term strikers would get their jobs back. It would take over three years to return all flight attendants to the line and this chapter conveys the level of solidarity and commitment that it took for the flight attendants to successfully bring back every last worker.

Chapter 8 turns to examine the legal dimensions of this strike. Although the number of court cases was extensive, three legal contests occupied much of the attention of both parties: bad faith bargaining, status quo/union security, and the crossover case. Though each is significant in its implications, the Supreme Court decision in the crossover case expanded the rights accorded employers in strike situations and consolidated the controversial hold that permanent replacement has in labor law.

The conclusion follows the events that happened in the period past the successful return of all full-term strikers in 1989. The pilots and machinists would later feel betrayed in their alliance with Icahn and what they saw as his failed promises and the eventual destruction of the airline. TWA would go into bankruptcy three times, and would be acquired by American Airlines. TWA would fly its last flight December 1, 2001. The chapter ends with a discussion of the impact of permanent replacements on U.S. workers and the significance of the solidarity that workers displayed in fighting for fair treatment.

NOTES

1. Joseph A. McCartin, *Collision Course: Ronald Reagan, the Air Traffic Controllers, and the Strike that Changed America* (New York: Oxford University Press, 2011); Arthur B. Shostak and David Skocik, *The Air Controllers' Controversy: Lessons from the Patco Strike* (New York: Human Sciences Press, 1981).

2. Peter Rachleff, *Hard-Pressed in the Heartland: The Hormel Strike and the Future of the Labor Movement* (Boston: South End Press, 1993), 3.

3. Rick Fantasia, *Cultures of Solidarity: Consciousness, Action, and Contemporary American Workers* (Berkeley: University of California, 1988).

4. IFFA v. TWA (W. D. Missouri, Bad Faith Bargaining 1988), Transcripts, 3156–3157.

5. Donna Steele, *Wings of Pride: TWA Cabin Attendants, A Pictorial History 1935–1985* (Marceline, MO: Wadsworth Publishing, 1985).

6. Ibid., 26.

7. Ibid., 199–223.

8. William A. Jolley, *Plaintiff IFFA's Suggestions in Opposition to Defendant TWA's Motion to Dismiss* (Kansas City, MO: 1986), 4.

9. Liesl Miller Orenic, *On the Ground: Labor Struggle in the American Airline Industry* (Urbana, IL: University of Illinois Press, 2009), 1, pointed out that airline organization has always been high even as overall union membership has declined.

10. Donna Steele, *Wings of Pride: TWA Cabin Attendants, A Pictorial History 1935–1985* (Marceline, MO: Wadsworth Publishing, 1985), 51–140.

11. Georgia Panter Nielsen, *From Sky Girl to Flight Attendant: Women and the Making of a Union* (Ithaca, NY: ILR Press, 1982). For comprehensive studies of the

complexities of the flight attendant occupation and their labor activism, see Kathleen M. Barry, *Femininity in Flight: A History of Flight Attendants* (Durham: Duke University, 2007); Drew Whitelegg, *Working the Skies: The Fast-Paced, Disorienting World of the Flight Attendant* (New York: New York University Press, 2007).

12. IFFA v. TWA (W. D. Missouri, Bad Faith Bargaining 1988), Transcripts, 3854.
13. Ibid., Exhibits AAAA.
14. Ibid., Exhibits 1.
15. Ibid., Transcripts, 4547.
16. Ibid.
17. David J. Walsh, *On Different Planes: An Organizational Analysis of Cooperation and Conflict Among Airline Unions* (Ithaca: ILR Press, 1994); David J. Walsh, "Strikes in the U.S. Airline Industry 1919–2004," in *The Encyclopedia of Strikes in American History*, ed. Aaron Brenner, Benjamin Day, and Immanuel Ness (Armonk, NY: M. E. Sharpe, 2009)
18. Rick Fantasia and Kim Voss, *Hard Work: Remaking the American Labor Movement* (Berkeley: University of California, 2004), 62; Bennett Harrison and Barry Bluestone, *The Great U-Turn: Corporate Restructuring and the Polarizing of America* (NY: Basic Books, 1988), 4.
19. Rick Fantasia and Kim Voss, *Hard Work: Remaking the American Labor Movement* (Berkeley: University of California, 2004), 15; Thomas Palley, "Reviving Full Employment Policy: Challenging the Wall Street Paradigm," *EPI Briefing Paper* #191 (June 22, 2007): 2. According to Palley, since 1979 there is a disconnect between productivity and compensation. "From 1959 to 1979 compensation moved with productivity. Since 1979 productivity has kept growing but hourly compensation has essentially flat-lined."
20. Bennett Harrison and Barry Bluestone, *The Great U-Turn: Corporate Restructuring and the Polarizing of America* (NY: Basic Books, 1988), 7–11.
21. Doug Rossinow, *The Reagan Era: A History of the 1980s* (New York: Columbia University Press, 2015), 18.
22. John Ehrman, *The Eighties: America in the Age of Reagan* (New Haven: Yale University Press, 2005); Bennett Harrison and Barry Bluestone, *The Great U-Turn: Corporate Restructuring and the Polarizing of America* (NY: Basic Books, 1988); Peter T. Kilborn, "Reagan Plan to Privatize Government is Gaining Support from Democrats," *New York Times*, February 15, 1988; Doug Rossinow, *The Reagan Era: A History of the 1980s* (New York: Columbia University Press, 2015).
23. Bennett Harrison and Barry Bluestone, *The Great U-Turn: Corporate Restructuring and the Polarizing of America* (NY: Basic Books, 1988), 91.
24. Michael A. Urquhart and Marillyn A. Hewson, "Unemployment Continued to Rise in 1982 as Recession Deepened," *Monthly Labor Review*, February 1983, 3.
25. Doug Rossinow, *The Reagan Era: A History of the 1980s* (New York: Columbia University Press, 2015), 87–95.
26. Robert Slater, *The Titans of Takeover* (Englewood Cliffs, NJ: Prentice-Hall, 1987), 18.
27. Frank Ackerman, *Hazardous to Our Wealth: Economic Policies in the 1980s* (Boston: South End Press, 1984), 125.

28. Stephen Franklin, *Three Strikes: Labor's Heartland Losses and What They Mean for Working Americans* (New York: Guilford Press, 2001), 42.

29. Joseph A. McCartin, *Collision Course: Ronald Reagan, the Air Traffic Controllers, and the Strike that Changed America* (New York: Oxford University Press, 2011), 341–42.

30. Jonathan D. Rosenblum, *Copper Crucible: How the Arizona Miners' Strike of 1983 Recast Labor-Management Relations in America*, 2nd ed. (Ithaca: ILR Press, 1998).

31. Ibid., 71–72.

32. Ibid., 10.

33. Ibid.

34. Hardy Green, *On Strike at Hormel: The Struggle for a Democratic Labor Movement* (Philadelphia: Temple University Press, 1990); Peter Rachleff, *Hard-Pressed in the Heartland: The Hormel Strike and the Future of the Labor Movement* (Boston: South End Press, 1993); Peter Rachleff, "They Say Give Back, We Say Fight Back," *Dollars & Sense*, August/September 2000.

35. Peter Rachleff, *Hard-Pressed in the Heartland: The Hormel Strike and the Future of the Labor Movement* (Boston: South End Press, 1993), 51.

36. Ibid., 125.

37. *Collective Bargaining and the Hiring of Permanent Strike Replacements: Hearings Before the Government Operations*, 102d Cong., 2d Sess. 1–105 (1992); Peter T. Kilborn, "California Strike Becomes a Battle Over Permanent Job Replacements," *New York Times*, April 17, 1994.

38. *Collective Bargaining and the Hiring of Permanent Strike Replacements: Hearings Before the Government Operations*, 102d Cong., 2d Sess. 1–105 (1992), 5.

39. Peter T. Kilborn, "California Strike Becomes a Battle Over Permanent Job Replacements," *New York Times*, April 17, 1994.

40. BBC News, "Nut Strike Cracks after 13 Years," *BBC News* (United Kingdom), March 3, 2005.

41. Julius Getman, *The Betrayal of Local 14* (Ithaca: ILR Press, 1998).

42. Ibid., 32.

43. Ibid., 45.

44. Rick Fantasia and Kim Voss, *Hard Work: Remaking the American Labor Movement* (Berkeley: University of California, 2004), 83–87.

45. Ibid., 70.

46. Jean T. McKelvey, ed., *Cleared for Takeoff: Airline Labor Relations since Deregulation* (Ithaca: ILR Press, 1988).

47. Steven A. Morrison and Clifford Winston, *The Evolution of the Airline Industry* (Washington, DC: Brookings Institution, 1995).

48. David J. Walsh, *On Different Planes: An Organizational Analysis of Cooperation and Conflict among Airline Unions* (Ithaca: ILR Press, 1994).

49. Robert Slater, *The Titans of Takeover* (Englewood Cliffs, NJ: Prentice-Hall, 1987), 6–7.

50. "The Raiding Game," *Dollars and Sense*, March 1987.

51. Ibid.

52. This book was written using a varied set of primary documents, supplemented by secondary sources. The research documentation for the 5-year period, 1984–1989, came primarily from union and company documents, extensive court documents, and interviews. For years after 1989, primary documents were union documents, supplemented by secondary sources.

Chapter 1

Setting the Stage

Prestrike Events

As an independent union, IFFA secured its first contract in 1978 under voluntary expedited negotiations which were concluded within ninety days.[1] Labor negotiations in the airline industry fall under the Railway Labor Act (RLA).[2] Essentially, this act was instituted to help smooth out industrial relations in the rail industry so that industrial conflicts would not halt rail transportation. One of the main tenets of the RLA is that labor contracts never expire, they can only be amended. Contract negotiations begin with each party presenting its proposals for change. Only those issues that are put on the table are up for negotiation; all other parts of the contract remain intact. If the parties cannot come to an agreement on their own, either one or both can request the assistance of a mediator from the National Mediation Board (NMB). Once a mediator is assigned, both parties will meet the mediator for further negotiations. If the negotiations are not moving toward a final agreement, the NMB may offer the possibility of arbitration to settle the agreement. If neither party accepts arbitration, and the NMB deems it appropriate at this time to allow the parties to move to the next stage, the NMB will release the parties to a thirty-day countdown. If no movement has been made toward agreement during this thirty-day period, both parties are released to self-help at its end. For the union, this means that they are released to strike if they so wish; for management, this means that they have the right to enact all of their proposals that are on the negotiating table.

In practice, RLA negotiations are a fairly long process. For each party to be perceived as bargaining in "good faith," it is important to show some kind of movement on the issues. What this means is that opening positions are perceived by both parties as being far off from what is actually needed in order to come to agreement. Initial positions are constructed to allow for movement. It is typical for the negotiating process to run eighteen months to twenty-four months, and it is not at all uncommon for agreement to be reached in the final days, even final hours, of the thirty-day countdown. It was within this structure of the RLA and the way it organizes labor negotiations that the 1986 labor conflict unfolded.

The very first contract, then, that IFFA concluded with TWA within a ninety-day period in 1978 represented a significant departure from what is referred to as the "interminably long" negotiations that are a hallmark of the structure of negotiations under the RLA.[3] More typical of RLA negotiations was the next agreement concluded by IFFA and TWA.

NEGOTIATIONS TO THE RED BOOK

The second set of negotiations between IFFA and TWA followed the more typical, and extended, pattern of negotiations under the RLA. Signed in April 1983 and referred to as the "Red Book," these negotiations took twenty-two months to complete and agreement was made only on the final day, final hours, of the thirty-day countdown to self-help. These were difficult negotiations that had primarily centered on work rule changes desired by TWA and IFFA. Abruptly, however, in the last month of negotiations, TWA replaced its proposals on work rule changes with a brand new comprehensive package that did not reflect any of the discussions or tentative agreements made on work rule changes during the course of the twenty-one months of prior negotiating. Instead, TWA offered increased wage and retirement benefits *higher* than were being requested by IFFA. IFFA attempted to make changes in the new package in the final days, but no changes would be made and this would be the agreement.[4]

William Hoar, who then was Director of Contract Administration of In-Flight Operations and who in the next years would rise to Chief Operating Officer, explained the change as an effort to bring about an agreement to avoid the possibility of a strike. According to Hoar, a strike by IFFA would ruin TWA's chances to take advantage of what appeared to be the first victim of the newly deregulated economy—Pan American Airways. If Pan Am failed, TWA hoped to pick up its Berlin routes. Any assurances given by Washington to that effect were contingent on TWA's uninterrupted flying during this time. Further, a strike at TWA could actually help Pan Am stay solvent by reaping financial gain from passengers diverted from the struck airlines.[5]

IFFA believed that TWA's abrupt change was part of a strategy to undermine their negotiations on work rule changes. And when TWA tried, almost immediately after the signed contract, to recapture these wage increases, IFFA saw this as evidence that they never really planned to give them in the first place.[6]

Later, both IFFA and TWA, reflected on these Red Book negotiations as early indicators of things to come in terms of difficult negotiations. The experience Hoar said he gained from these negotiations was of IFFA intransigence.[7] William Jolley, IFFA lead counsel from the Kansas City firm of Jolley, Walsh, Hager and Gordon, argued that these negotiations were:

> not a product of negotiations or mutual deliberations. On the contrary, it was doled out solely as the result of TWA's unilateral deliberations, without input from the Flight Attendants' elected representatives. . . . Indeed the nearly two years of negotiations . . . were rendered a monumental waste of time and effort—a harbinger of things to come.[8]

MIDTERM WAGE NEGOTIATIONS

It was just shortly after the signing of this contract that TWA initiated what they called midterm discussions with both their organized labor and unorganized employees to seek voluntary wage concessions. Reflecting both specific financial losses and the financial stress placed on all major carriers in the competitive post-deregulated period, TWA sought $100–150 million in concessions from its overall workforce. Hoar talked of a two-phase approach: Phase 1 would focus on a voluntary commitment of employees to wage concessions, and Phase 2 would focus more heavily on work rule changes which would be sought during the next contract negotiations. According to IFFA, Hoar told IFFA representatives early on that Phase 2 would be "a substantial restructuring of the Flight Attendant Agreement," and that "TWA was seeking to change Flight Attendant lifestyles."[9]

Of the $100–150 million, TWA sought about $40 million from the flight attendants.[10] IFFA offered what was determined to be about $28.5 million in concessions.[11] In return, IFFA wanted TWA to rescind a furlough announcement of 400 flight attendants—a furlough that they believed was a "hammer to force IFFA to accept TWA's unacceptable and unreasonable demands."[12] William Borden, Vice President of In-Flight Services, had written to all flight attendants advising that "lacking an agreement, we will be sending furlough notices to four hundred (400) Flight Attendants effective January 31, 1984, with the potential for additional furloughs in March of 1984."[13]

The major stumbling was not the financial difference between the two parties. IFFA offered a substantial amount of money, what they determined to be about $5600 from each flight attendant over a fifteen-month period.[14] This was in part an acknowledgment of the economic problems facing TWA as well as the other major carriers. From these midterm concession talks, all negotiations accepted as given that they were concessionary on the part of workers.

The obstacle in these voluntary talks, and one that was never overcome, was IFFA's desire to extend the date of expiration of their existing Red Book contract by one year.[15] TWA's best offer to IFFA was a five-month extension, responding that a year would conflict with their contract negotiations with the International Association of Machinists and Aerospace Workers (IAM). TWA gave the pilots, ALPA, an eighteen-month contract extension in return for a temporary 10 percent wage cut. And, TWA imposed a temporary 10 percent wage cut on noncontract employees and management.[16] In the *TWA Skyliner* magazine for employees, President "Ed Meyer Says Thanks You" to the employees who took wage cuts. In a companion piece, TWA pointed out that the financial situation could have been even better had the nonparticipating groups contributed, referring to their failed midterm negotiations with both IFFA and IAM.[17]

According to Teolis, IFFA had hoped as well that a successful conclusion of voluntary concessions would also accomplish a new relationship between the two parties. "[I]t's important here to remember that what we originally sought to accomplish with these concession talks was a new attitude in our relationship with the company—one that would avoid confrontation, not just delay it by a few months."[18] Whether IFFA believed greater cooperation would have come from successful midterm negotiations or not, in the absence of agreement, relations that had always been difficult, turned worse.

NEGOTIATING TO STRIKE: THE FIRST PHASE

The negotiations that resulted in a strike in March 1986 began out of the ordinary and started on a confrontational note. IFFA's negotiating team was taken by surprise by TWA's earlier than normal contract openers. By agreement, a Section 6 notice that initiated contract talks had to be filed *no later* than ninety days prior to the amendable date of the contract. For a contract date of July 31, this meant that contract negotiations would typically get under way between the flight attendants and TWA in late April, early May. As IFFA told its members:

> TWA jumped the gun by serving its Contract Reopeners on us on February 29 [1984]—two months earlier than ever before. The Company is obviously attempting to create a false feeling of urgency about the need for a quick agreement and is even criticizing us for not having already commenced formal talks concerning TWA's concession requests.[19]

This early notice caught IFFA in the midst of a change in leadership. Teolis, who had a long history of leadership of TWA flight attendants and was President of IFFA since its inception, resigned. In a taped interview distributed to all flight attendants, Teolis explained his resignation as a response to the persistent conflictual relations with TWA, resulting in personal burnout and an organizational identity too fused to one person. In response to a question about his resignation, Teolis responded:

> I can't continue because, very simply, I have little left to give. I've been involved in TWA flight attendant union work for fourteen years. During these fourteen years, my work was never just a job. It was a crusade and a religion. I've always been deadly serious about my work, and I've always thrown myself into it 1000%.
>
> I'd like to think that I've played a big part in what we've accomplished, but I'm not so naive or egotistical to think that I've done it all myself. The directions we've taken, and the decisions we've made have been team decisions. I think it's really a shame, but TWA, along with the help of some of our own members, has been really successful lately in putting way too much focus on Arthur Teolis, the individual. They're still trying to totally divert your attention away from the real issues, simply by zeroing in on Teolis. To be perfectly honest, that's a really big part of why I truly think it best for me to resign. A union is not one person. It can't be. A union is all of its membership acting collectively and with one voice.[20]

During this same time frame, TWA was in transition itself. As of February 1, 1984, TWA became a separate company from Trans World Corporation.[21] In an "Independence Day" Newsgram, TWA announced their new identity but quickly pointed out that "nothing has really changed for us, including the fact that our future depends solely on our collective will and talent."[22]

Things had changed with its private ownership and it was the first step in looking attractive to the new airline raiders. In the short run, TWA would be infused with $23.5 million in tax benefit compensation from Trans World which reduced TWA's 1983 losses.[23] In the long run, financial analysts uniformly believed the spinoff was good news for Trans World as it shed the "chronically unprofitable airline."[24]

In one of the last letters that Teolis wrote to TWA as President, he requested a May 1, 1984 date to commence negotiations as opposed to TWA's proposed March 6, 1984 date. Teolis explained IFFA's timetable for negotiations had been disrupted by the early notice. IFFA followed a specific procedure for the development of its contract proposals. Anticipating a late April exchange of Section 6 notices, they had just begun this process which included the development of a lengthy questionnaire for the membership and a twenty-one day time period for return of the responses. These results would then be used to formulate their proposals for contract negotiations. Because they were in the early stages of preparation and TWA's proposals dealt with issues that IFFA would be focusing on as well, "To meet with you for the purpose of negotiating over these Articles without IFFA's proposals on the same subject matters, would be futile, time-wasting and wholly unproductive."[25] Teolis saw the May 1 date as giving them "three full months before the contract becomes amendable. These negotiations are simply too important to get into without membership input. I'd be surprised if the company or any of our members honestly disagreed."[26]

In a hand delivered letter, TWA responded that the May 1 date was "unsatisfactory and unacceptable." Citing both the economic situation at TWA and refuting Teolis' reasons for an extension, TWA proposed March 26, and closed their letter, "If you continue to decline to commence conferences until May 1, TWA reserves the right to declare that you have forfeited the right to conferences on its proposals and to take whatever other steps may be necessary to enforce our rights under the Railway Labor Act."[27] There would be a couple more skirmishes before they eventually sat down at the table for the first time.

This mini-dispute goes public as well. In a management newswire, TWA interpreted the timing of Teolis' resignation as an attempt to cause an "unjustified delay." Meyer sent a letter to all flight attendants, a strategy that TWA often employed and IFFA saw as a tactic to undermine their leadership, which implied that contract openers were worse because of the failed midterm concessions. "Absent Phase I concessions, your Union has forced us to enter contract negotiations in order to reduce these costs."[28] Teolis' countered, "pure hogwash," arguing that TWA had always talked in terms of money first, work rules next. "Mr. Meyer and TWA's negotiators made it clear that whether or not we gave midterm economic concessions had no bearing whatsoever on the new contract demands for work rule changes that the company would make in Phase II. For him to imply otherwise now is downright deceitful."[29] IFFA explained their position and desire to wait to commence negotiations to flight attendants, "IFFA has NEVER started negotiations without having first put out a questionnaire to find out what WE want."[30]

Although the start of negotiations between TWA and IFFA was a rocky one, the transition in leadership within IFFA was a smooth one. Frankovich moved from Vice President to President. She had been involved in the flight attendant labor unions since 1974 and had been the lead person in the day-to-day contract negotiations with TWA.[31] She would remain as chairperson of the negotiating committee.

IFFA and TWA would meet on March 29, 1984, for the first of what would be 100 negotiating meetings. Having sent out their questionnaire just days earlier, the first set of meetings would focus solely on TWA's twenty proposals.

TWA's PACKAGE

TWA's February 29 package was comprehensive, requesting both pay reductions and extensive work rule changes. TWA wanted a 13 percent wage cut plus the elimination of a 3 percent wage increase that was slated for July. Combined with other monetary reductions and work rule changes, the package was estimated to be about a 23–25 percent reduction in flight attendant labor costs, representing about $60–64 million.[32] IFFA described the package:

> When you read their [TWA's] proposals, you'll see that in addition to the monetary concessions they've already asked for, they want to strip us of all our important work rules. It would be turning the clock back. It would be like flying in the 1950s and early 1960s. When they said they wanted to change our lifestyle, they weren't kidding. What the company really wants from us is everything they can possibly get, and soon.[33]

TWA as well saw this proposal as a high one. Chief TWA negotiator Hoar later explained in a court deposition how they put the package together:

> Proposals would be formulated, and, you know, you would kind of shoot for that as a nice-to-get opening position if we could get it, unrealistic as it might be.
>
> . . . we would have looked at ASM [available seat mileage] costs and we would have said okay, it is about 23 percent and it is about 60 million, in that ballpark, how can we achieve it if indeed we could get everything that we would ask for in an opening position?[34]

TWA admitted that they were asking for "major" work rule changes and stated "TWA's proposals were intended both to reduce flight attendant costs and to achieve increased operating flexibility and efficiency through greater control over the work force."[35] TWA's then Executive Vice President, Richard Pearson, later referred to some of these proposals as "simply not doable," "a waste of time," and "brutally hard."[36] The twenty proposals had the cumulative effect of reducing wages and benefits while increasing the workload and decreasing worker discretion and employment stability. Coupled with worker concessions were proposals that directly addressed and withdrew union rights.

TWA contract demands, concessionary and with union animus, replicated what was happening throughout industries in the 1980s. It was nothing short of a transformation of both occupations and labor-management relations. For flight attendants, this issue had particular significance because it meant that they were being "thrown back" to an earlier era where the expectation was that they were single, temporary workers. As a senior labor force, many with families, and all affected by the growing awareness of U.S. women about the inequities faced by women workers, this retreat to the past felt impossible.

PROPOSED CHANGES IN A COMPLEX CONTRACT

At the time of contract negotiations, about 90 percent of flight attendants' work time was done away from their "domicile," the place where they reported for work and were released from work. TWA was organized on a seven domicile system: New York City, Boston, Chicago, Kansas City,

St Louis, San Francisco, and Los Angeles. The contract for a constantly moving workforce was complex and detailed.

TWA flight attendants were paid a base salary of sixty-five hours, and an incentive rate of 15 percent more for additional hours. *Duty period* was calculated from the time flight attendants reported for duty until they were released for an intervening rest. A *trip* could consist of one or more duty periods. For example, "A trip can be two legs from New York to Chicago and back or a trip can be ten days in length and as many as ten or more legs, taking the flight attendant from New York to Paris to Cairo and Kuwait to Bombay [Mumbai] and the same route back."[37] A flight leg was the closet calculation to in-air time and it was calculated using "block to block" time. A flight leg began when ground personnel removed the wedge beneath the plane tire and the leg ended after the plane landed and the wedge was replaced behind the tire.

One of the gains the flight attendants had made over the years was in expanding the alternative ways to calculate the hours that they worked. Block to block in-air time may not adequately reflect the sheer number of hours a flight attendant was "working." How do you determine what the pay of flight attendants should be: block to block in-air time; actual time on duty (duty rig); or, from the time that flight attendants reported for a trip until they were released from that trip whether it be ten hours or ten days (trip rig)? Duty rig and trip rig were two alternative methods to a block to block calculation to determine "work" time for purposes of compensation. For TWA flight attendants, duty rig was a 1:2 ratio which meant that for every two hours on duty, the flight attendant would receive one hour of pay (with a minimum of four and a half hours). Trip rig was set at a 1:3.5 ratio. For compensation, the *highest* amount would be credited to the flight attendant. For example, a flight attendant reported for duty at 12:00 noon and was released at 10 PM. In-air block time was six hours. Computed on an in-air block time, one for one, the flight attendant would receive six hours of compensation. Duty rig computed on the basis of ten hours on duty at a rate of one for two, would yield five hours. Trip rig would yield less than three hours and so the minimum of four and a half hours would be applied. In this case, block to block would give the best pay and therefore would be the basis of compensation.

Once the flight attendant left the domicile, they were under TWA's "Away From Domicile Scheduling Policy" which was not a part of the collective agreement but determined solely by TWA. According to IFFA counsel:

> TWA was free to, and did, change the policy with its only obligation being to "consult" with the Union about such changes . . . [It] allows the Company to change a Flight Attendant's schedule, reassign the Flight Attendant to different flight parings, lengthen or shorten a Flight Attendant's trip or number of days away from home, as determined solely by TWA in the formulation of its policy.[38]

This policy created a certain amount of uncertainty. A three-day trip might turn into a longer one because of flight delays, aircraft problems, etc. Work rule changes desired by IFFA were directed toward creating stability in an occupation that has a certain amount of inherent unpredictability and that had historically softened the blow of that uncertainty by a revolving door labor force. Any of the work rules that flight attendants had achieved slowly over the years which gave stability to the occupation were especially significant to them. Despite the fact that it had taken years to make certain changes, these changes were made during the employment lifetime of the then active flight attendants. They possessed a keen sense of both the past and the progress made. When TWA presented its package of sweeping changes, they were not just perceived as *changes* in the work rules, but changes that returned the occupation to its former days.

One important proposed change was *Same Calendar Day Balance*. This protection meant that if something went wrong in a bid schedule, for example a trip was canceled, TWA could only "balance" a flight attendant within the same days that the flight attendant was scheduled to fly in that bid period. TWA wanted to eliminate same calendar day balancing and use flight attendants any time during a bid period with the exception of guaranteed days off. According to IFFA, flight attendants had worked for forty years to get same calendar day balancing and it was their "lone schedule protection." "[U]nder our *current* contract, we have some ability to have time we can call our own, to know when we work and when we don't to make plans and keep appointments, and to be around at times important to us and our families."[39] As a flight attendant explained, "Same calendar day balance is as close a control as we can get to a set schedule."[40] Same calendar day balance was the major point in TWA's Proposal 5, but there were further proposed eliminations of last trip guarantee, inversal protection, and move-up protection—all of which were seen as increasing disruptions in scheduled bids.

TWA's proposed change to the *Flexible Monthly Credit Cap* would affect both flexibility and compensation. Flight attendants had a base rate of sixty-five hours and a maximum cap of seventy-five hours that they were required to fly, with "incentive pay" of 15 percent above base hourly pay for the last ten hours; flight attendants could exceed seventy-five hours of time but only at their own discretion. Under "Flex Cap," the company could vary the amount of hours flight attendants were required to fly on a monthly basis (65–85) requiring higher flying time during their peak season and lower flying time during their off seasons. Flex cap meant that monthly salary would fluctuate and create less stability in pay, their ability to work at incentive pay would be curtailed, and the amount of flying time they would be required to fly would be raised. For IFFA, it had numerous ramifications. "It could mean lower pay for our work force because of the reduction in the hours that you would be flying. It could be an increased work load on our work force. It basically gave the company total ability to change the work schedule or conditions from month to month."[41]

Two other aspects of this proposal decreased the control flight attendants had over their work life, and correspondingly, increased TWA's. For example, if a flight attendant had been scheduled to fly seventy-five hours but a four-day trip turned into a five-day trip, the extra hours or "bow wave" could be paid to the flight attendant at incentive pay or banked for use in the next month as a credit on flying time. TWA wanted discretion over which method was employed. They also wanted to eliminate the rights of the Simms arbitration which gave flight attendants the discretionary right to determine if they flew over seventy-five hours.

In addition to base and incentive pay, there were a variety of other forms of compensation (e.g., pay for language on international system, night pay, extended on-duty pay, holding time pay, understaffing penalty pay), but probably the most important was the expenses paid for time away from the domicile. Expense money for time away from domicile was tax-free and, after "years of hard fighting," they had expense parity with the pilots. The contract proposed a reduction from $1.75 to $1.50. "Have you ever ordered from the 'Flight Attendant' menu?"[42] In addition, the company wanted to select layover hotels for flight attendants "in all instances" versus the negotiated input from IFFA's Housing Committee, eliminate the $7.00 crew meal penalty payment, and combine the ground transportation for pilots and flight attendants.

The issue over combined ground transportation was a sensitive one for the flight attendants. Prior to IFFA, domestic flight attendants did not have ground transportation provided by the company in cases where the hotel did not have pick-up. International flight attendants had combined ground transportation with the pilots. It was their experiences with the pilots that had led them to negotiate separate company provided ground transportation. As flight attendant and member of the negotiating team, Cynthia de Figueiredo explained:

> On International, there frequently had been problems about who was in charge of the crew bus, who would determine when it left, where it stopped, whether or not to wait for someone. This was an emotional issue with many of the people who had flown and who had experience with the combined transportation on International.[43]

Two other proposed changes touched a sensitive cord in flight attendants: XCAP (extra cabin attendant position) and management seniority. XCAP was the right of flight attendants to use the jump seat for flights free of charge; it was based on a first-come first-served basis for flight attendants in uniform.

The XCAP was particularly helpful to flight attendants as displacement had increased and more and more flight attendants were having to commute to their new points of departure. Displacement affected junior flight attendants who were least likely to have unlimited passes; and, even with a pass, a full plane made them unusable if you needed to get to your destination in a timely fashion.

TWA's proposal was to allow management the use of jump seats. IFFA had already gone to arbitration with the pilots over XCAP, and won, but the dispute between them and the pilots had further eroded their relationship. To now have management taking the jump seats was an intrusion on a privilege they saw as helping them to soften the difficulties of displacement. Management travelling for business could get passes.

Even more contentious was TWA's proposed change involving management seniority. In their 1983 Red Book contract, IFFA had negotiated a freeze plus one year for flight attendants who went into management and then, at a later date, wanted to return to their flight attendant positions. In the 1984 contract negotiations, TWA wanted to restore all seniority and allow accrual of seniority for flight attendants while in management positions. IFFA wanted to go one step farther than their 1983 agreement and remove them entirely from the seniority list. As a TWA executive explained, "It was presented to me during the discussions as a strike issue by both sides."[44] Questioned in court by IFFA counsel, flight attendant de Figueiredo explained its significance:

> This is an emotional issue for our work force. You are dealing with seniority entitlements, and what this provision would allow is for an individual to enter—to enter management, to discipline and discharge flight attendants, to work directly against our work force and the union and then return to the line and reap the benefits that our work force and our organization had managed to gain.
>
> Question: Would it also affect the seniority of the flight attendants?
>
> Answer: Yes it would. . . . If the individual that I mentioned had their full seniority restored, it would—well, most everything in the airline industry as far as the flight attendant is concerned is governed on the basis of seniority. The order in which you board an aircraft in the event that you are riding on a pass on your personal time, the order in which you are awarded vacation, your retirement, everything is based on seniority. The awarding of bids is done entirely by seniority, and this would allow someone who had their full management seniority, that is, the time they had spent in management reinstated, an advantage over those who had continued to work as flight attendants when they returned to the flight attendant position.[45]

The issue of seniority rights has always been a central unifying concepts for organized labor, and IFFA was well versed in its significance and complexity. They had recently dealt with the issue of seniority in terms of a returning mothers' case and would in the not too distant future have to deal with the seniority issues of merging with flight attendants from Ozark. These all formed a backdrop to the multiple attacks on seniority that IFFA members were to face in 1986 and beyond. IFFA was clear on its position on seniority rights and operated under the idea that "seniority interests of those who earned their seniority working as Flight Attendants to be superior to, and more legitimate than, those seeking seniority for time not spent as working Flight Attendants. A refusal to advance the legitimate and deserved contract interests of some employees, to avoid offending others, is not only irresponsible and neglectful, but unlawful."[46] IFFA made their position clear:

> Make no mistake about it, the interests of supervisors are contrary to the interests of working flight attendants. Supervisors investigate and discipline flight attendants. Supervisors actively work on behalf of management to defeat flight attendant efforts at a better contract. Supervisors will cross flight attendant picket lines, take their jobs and seek to replace them in any strike. Supervisors terminate flight attendants.[47]

TWA's comprehensive proposals also reshaped established labor-management relations. TWA introduced a *two-tier wage structure*. Also known as the b-scale, or "killer bees," this system operates by bringing in new employees at a reduced wage rate which may or may not merge at a later date with the pay structure already in place for the more senior workers. The newly deregulated airline industry was one of the hardest hit with the two-tier wage system.[48] American Airlines led the way and the practice spread rapidly. "In the U.S. airline industry, two-tier plans were virtually nonexistent in 1982, began appearing in numbers in 1983, and by 1986 were an established industry practice."[49]

TWA actually was requesting both a b-scale for new hire flight attendants in both wages and benefits *and* a comparable c-scale for flight attendants who were currently on furlough to be implemented when they returned to the line. Over the course of negotiations, IFFA explained to members their opposition to the two-tier wage structure and referred to it as a "massive restructuring" of the workforce and highlighted the dangers of creating two differentially paid populations:

> The most devastating effect of two-tier systems . . . is a permanent division of the work force. An establishment of "haves" and "have-nots" within one bargaining unit runs contrary to basic principles of equal pay for equal work.
>
> [It] would create a very real potential for dividing the work force on a permanent basis with strong negative impact on employee morale and productivity heightened by animosity between those hired before and those hired after the agreement.[50]

There were more direct attacks on the union itself in the package. These came in the form of the withdrawal of payment for union representatives, and even more significantly, the elimination of union offices on property. IFFA saw the elimination of offices as severely affecting their ability to perform their job as a union, in terms of handling grievances, overseeing contract compliance, answering contract questions, representing flight attendants in discipline and dismissal hearings, etc. The fact that TWA paid for union representatives and office space for IAM and did not attempt a massive change in that relationship when they underwent negotiations opened TWA's position with IFFA to claims of unequal treatment and inconsistency.[51]

The contract package also included something new to the agreement which was an amendment that the company would not continue dues check-off on flight attendant paychecks in the event of a strike. Something else that did not appear in the 1983 Red Book: TWA asked for a no-strike clause that would prohibit IFFA from striking during the length of the contract. The sum of these proposals, if put in place, would severely weaken IFFA's ability to represent its workers.

The fate of the union was very much on the mind of IFFA's leadership and negotiating team when assessing this concessionary package from TWA. On a very concrete level, how IFFA managed this concessionary package, i.e., the extent to which they were successful in securing the best contract they could under these conditions, reflected on their sustained credibility with the labor force. The combined proposals were so extensive, however, that it put IFFA in a very difficult position. There was certainly industry-wide recognition by unions that they had to come to grips with the new era of concessionary bargaining. But, the question was how much and what impact such give-backs would have on the members and the union itself. Concessionary bargaining, in and of itself, tested the strength of the union.

As they enumerated their proposals, the overall design of TWA's contract openers was a substantial restructuring of the flight attendant occupation. From February 1984–1985, this would be the comprehensive package on the table for TWA. The first four meetings between the two parties focused solely on TWA proposals because IFFA was still in the process of developing their proposals. Similar to the dispute over starting the negotiations early, the tenor of the negotiating meetings maintained and even escalated that confrontational atmosphere. At the very first meeting on March 29, TWA stated that it wanted a 25% reduction in flight attendant costs and it wanted a contract by July 1984, a swift resolution by RLA standards.

The meetings began with an explanation of TWA's proposals. Although TWA explained the proposals in terms of how they would operate, IFFA wanted an explanation of how TWA arrived at a 25% reduction in flight attendant costs and how each proposed savings would add to the whole. Although

TWA had an answer to this based on their perceived advantage of TWA flight attendants over flight attendants at other carriers, Hoar and the negotiating committee would only respond that 25 percent was necessary for the viability of the company.[52] Hoar said that it was "Absolute" and another negotiator for TWA backed it up, "25 percent is not a goal. It is a REQUIREMENT."[53]

TWA negotiators balked at giving specific information on savings either in terms of money or headcount. TWA saw the request for information on finances and numbers as IFFA's strategy for delaying the negotiations and referred to a memo that IFFA legal counsel had written about deliberation. IFFA argued just the reverse: without such data they could not negotiate. TWA sent out a "newswire" to employees, announcing that "IFFA talks resumed in New York, but regrettably with the union representatives continuing to demonstrate a marked lack of enthusiasm for anything other than 'due deliberation' and 'analysis'—in other words, delay."[54]

These early meetings were filled with struggles over information. IFFA questioned the necessity of a 25 percent reduction and how each part of the package figured into the overall price tag. TWA tried to convince IFFA that the information they requested was neither relevant nor productive and attempted to move the negotiations along quickly to a contract. IFFA complained about the lack of information presented by TWA on the detailed costs of its particular proposals; TWA saw this as a tactic to stall the negotiations. As a TWA negotiator was recorded as saying, "We have never been able to communicate on numbers—U put ur numbers on them/we put our numbers on them."[55]

In later court hearings that elaborate the negotiating meetings in detail, there are numerous examples of combative exchanges between the two parties. Reflecting on these, U.S. District Court Judge Howard Sachs, who will oversee many of the court cases that were generated out of this dispute, commented on the tenor of negotiations as of April 19, only five days into negotiations: "All this trouble before Mr. Icahn got into it?"[56]

IFFA PACKAGE

IFFA would present their section 6 notice and proposals to TWA on April 27, 1984, and early May negotiations would revolve around IFFA's package. In their presentation, IFFA postponed discussion of economic items and focused the discussion on their proposals on work rule changes, improvement in benefits, and issues of seniority.[57] IFFA said they would give a full presentation of proposals 15 (retirement), 16 (insurance), and 17 (aircraft and domicile staffing) at a later date, but according to IFFA Hoar rejected them without a presentation. "Don't even bother to bring it up (proposals 15 and 16)." "Item

17 is rejected. Don't bother to bring it up." Frankovich said, "We will talk about them." Hoar responded, "TWA rejects these proposals."[58]

TWA, accused by IFFA of dragging its feet on financial price tags on its proposals, quickly determined that the IFFA proposal was around $75 to $80 million and "so divergent" from the goals of TWA that they quickly requested mediation. Borden sent a letter to all flight attendants informing them of TWA's decision to file for a mediator. In his May 8, 1984 letter:

> Last week, IFFA presented us with their openers, and frankly we were shocked at what we saw. . . . Now that we've had time for reflection, analysis and discussion, I must tell you that we're still in a state of astonishment. . . . What's now clear is that the presentation of IFFA's openers has not advanced the negotiating process but actually moved it backwards.[59]

Frankovich quickly wrote to the NMB on May 8 objecting to the premature request for a mediator: "We believe it is far too early to request the services of the Mediation Board as we have not yet fulfilled the statutory requirement to exhaust the possibilities of reaching an agreement through direct negotiations." Frankovich and the negotiating committee addressed the flight attendant workforce: "You should be aware that this action is both unnecessary and premature, since it implies that we have exhausted the possibilities of reaching an agreement through direct negotiations. This is simply not true."[60]

Negotiations were recessed, however, and there would be no negotiating meetings from May 9 until July 19 when negotiations would start up again in the presence of the first of what would be four mediators from the NMB. Despite the fact that IFFA had felt that the decision to bring in a mediator was premature, they acknowledged that the "company tone at the negotiating table has improved considerably since the mediation process has begun."[61]

THE FIRST PHASE CONCLUDED

In this period of negotiations, TWA proposals were quite high with significant concessionary demands. Although IFFA presented a package that would increase labor costs, they did not press the purely financial aspects of their proposal, to the point of not actually having a suggested pay increase rate. It would be an error to disregard IFFA's proposals and the contentious exchanges that occurred over their package. But, in the economic climate of the early eighties coupled with the impact of deregulation on airline workers, it was clear that TWA's demands for concessions predominated. In negotiations in the airline industry after deregulation, "Management seizes initiative in bargaining."[62]

While negotiations are recessed between the two parties, Meyer put together a financial presentation for IFFA's negotiating team. His June 5 presentation did not address the specific company proposals, but focused on the severity of the economic situation for TWA. He presented a series of slides illustrating TWA's financial position compared to the traditional major carriers as well as the successful expansion of Southwest Airlines and new low-cost carriers such as People Express Airline. Meyer claimed that they were not to be compared to these new entrants but to the major carriers. His presentation which included both, probably more accurately reflected the situation for TWA. They found themselves in the deregulated, recessed economy caught between other major carriers attempting to weather the period by concessionary and growth strategies and the proliferation of low-cost carriers. American Airlines CEO Robert Crandall's decision to create a carrier within a carrier at American which would be a permanently lower paid workforce through a two-tier wage system had got the attention of all of the major carriers.[63] When TWA recessed negotiations between IFFA and TWA and Borden wrote to all the flight attendants informing them of their request for a mediator, he cited American: "Time is running out on us, as each day we read new details of the plans American and others are shaping to build their futures at our expense." And, similarly, Meyer made reference to the transformation of American: "We now have *another* kind of low-cost rival to contend with, in the form of one of our former high-cost rivals."[64]

TWA did have one of the poorest financial outlooks of any of the major carriers in the early eighties and Meyer's presentation detailed that picture. Looking at the deregulated period 1979–1983, TWA had lost $476.1 million and that placed them in the middle of the loss pack of major carriers for that period. The *only* airline that recorded a greater loss during this period *and* survived the 1980s was United Airlines.

The first quarter of 1984, which typically was TWA's lowest quarter because of its seasonal nature and strength in summer international travel, showed TWA operating *loss* to be greater than any of the major airlines. Or as Meyer described it: "dead last."[65] In this same time period, American, United, and Delta would top the list of profitable airlines. Even Pan Am, which would not eventually show a profit for the 1984 year, placed ahead of TWA. The point of Meyer's presentation was that TWA's poor economic showing was due to labor costs. At the end of his presentation:

> Let's come to the point, now. What is it we're after?
>
> We want to achieve a level of profitability that will enable us to start growing again, instead of shrinking and shrinking in search of an elusive level at which we can make money.

> There's just one area where in many cases we're forced to pay *more* than the current average going rate in our industry.
>
> It also happens to be the *largest* single cost item on the list—payroll and benefits . . . there just isn't any other place to look.
>
> My purpose is simply to inform the representatives of IFFA and the NMB of TWA's severe labor-cost problem and how it adversely affects our current competitive position in the industry.
>
> TWA wants and badly needs a new agreement at the earliest possible moment.[66]

According to Meyer's presentation, TWA's 1983 employment expenses were 39.1 percent of operating costs compared to 38.2 percent average of other major carriers, which IFFA argued during negotiations could be accounted for in a variety of ways, e.g., different beginning and ending dates of labor contracts, some of which had already undergone some form of concessionary bargaining. TWA compared less favorably to Southwest (30.4%) and such new entrants as People Express (20.8%). According to Meyer, TWA flight attendants base salary and incentive pay was $31,597, 12.7 percent higher than other major carriers ($28,024). Including benefits and payroll taxes, the gap grew to 13.8 percent ($38,592 versus $33,884).[67]

The economic difficulties for TWA were real and IFFA had garnered the best flight attendant contract in the industry in their 1983 Red Book contract negotiations. They had offered midterm concessions of $28.5 million (estimated at $5,600 per flight attendant) in early 1984, rejected by TWA primarily because IFFA wanted an extension of the next contract negotiations. With TWA's openers, and the Meyer presentation, questions remained not only related to how much of the financial problems of TWA should be laid at the doorstep of labor, but specifically, what does this financial situation mean for IFFA's negotiating position. IFFA clearly wanted to negotiate the way former President Teolis explained negotiating:

> I've been active in unions for a long time. I know I'm absolutely right when I say that a union's job—its goal—is to protect its members and to get as many improvements in working conditions as possible. When improvements aren't possible, we try to keep what we have. And, if we can't keep what we already have, we try to minimize what we're forced to give back. We try to minimize our losses. That's exactly what IFFA's been doing.[68]

There were discrepancies in the presentation by Meyer and the position of the TWA negotiating team. Meyer showed the analyses for both the *major carriers* and *new entrants*, but stated clearly that they were not expecting to match the new entrants. Hoar and the negotiating team used the low-cost carriers, and stated that the comparison of cost should be with People Express.[69]

IFFA would meet with Meyer twice in June and though they told their membership they were "somewhat dismayed" that they had not received specific information about the cost of individual proposals, they "were pleased that the meeting gave us an opportunity to present a frank and direct message to TWA Corporate officers . . . but IFFA also reiterated that a quick settlement of our dispute would be in jeopardy as long as TWA continues to 'point the finger' at flight attendants and contract labor as the single source of the company's financial woes."[70]

With IFFA and TWA recessed, with the presentations by top TWA executives over, the next step was extended mediation.

NOTES

1. William A. Jolley, *Plaintiff IFFA's Suggestions in Opposition to Defendant TWA's Motion to Dismiss* (Kansas City, MO: 1986), 10.

2. IFFA, *The 630 News: The Official Publication*, Spring 1985, 3. This primary IFFA publication gets its name from the address of IFFA Headquarters in New York City.

3. William A. Jolley, *Plaintiff IFFA's Suggestions in Opposition to Defendant TWA's Motion to Dismiss* (Kansas City, MO: 1986), 10, referencing Detroit & Toledo Shore Line Railroad Co. v. United Transportation Union, 1969.

4. IFFA v. TWA (W. D. Missouri, Bad Faith Bargaining 1988), W. Hoar Deposition, 185. In the deposition of Hoar, chief negotiator, he affirmed that the package represented a change and did not include the work rule changes that had been tentatively agreed on, and that TWA did not alter its final package at all in the remaining days of the thirty-day countdown.

5. Ibid. According to Hoar, the internal negotiations with IFFA were very much part of the larger picture of jockeying for position to take advantage of Pan Am losses and affected their switch in negotiations to bring about agreement. He went on to say that "if we had a strike, we were going to infuse Pan Am immediately with tons of cash over the North Atlantic, which would be their salvation."

6. IFFA v. TWA (W. D. Missouri, Bad Faith Bargaining 1988), Transcripts, 4590–93. As Frankovich testified, "I thought the offer of a wage increase which we had not requested, an immediate request for wage concessions as soon as the contract was signed, was a plan . . . It was a plan to take back that which they had never intended to grant to start with."

7. IFFA v. TWA (W. D. Missouri, Bad Faith Bargaining 1988), W. Hoar Deposition, 184.

8. William A. Jolley, *Plaintiff IFFA's Suggestions in Opposition to Defendant TWA's Motion to Dismiss* (Kansas City, MO: 1986), 14.

9. Ibid., 15–16.

10. Ibid., 17.

11. IFFA, *Hotline*, January 20, 1984. As a way to communicate on a daily basis, IFFA used a phone message system that flight attendants could call to get updated information.

12. Ibid., January 5, 1984.

13. IFFA v. TWA (W. D. Missouri, Bad Faith Bargaining 1988), Exhibit 224.

14. IFFA, *Hotline*, February 8, 1984.

15. *Message to IFFA Membership*, by Arthur Teolis, 1984, audiocassette.

16. Murray Gartner, *Defendant TWA's Suggestions in Support of Its Motion to Dismiss* (NY: 1987), 13.

17. TWA, *TWA Skyliner*, February 11, 1985, cover, 8. This magazine was an official publication of TWA for all TWA employees.

18. *Message to IFFA Membership*, by Arthur Teolis, 1984, audiocassette.

19. IFFA, *Hotline*, March 26, 1984.

20. *Message to IFFA Membership*, by Arthur Teolis, 1984, audiocassette.

21. "Spinoff Approved at Trans World," *New York Times*, December 29, 1983, Financial Desk.

22. IFFA v. TWA (W. D. Missouri, Bad Faith Bargaining 1988), Exhibit 235.

23. TWA, *TWA Skyliner*, February 1985. "The corporation compensated the airline for tax benefits generated by TWA that Transworld made use of in its consolidated tax returns—in the amount of $23.5 million, after applicable taxes—thereby reducing TWA's 1983 loss of $35.9 million to $12.3 million."

24. "Trans World Corp. Expected to Approve Spinoff of Airline," *The Wall Street Journal*, October 25, 1983.

25. IFFA v. TWA (W. D. Missouri, Bad Faith Bargaining 1988), Exhibit 7.

26. *Message to IFFA Membership*, by Arthur Teolis, 1984, audiocassette.

27. IFFA v. TWA (W. D. Missouri, Bad Faith Bargaining 1988), Exhibit 8.

28. William A. Jolley, *Plaintiff IFFA's Suggestions in Opposition to Defendant TWA's Motion to Dismiss* (Kansas City, MO: 1986), 34.

29. *Message to IFFA Membership*, by Arthur Teolis, 1984, audiocassette

30. IFFA, *Hotline*, March 26, 1984.

31. IFFA v. TWA (W. D. Missouri, Bad Faith Bargaining 1988), V. Frankovich Deposition, 6.

32. William A. Jolley, *Plaintiff IFFA's Suggestions in Opposition to Defendant TWA's Motion to Dismiss* (Kansas City, MO: 1986), 18–21.

33. *Message to IFFA Membership*, by Arthur Teolis, 1984, audiocassette.

34. IFFA v. TWA (W. D. Missouri, Bad Faith Bargaining 1988), W. Hoar Deposition, 53.

35. William A. Jolley, *Plaintiff IFFA's Suggestions in Opposition to Defendant TWA's Motion to Dismiss* (Kansas City, MO: 1986), 21.

36. Ibid., 310.

37. IFFA v. TWA (W. D. Missouri, Bad Faith Bargaining 1988), Transcripts, 81.

38. William A. Jolley, *Plaintiff IFFA's Suggestions in Opposition to Defendant TWA's Motion to Dismiss* (Kansas City, MO: 1986), 10.

39. IFFA, *Information Representative Cards*, 1985. IFFA's structure included flight attendants who served as Information Representatives to help disseminate information to other flight attendants. These cards were parts of packets that they would be given to help answer questions.

40. IFFA v. TWA (W. D. Missouri, Bad Faith Bargaining 1988), Transcripts, 159.

41. Ibid., 152–53.

42. IFFA, *Information Representative Cards*, 1985.

43. IFFA v. TWA (W. D. Missouri, Bad Faith Bargaining 1988), Transcripts, 142.

44. IFFA v. TWA (W. D. Missouri, Bad Faith Bargaining 1988), R. Pearson Deposition, 87.

45. IFFA v. TWA (W. D. Missouri, Bad Faith Bargaining 1988), Transcripts, 238–39.

46. IFFA, *The 630 News: The Official Publication*, Fall 1984, 6–7.

47. IFFA, *Information Representative Cards*, 1985.

48. Bennett Harrison and Barry Bluestone, *The Great U-Turn: Corporate Restructuring and the Polarizing of America* (NY: Basic Books, 1988).

49. David J. Walsh, "Accounting for the Proliferation of Two-Tier Wage Settlements in the U.S. Airline Industry, 1983–1986," *Industrial and Labor Relations Review* 42, no. 1 (October 1988): 50–62.

50. IFFA, *The 630 News: The Official Publication*, Fall 1984, 22.

51. William A. Jolley, *Plaintiff IFFA's Suggestions in Opposition to Defendant TWA's Motion to Dismiss* (Kansas City, MO: 1986), 90.

52. Ibid., 40.

53. William A. Jolley, *Plaintiff IFFA's Suggestions in Opposition to Defendant TWA's Motion to Dismiss* (Kansas City, MO: 1986), 40, 45.

54. Ibid., 42.

55. Ibid., 47.

56. IFFA v. TWA (W. D. Missouri, Bad Faith Bargaining 1988), Transcripts, 387.

57. William A. Jolley, *Plaintiff IFFA's Suggestions in Opposition to Defendant TWA's Motion to Dismiss* (Kansas City, MO: 1986), 60.

58. Ibid., 62.

59. IFFA v. TWA (W. D. Missouri, Bad Faith Bargaining 1988), Exhibit I.

60. IFFA, *Hotline*, May 9, 1984.

61. Ibid., May 9, 1984 and October 2, 1984.

62. David J. Walsh, *On Different Planes: An Organizational Analysis of Cooperation and Conflict among Airline Unions* (Ithaca: ILR Press, 1994), 39.

63. Thomas Petzinger, Jr, *Hard Landing: The Epic Contest for Power and Profits that Plunged the Airlines into Chaos* (Armonk, NY: M.E. Sharp, 1995).

64. IFFA v. TWA (W. D. Missouri, Bad Faith Bargaining 1988), Exhibits I and 14.

65. William A. Jolley, *Plaintiff IFFA's Suggestions in Opposition to Defendant TWA's Motion to Dismiss* (Kansas City, MO: 1986), 23.

66. IFFA v. TWA (W. D. Missouri, Bad Faith Bargaining 1988), Exhibit 14.

67. Ibid., Exhibit 69. Using available seat miles (ASM's) for determining the cost of flight attendants, Meyer also presented a comparison of TWA flight attendant costs across carriers in 1983. TWA cost per ASM for TWA flight attendants was $0.551, and for the average of the other majors, $0.447. According to Meyer, this represented a $44.2 million gap (23.3%) between TWA flight attendants and other major carriers. Meyer also showed the rise in flight attendant costs over the past years. In 1978, the average TWA flight attendant base salary and incentive pay was $16,211. By 1984, this same figure was estimated at $35,082. Adding retirement, insurance and payroll taxes, the figure in 1978 was approximately $20,000 compared to a $44,000 estimated

figure for 1984. This represents a $120 percent increase in salary and benefits. One of the interesting and dramatic increases for the flight attendants is in the area of retirement benefits, reflecting the changing character of the labor force. By 1984, the average seniority of flight attendants was fourteen years. Retirement benefits went from $775 per year to $3,529 per year, a 355.4 percent increase.

This 120 percent increase is the highest of all employees during this time period. For example, TWA calculated the average increase in pay and benefits of all of its employees to be 62 percent; this figure is conservative in that it counts the wage concessions of the pilots and noncontract employees which were slated to snap-back. With a 62 percent consumer price index, this represented a 2 percent above inflation rate. For the flight attendants, it represented an increase of 62 percent above inflation for this time period.

A comparison on real dollars showed that IAM's increase of 81 percent meant a $21,000 increase between 1978 salary and benefits ($26,000) and 1984 ($44,000); for pilots, their 49 percent increase which does not include their 10 percent snap-back concession represented an increase of $34,000 per year from a salary and benefit package of $70,000 in 1978 to a salary of $104,000 in 1984.

68. *Message to IFFA Membership*, by Arthur Teolis, 1984, audiocassette.

69. IFFA v. TWA (W. D. Missouri, Bad Faith Bargaining 1988), Transcripts, 299–300; William A. Jolley, *Plaintiff IFFA's Suggestions in Opposition to Defendant TWA's Motion to Dismiss* (Kansas City, MO: 1986), 36.

70. IFFA, *Hotline*, June 6, 1984.

Chapter 2

Lost Chances

Unintended Consequences of Improved Conditions

Negotiations between TWA and IFFA were recessed from May to July 1984. They started up again in the presence of the NMB mediator, Dick Cosgrove, who was replaced early on by Gale Oppenberg.[1] IFFA negotiators reported back to the membership, "While both sides are gaining a better understanding of each other's positions on a variety of subjects, to date, *not one* of the dozens of bargaining items on the table has been agreed to. We are still far apart, and the likelihood of a quick settlement of our differences is, at this point, remote."[2]

While negotiations moved slowly, developments outside the negotiating room, altered the process. After years of struggle, the financial outlook for the major carriers improved. The airline industry as a whole reported greater operating profit margins in 1984 than in any year since deregulation.[3] Just as IFFA and TWA returned to the negotiating table in July, TWA announced profits for the second quarter of 1984 and there was the anticipation that TWA would have an end of the year profit. This early good news would be strengthened by President Meyer's prediction that this trend would be long term.[4] His forecast proved correct and TWA reported the first after-tax profit ($29.9 million) since 1978. The company credited its employees who took wage reductions, an improved economy and strong dollar, and the 1984 oil glut which dropped jet fuel prices. There was a decline in the number of domestic passengers but each passenger was more valuable because there had been some relief in the competitive fare wars. This decline was more than offset with an increase in system-wide traffic from their international route expansion to five new destinations. For the second year, their international operation was doing very well and, by April 1985, TWA planned to serve "19 points in 15 countries of Europe, Asia and the Middle East, operating 207 weekly flights in each direction. The airline will offer 71,649 seats across the Atlantic each week this summer, up from some 60,835 seats weekly in 1984, an 18 percent increase. That in turn was 21 percent ahead of the 50,257 weekly seats offered in 1983."[5] Although they labeled their profit picture as "pale by comparison" to competitors American and United, they believed that the profit picture would continue in 1985.

The major carriers as a group were doing better. The eleven major carriers collectively recorded an operating profit in 1984 eight times greater than 1983 ($1.9 billion versus $228.9 million). They had a net profit in 1984 to a net loss in 1983. *All* of the major carriers had an improved financial position in 1984 over 1983, *except* Pan Am. TWA had both an operating and net profit in 1984.[6]

As TWA recorded profits and anticipated future growth, they still demanded high concessions from the flight attendants and called for "overall employment cost relief through productivity improvement."[7] Although TWA stated that its profits would be even greater if "non-participating" groups, i.e., IFFA and IAM, had given midterm concessions, IFFA countered by adding the contributions its labor force had made through increased productivity:

> 1984 year end TWA profits announced this week bode well for all of us. The sacrifices of the Flight Attendant workforce in increased productivity in view of reconfigured aircraft, high passenger load and reduced crew complement contributed greatly to this financial turnaround. We expect this financial upturn should have a positive impact on the progress of negotiations.[8]

AN OPENING: NEW MANAGEMENT, NEW POSITIONS

Almost a year to the date of TWA's original contract openers, TWA presented a new comprehensive package to IFFA. This February 22, 1985 package was a much reduced one, estimated at around $30 million versus the $60 million of the former package. Although it carried some of the critical work rule changes that IFFA opposed, it was a package that held the possibility of a negotiated agreement. TWA claimed that this package was the result of the improved economic situation in 1984.[9] It was not clear that such a package would have been presented to IFFA, even with the improved economic situation, had there not been a change in management as well.

In late summer 1984, there would be what IFFA referred to as "a major corporate shake-up" at TWA which would have significant bearing on their labor negotiations.[10] TWA created a new position of Executive Vice President and Chief Operating Officer and promoted Richard Pearson to what was the second most important job to Meyer's presidency. Dick Pearson, who had been with TWA since 1967, and in his earlier years had worked under Crandall at American Airlines, came to the New York corporate offices from heading the Kansas City maintenance operation. While Meyer was to focus on long range planning, Pearson's job was to restructure the airline to be a competitive player in a deregulated economy and to regain its historical prominence in the industry. Pearson would report to Meyer and have "authority over the day-to-day operations of the airline: flight operations, maintenance and engineering, airport operations, marketing and sales, the international division, human resources, corporate information services, and the controller function."[11]

Early on, Pearson became directly involved in the labor negotiations that were going on with both IAM and IFFA. He already had a good deal of experience in labor negotiations with IAM because of his position at the maintenance base in Kansas City. And, he had definite ideas about how negotiations should proceed at TWA. Pearson was focused on the long-term effects of work rule changes rather than pay cuts. Wage cuts in the airline industry during this time typically gave the employees something in return, such as stock ownership plans. TWA did not want to give these two labor groups equity, and therefore, Pearson thought that a pay pause was more appropriate for negotiations.

Pearson's experience with IAM shaped his approach with IFFA. He wanted continuity between the demands made of IAM and IFFA. In IAM negotiations that he had recently been involved in, TWA had requested a pay pause, and he wanted the same for IFFA. "I felt that the company strategy should be to pursue the same consistency, if you will, of approach with all of its laborers."[12]

He was also influential in removing some of what were seen as the harsher earlier proposals. Pearson referred to some of these proposals as "simply not doable," "a waste of time," and "brutally hard."[13] In the new TWA package of February 1985, TWA had withdrawn their demand for the elimination of paid representatives and union offices on the property, as well as the elimination or reduction of a number of work rule changes.[14]

This was Pearson's deal, and members of the negotiating team and TWA management were dissatisfied with the level of cutbacks made in this package. Hoar and Borden, both playing major roles in the negotiations, were opposed to returning paid representatives and union offices on the property to IFFA. Pearson referred to this new package as "more consistent with the realism approach as opposed to the wish list approach." He explained, "We were trying to put a package out in a comprehensive sense that we could get a settlement with. . . . I think our credibility would have been questioned if we left in what I considered unrealistic approaches at that point."[15]

Pearson's job was to guarantee that TWA would make it through this volatile era and his approach was to move away from pay concessions to focus seriously on two-tier wages and major work rule changes that they had a reasonable chance to negotiate to settlement. "[I]t was formulated to get an agreement."[16]

Some of the major items still remained in place, some with modifications: same calendar day balancing, flex cap, reduced employee expenses. Despite Pearson's stated opposition to the accrual of management seniority, that proposal remained in. TWA also added a no furlough agreement for all flight attendants hired prior to January 1, 1985 and a buyout proposal for flight attendants. TWA would later view the elimination of the wage cut (13% and another 3% which had been slated to go into effect) to be the most significant change in their new package.[17]

Prior to sending out the proposal, Pearson called Frankovich and set up a luncheon meeting, including TWA's Borden and IFFA's Jolley. According to Frankovich, Pearson said it was "time to make an agreement" and he had looked at the package and "thought some of them were very harsh and he knew we would never agree with them, so he told the company to get rid of them."[18]

IFFA's NEW RESPONSE

IFFA presented a new package to TWA January 22, 1985 which was referred to as the "big six" items: scope which included items such as protections in the event of sale, merger, etc. of the airline as well as seeking a commitment not to start a nonunion carrier, "expedited arbitration, computer access, increased crew complement, retirement improvements and elimination of management seniority."

After TWA's presentation of its new package in February, IFFA again revised their proposals on March 8. From February to May 1985, IFFA and TWA would exchange a variety of proposals and counterproposals. IFFA agreed to a b-scale that merged over time, and accepted a wage pause until the end of 1985 followed by a wage increase.[19]

With profits up, load factors up, expansion up, and packages down, there was no period where agreement was closer than in the first half of 1985. Despite strong statements on the part of both IFFA and TWA about the lack of sufficient movement on the other's part, there were a lot of indications that this was posturing to move into the final phase of negotiations—the release to self-help and the thirty-day countdown when the "real" negotiating would finalize in an agreement. As Pearson explained:

> [I]t's traditionally documented in our industry that strategies in the labor relations area on both sides tend to—that both parties hold back, to a large degree, much of their bottom line or where they're only going to settle position until

such time as you get into a structured time frame; that is, the proffer for mediation and the resulting thirty-day period in which intensive negotiations go on and you are arriving at a final date in which either agreement is reached or either party is free to seek relief. At least in my opinion, it seems to me that in many cases, certainly in my experience with IAM, in particular, that little, if any, real, final progress was made until there was actually a deadline date and a structured time remaining for those negotiations.[20]

Pearson wrote in a management newswire on April 30:

In my opinion, neither union's [IAM and IFFA] leadership shows any inclination to help in a constructive way and our few remaining options now involve asking the NMB for release into a cooling off period, in the hope that either that added urgency will get discussion moving or we will reach a point at which we can seek self-help through continuing the operation of our airline.[21]

When Jolley asked him in a deposition, "was it your belief or opinion that the parties had, in fact, gotten their positions to a manageable basis where further pressure from the government could bring an agreement," Pearson responded, "Yes, sir."[22]

IFFA as well presented a firm position on the "outrageous" level of TWA demands at the negotiating table but at the same time prepared its membership for a countdown to what they believed was an opportune time to come to agreement. In responding to the proposals TWA had on the table, Frankovich in a taped message to the membership listed these demands and stated:

These demands are unreasonable and outrageous, and only show that TWA is trying to push us to see how far we'll go. There is no question in my mind that what we've offered is more than reasonable and more than what is needed for TWA to remain in a strong competitive position. I think this is the time to draw the line. I'm betting you'll agree.

What we've asked for in return for these substantial savings are low-cost items, and items requiring a change in TWA's attitude towards labor relations. We've asked for a guarantee against TWA starting a nonunion airline; removal of supervisors from our seniority list; an expedited grievance and arbitration machinery; computer access to allow IFFA equal footing with supervisors in handling grievances; a commitment to put the required number of cabin attendants on the aircraft when loads are high and service is full; the assurances that service managers work as service managers, not as cabin attendants; no cost improvements in furlough, displacements, and recall procedures; the recall of 159 furloughed flight attendants dropped from the seniority list last October because of the five-year recall limitation; and enhancement of our retirement plan. TWA has rejected our offer and refuses our compromise.

> TWA's response to IFFA's offer: "It's not enough." "It's woefully inadequate and doesn't even come close." "It's TWA's turn." TWA will not give IFFA what it asked, and demands far more than what IFFA offered.
>
> IFFA is drawing the line with TWA, and we're asking every member to join in our effort. TWA will go as far as we let it . . . but it has too much to lose to push too hard. We need to convince the company that we will not be pushed.[23]

Conditioned on displaying a strong negotiating position, IFFA believed this was a good time to make an agreement. In early March 1985, "We at IFFA Headquarters are convinced that we're finally heading toward a resolution of our contract dispute with TWA." As TWA approached its busiest season—what was predicted to be a record breaking season—IFFA thought that it might even be possible to make an agreement prior to requesting a release to countdown. TWA anticipated hiring new flight attendants in April and this gave TWA an added incentive to settle in order to take advantage of the b-scale. "In this round of negotiations, TWA is pressured to settle SOON . . . before it fully implements its expansion and before it hires new flight attendants. We may well be able to get our most favorable contract terms Soon . . . and before a strike countdown."[24]

BOTH SIDES MOBILIZE

While hopeful of an agreement, each of them expressed their reluctant willingness to take a strike or withstand one. "The question of a strike called by the representatives of either or both unions would be the worst imaginable door to try to use to reach new agreement. But your airline is prepared to operate if struck."[25] TWA was developing a contingent labor force in the event of a strike by either IFFA or IAM:

> As you know, we now have trained and in the pipeline sufficient flight attendants, license A & P mechanics and non-contract employees standing ready to perform a variety of essential tasks if needed.[26]

TWA told its stockholders that "The company hopes and expects to reach mutually acceptable agreements with both unions through the normal bargaining process, but has thoroughly prepared contingency plans in the event that proves impossible." Among its plans was the preparation of contingent flight attendants from its noncontract airline employees. The requalification of personnel who had previously been qualified plus any new volunteers, both domestic and overseas employees, were to undergo "Flight Attendant Safety/ Service Training"[27] To increase the contingent workforce further, TWA contacted Clipped Wings, the organization for former TWA flight attendants, offering them the chance to fly again.

Frankovich called upon members of Clipped Wings to honor their picket lines and refuse to cross. In a letter to chapter presidents, Frankovich spoke of their collective interests as former and current flight attendants, and acknowledged these former flight attendants for laying the groundwork of the gains that they had made over time. She asked them not to allow TWA to "pit one group against the other by enlisting the aid of Clipped Wings to undermine our Unions effort to obtain a fair contract. As I understand it, your members are being asked to cross our picket lines and work against us in the event we find it necessary to strike." At the end of her letter, Frankovich acknowledged, "As you can see, I am asking your help and am offering nothing in return other than our appreciation and admiration and the knowledge that what you started can continue to grow."[28]

IFFA discounted that TWA could actually use any of these populations: with flights up, their other employees were busy, new hire flight attendants were already being brought on the line so could not be a replacement force waiting in the bleachers, and Frankovich reported that they were receiving support from the Clipped Wing. She reasoned:

> TWA claims it has 1500 in its scab work force. Most of these are ticket agents, reservations, and supervisors, all necessary in their current positions. . . . And 1500? Right now we're operating at 6,600 active flight attendants and the number is increasing. . . . You tell me what kind of operation TWA can realistically maintain with 1500 inexperienced, nonflight attendants.[29]

IFFA mobilized the support of its membership through involvement and information. IFFA had instituted what was called an Information Representatives Program (Info Reps) in the summer of 1984. Already in the June of 1984, "The Information Representatives Program is in full swing. We urge you to keep in touch with these representatives for up-to-date information on negotiations and also to pass along to us any relevant items which you think we should know."[30] In Spring 1985 there were 500 IFFA representatives "ready to discuss [negotiating items] with you at length." With special mailings, Info Reps would be given additional information in letters, on cards, to use in their discussion with other flight attendants. Hotline messages, taped messages that flight attendants could call were routinely available as well. Because of the domicile system, IFFA leadership and negotiators would also visit domiciles for discussions of negotiations.

The organizational structure of IFFA was borne out of past experiences and proved an effective one for the mobilization of flight attendants. They had become an independent union precisely because of the experiences they had with other affiliations where information was not forthcoming, where decisions were made without their input and often not in their best interests. IFFA had developed numerous avenues to disseminate information to members and encouraged participation. As an independent union, there was not much distance between the leadership and the rank and file. They all identified as flight attendants.[31] What this meant on the day-to-day was that the leadership understood what it meant to be a flight attendant, what they had been through as they redefined the occupation, and what the pressing issues were. What this meant in the long run, and became so effective, was that members identified with the union and believed that it represented their best collective interests.

In the year of negotiations prior to Spring 1985, IFFA kept the membership generally informed about the continuing negotiations and in the final months of Spring 1985 they stepped up that information, and actually "broke" with past tradition by disclosing specific bargaining positions. According to Frankovich, they articulated each party's positions because of "false charges" made by TWA. "Ed Meyer's statement that TWA is offering us roughly the same kind of deal given to unions at other airlines is not true. . . . The truth is that TWA is asking MORE from us than what those carriers got. And TWA is offering us LESS in return."[32]

IFFA compiled a comparative look at other flight attendant contracts at American, United, Northwest, Ozark, and Piedmont. Each of these contracts with ending dates in 1986 and 1987 had a lot in common. Each of them contained two-tier wage structures and pay increases. IFFA agreed to a b-scale that would merge over time despite a reluctance to do so with the knowledge that they were setting a precedent at TWA as the first large union group to accept a b-scale.[33] IFFA also incorporated a pay increase, following a pay pause. "If we kept our 1984 pay rates in effect until 1989, we would fall behind the cost of living, other Flight Attendants in the industry and other TWA work groups. And it would be difficult to catch up in furtures [*sic*] negotiations."

Most of these comparable contracts carried an early buyout provision which TWA was now offering IFFA. IFFA valued the early buyout, however, as an advantage *for TWA* not necessarily for the flight attendants IFFA represented who stayed within the corporation, and she gave the following rationale:

> If TWA wants to encourage senior workers to retire so that they can hire lower paid employees, retirement plan improvements are the way to go about it. A buy-out is a benefit to TWA, not the working flight attendants. We will accept it for those planning to leave [offer is only good for a short period after agreement], but we shouldn't have to pay for it with concessions.[34]

The "staggering list of additional productivity concessions" in the form extensive work rule changes requested by TWA, according to IFFA, were not part of these other contracts.[35]

IFFA compared themselves to flight attendants at other *profitable* airlines and TWA to other *profitable* carriers and kept up-to-date on negotiations throughout the airline industry. During the Spring 1985, they also watched closely the unfolding of difficult labor negotiations at Pan Am. The machinists, organized under Transport Workers Union (TWU), went on strike February 28, 1985. In a show of interunion support, ALPA and IUFA (Independent Union of Flight Attendants) honored their strike and effectively shut down the airline. ALPA returned to work in about a week, with President Duffy citing "Continuation of the strike posed a serious threat to the longterm viability of the airline." The flight attendants remained out until a couple days before TWU and Pan Am reached an agreement, March 23, 1985.[36] The problem for the flight attendants was that they were less than ten days away from their *own* strike deadline. Having just come off of a strike did not bode well for their willingness to initiate a strike for their own contract. And, it proved disastrous for them.

The Pan Am flight attendants had ended up with a massive work rule concessionary package and a starting monthly salary for new flight attendants at $784, the lowest in the industry. IFFA knew that this contract could potentially have bearing on their own negotiations. "Pan Am Flight Attendants just concluded a heavily concession laden agreement. As you would suspect, TWA is already trying to hold it over our heads." IFFA argued how:

> Pan Am is very different from TWA. Pan Am lost $220 million dollars in 1984. TWA made a $70 million operating profit and a $30 million net profit. Pan Am is alleged to have had $600 million in unpaid debt to its employees (refused wage snap-back, refused payment on retirement funds etc.) TWA has no such debt. Pan Am brought to you by the same man who brought you Braniff and Air Florida—Ed Acker, Former Chairman of the Board for these two bankrupt airlines. TWA is in good financial shape and there is no consideration of bankruptcy. Pan Am's Flight Attendant's Union (IUFA) was led by a well meaning but inexperienced President. He had no previous negotiating experience. It would seem that he or his negotiating team panicked, fearing no support existed in his Flight Attendant ranks. The night of the strike deadline he walked out of negotiations leaving the IUFA Negotiation Team leaderless.[37]

The Pan Am strike was costly for both sides. According to IFFA, Pan Am lost $5 million a day in the twenty-seven day strike, and shortly after the strike, Acker sold Pan Am's Pacific route for $750 million to Richard Ferris at United. Both TWA and United gained passengers from the strike at Pan Am.[38]

For both IFFA and TWA, for good reasons (improved economic outlook) and bad (cost of a strike for both sides), it was a good time to make an agreement. IFFA was ready for final countdown negotiations, and stated that in their messages to Info Reps and the membership as a whole. One of the things that IFFA did was educate its members on the things that they could do to "send a message" to TWA: vote yes to a strike vote, don't let TWA compare itself to Pan Am, don't let them engage in "mail-order negotiations" as a way to bypass IFFA negotiators, don't be influenced by TWA's threats of downsizing, furloughs, and replacement of flight attendants, and don't get caught in the rumor mill.[39]

On May 3, 1985, IFFA relayed to their membership that the NMB had officially recessed their negotiations and were reviewing their case. IFFA informed its membership that NMB was not likely to do anything until they knew what would happen between United and its pilots which were presently in a countdown to strike, with the thirty-day cooling-off period to end on May 17. They anticipated release:

> The National Mediation Board has scheduled the resumption of negotiations between IFFA and TWA for Tuesday, May 21. At this point, we believe it is very likely that a release to a thirty day countdown for a strike will come very soon. We will shortly be mailing a strike ballot to all IFFA members. We urge you to use this ballot to send the message to TWA that we will not be pushed further. Your IFFA Negotiating Committee will continue, in the days ahead, to attempt to reach an equitable agreement. However, we will immediately begin preparations for a strike. All IFFA domiciles will need assistance in setting up the strike headquarter offices and will need volunteers to aid in this endeavor. If you are willing to volunteer your services to help, please call the domicile IFFA office as soon as possible.

IFFA sought release to self-help on May 21, 1985.[40] It may very well have been that if they had been released, the thirty-day countdown would have provided the necessary impetus to final resolution. There was no other time when the chances for agreement appeared greater. TWA's economic situation was improved and looking sustained, and both packages had "dramatically narrowed." A negotiated conclusion without a strike was a real possibility.

Under normal circumstances, summer would have been an opportune time for IFFA to be given a release to self-help. In preparation for the possibility of a release, IFFA sent out ballots to its membership, which when returned and tallied, gave IFFA's negotiating committee a 96.6 percent positive strike vote.[41] Being able to strike in the summer would have put added pressure on TWA because the threat of a strike during peak travel would have been extremely costly. There was not, however, anything normal about the circumstances of this labor struggle.

NOTES

1. The replacement was due to an industrial accident.
2. IFFA, *Hotline*, September 28, 1984.
3. Steven A. Morrison and Clifford Winston, *The Evolution of the AirlineIndustry* (Washington, DC: Brookings Institution, 1995), 31.
4. IFFA, *Hotline*, August 10, 1984.
5. TWA, *TWA Skyliner*, February 1985.
6. IFFA, *The 630 News: The Official Publication*, Spring 1985, quoting from an article in *Aviation Daily*.
7. Murray Gartner, *Defendant TWA's Suggestions in Support of Its Motion to Dismiss* (NY: 1987).
8. IFFA, *Hotline*, January 25, 1985.
9. Murray Gartner, *Defendant TWA's Suggestions in Support of Its Motion to Dismiss* (NY: 1987).
10. IFFA, *The 630 News: The Official Publication*, Fall 1984.
11. IFFA v. TWA (W. D. Missouri, Bad Faith Bargaining 1988), Exhibit 511.
12. IFFA v. TWA (W. D. Missouri, Bad Faith Bargaining 1988), R. Pearson Deposition, 71.
13. William A. Jolley, *Plaintiff IFFA's Suggestions in Opposition to Defendant TWA's Motion to Dismiss* (Kansas City, MO: 1986), 86.
14. IFFA v. TWA (W. D. Missouri, Bad Faith Bargaining 1988), R. Pearson Deposition, 74.
15. Ibid., 73–76.
16. William A. Jolley, *Plaintiff IFFA's Suggestions in Opposition to Defendant TWA's Motion to Dismiss* (Kansas City, MO: 1986), 87.
17. Murray Gartner, *Defendant TWA's Suggestions in Support of Its Motion to Dismiss* (NY: 1987), 43.
18. IFFA v. TWA (W. D. Missouri, Bad Faith Bargaining 1988), Transcripts, 3864–65.
19. IFFA v. TWA (W. D. Missouri, Bad Faith Bargaining 1988), Exhibit HH.
20. William A. Jolley, *Plaintiff IFFA's Suggestions in Opposition to Defendant TWA's Motion to Dismiss* (Kansas City, MO: 1986), 103–4.
21. Ibid.
22. Ibid.
23. *Draw the Line*, narrated by Vicki Frankovich, by IFFA, audiocassette, recorded Spring 1985.
24. IFFA, *Information Representative Cards,* March 1985.
25. *Draw the Line*, narrated by Vicki Frankovich, by IFFA, audiocassette, recorded Spring 1985, quoting TWA management's Jerry Cosley, speaking on the TWA response line, April 25, 1985.
26. IFFA v. TWA (W. D. Missouri, Bad Faith Bargaining 1988), Exhibit 261; William A. Jolley, *Plaintiff IFFA's Suggestions in Opposition to Defendant TWA's Motion to Dismiss* (Kansas City, MO: 1986), 102–3.
27. IFFA v. TWA (W. D. Missouri, Bad Faith Bargaining 1988), Exhibit, 229; William A. Jolley, *Plaintiff IFFA's Suggestions in Opposition to Defendant TWA's Motion to Dismiss* (Kansas City, MO: 1986), 28.

28. IFFA, *The 630 News: The Official Publication*, Spring 1985, 21.

29. *Draw the Line*, narrated by Vicki Frankovich, by IFFA, audiocassette, recorded Spring 1985.

30. IFFA, *Hotline*, June 15, 1984.

31. Interview, Mary Ellen Miller, IFFA Director of Safety and Legislation, 2016.

32. *Draw the Line*, narrated by Vicki Frankovich, by IFFA, audiocassette, recorded Spring 1985; IFFA, *Information Representative Cards*, Spring 1985.

33. IFFA v. TWA (W. D. Missouri, Bad Faith Bargaining 1988), Transcripts, 1025.

34. *Draw the Line*, narrated by Vicki Frankovich, by IFFA, audiocassette, recorded Spring 1985.

35. Ibid.

36. David J. Walsh, *On Different Planes: An Organizational Analysis of Cooperation and Conflict among Airline Unions* (Ithaca: ILR Press, 1994), 58–59.

37. IFFA, *Information Representative Letter*, April 26, 1985.

38. IFFA, *The 630 News: The Official Publication*, Summer 1985, quoting an article from *Aviation Daily*; April 19, 1985 and April 12, 1985.

39. IFFA, *The 630 News: The Official Publication*, Spring 1985, 6–8.

40. William A. Jolley, *Plaintiff IFFA's Suggestions in Opposition to Defendant TWA's Motion to Dismiss* (Kansas City, MO: 1986), 102–3.

41. IFFA, *The 630 News: The Official Publication*, Fall 1985, 5. The strike ballots went out at the end of May and June 19 at 10 AM was the deadline for return.

Chapter 3

Things Worsen

Carl Icahn Enters the Picture

The Summer of 1985 proved to be an awful time. Just as IFFA was in the process of requesting a release to a thirty-day countdown, the most significant airline strike of 1985 was getting under way, the ALPA strike at United Airlines. The NMB would not grant a release that would open the possibility of another strike in the airline industry at the same time.

Days after the United Pilots concluded their strike, havoc was wreaked on TWA with the hijacking of the Athens/Rome Flight 847. And, the international crisis is further complicated on the domestic side by the heating up of an air war between Frank Lorenzo and Carl Icahn for the ownership of TWA.

The NMB did not grant a release and instead responded to a request by TWA and put negotiation talks in recess on May 21, 1985. Formal collective bargaining would be put on hold for a full half year.[1] Formal collective bargaining negotiations would not resume again until December 2, 1985, in a totally new, and substantially more ominous, climate for the flight attendants under the new ownership.

TWA'S TAKEOVER AND ITS IMPACT ON IFFA

Questions of the ownership of TWA began to surface in the spring of 1985. Around this time it became clear that someone was slowly buying up TWA common stock and gearing up for a takeover. It was alarming to TWA to find out that it was Icahn who had made TWA his next takeover pursuit.

IFFA first mentioned the "rumor" of a takeover by Icahn on May 10, 1985, and relayed to the membership that they had been in contact with IAM and ALPA and would be meeting with TWA.[2] Their position was that they were the representatives of the flight attendants and would negotiate to agreement no matter who was owner:

> We have received many inquiries regarding the attempted "takeover" of TWA by Mr. Carl Icahn. We want to assure everyone that no matter the outcome of that confrontation, IFFA's position as the Representative of Flight Attendants remains unchanged. Our contract is still valid and we will continue to negotiate with TWA, regardless of who owns or controls the Company.[3]
>
> Our interests lie in obtaining a contract with TWA that will afford the protection we need no matter who is the eventual owner of the Company. We must all avoid panic and concentrate on obtaining a new contract and providing the same quality service our passengers have come to expect from us.[4]

The question of ownership quickly took center stage at TWA. Although TWA had only become aware of it in late April 1985, the idea of a takeover had actually originated in a discussion Icahn had in the Summer of 1984 with Sanford Rederer, an economist and formerly of the Civil Aeronautics Board (CAB).[5] Icahn later recounted that Rederer's advice was "instrumental" in his decision to acquire TWA, and Icahn would appoint him as a vice president of strategic planning at TWA.[6] By September 1984, Icahn had been secretly buying TWA stock and by late April 1985 had accumulated enough (5%) of the outstanding shares to be required to file with the Securities and Exchange, revealing his name and intentions. Icahn, set up by the investment firm of Drexel Burnham Lambert met with Meyer for the first time on May 3, 1985.[7] He told Meyer, and the other TWA members present, about the "Rederer" plan which included among other things the elimination of flights and the domestic operation, the selling off of such assets as the maintenance base in Kansas City, the selling of aircraft, and the selling of selected airport facilities (e.g., O'Hare, LaGuardia, Philadelphia, and Boston). Management was less than enthusiastic about this and pointed out that they had already discarded such ideas. In particular, TWA had researched the idea of eliminating their domestic operation and focusing solely on their very successful international route structure. But as Meyer explained their commissioned research affirmed the connection between the domestic and international operations:

> [O]ur domestic operations are in fact inseparable from and indispensable to the success of our international services, and that an even more substantial feeder system centered on St. Louis was not only distinctly preferable to a further domestic contraction but actually imperative for our competitive development. Accordingly, we will expand our domestic operations at St. Louis substantially in 1985, and will also for the first time, offer transatlantic services there, as an initial step in developing St. Louis into a major interior gateway for our international operations as well.[8]

Because TWA had not been a money maker for many of the past years, management was not at all prepared for TWA being seen as a potential takeover target and the attempt took them by complete surprise. Other companies had put safeguards in place against takeovers, but TWA had none.[9] The fact that TWA had been spun off from Trans World Corporation and was now a sole and independent enterprise, had actually made a profit in 1984, and their stock was perceived as undervalued, made TWA a potentially attractive candidate for takeover:

> T.W.A. was caught with its takeover defenses down. Unlike many other major companies, it had taken no steps to stagger the terms of its directors or to introduce other routine "shark repellants" to make it harder to gain control. "We were fighting with an unloaded gun," explained James Freund, a partner of Skadden, Arps, Slate, Meagher & Flom, which advised T.W.A. on takeover defense.[10]

TWA management was actively opposed to Icahn and quickly delivered the message that he and his plans were "uninvited and undesirable."[11] They were specifically opposed to his expressed plans for the airline but generally opposed to his reputation for not running companies but for selling them off in bits and pieces.[12] They filed a suit in the U.S. District Court, Southern District of New York, arguing violations in federal securities law in Icahn's dealings with TWA; a Department of Transportation (DOT) filing stating, "Icahn's exercise of control over TWA would seriously threaten the Company's continued fitness;" and, a Missouri suit citing state violations on Icahn's part.[13]

TWA, in a special edition, "TWA vs ICAHN," informed their employees that they had "launched an aggressive counterattack" and wrote:

> The one strategy that Icahn is not willing to pursue is to manage TWA in a competent, responsible manner or to maximize the long-term interests in TWA, its public shareholders, its employees and the traveling public. Accordingly, he should not be permitted to exercise unfettered control over TWA.[14]

Not incidentally, they were also concerned about their own longevity as managers. By Spring 1985, Icahn was already a well-known corporate raider and greenmailer who openly displayed little respect for management. He was known for his "anti-Darwinian" theory:

> Unfortunately, many of today's chief executives have spent the first 20 or 30 years of their business careers studying how to please their boards rather than concentrating on how to increase their corporations' profitability. Top management in America, with many notable exceptions, is sadly lacking in knowledge and leadership.[15]

And:

> It's what I call the anti-Darwinian theory, the survival of the unfittest. In a lot of corporations, a guy gets to the top by kowtowing, and then picks somebody to succeed him who has done the same.[16]

Icahn's growing interest in TWA came on the heels of his controversial takeover bid of Phillips Petroleum where the management was so outraged that they took out full page newspaper ads, "Is Icahn for Real?"[17] Phillips had just repelled the hostile takeover by T. Boone Pickens when Icahn went after the company. Pickens left the fight with $89 million in pretax profits and Icahn made $50 million for thirty days work.[18]

Similar to Phillips and as part of their counterattack, TWA's Meyer and Pearson took out full page ads in the *New York Times* and the *Wall Street Journal*:

> *If you thought we'd just stand by and do nothing while you try to take over our company—think again.*
>
> You secretly accumulated our stock for several weeks. Finally, you disclosed that you have bought one-fourth of our shares.
>
> You have also been, as usual, vague about what your real intentions are—and, characteristic of your past actions, you have threatened to take over our company.
>
> *Well, Mr. Icahn, we have no intention of standing by and doing nothing while you play your Wall Street games with us.*
>
> TWA is a vital part of this nation's economic well being. And because we view that role seriously, we are going to take whatever steps are necessary to protect the constituencies and communities we serve . . .
>
> You see, Mr. Icahn, running a major airline is a big job, one that we don't take lightly. It's not like speculating with paper on Wall Street. You have to be proved "*fit*" to operate an airline—"*fit*" to own; "*fit*" to raise the vast sums of money needed to maintain equipment safely and invest in new, modern aircraft; "*fit*" to comply with the many important rules and regulations that the various federal, state, municipal and international agencies demand of an air carrier.
>
> In fact, we think you are so unfit we are asking our government's Department of Transportation to rule on your fitness to control an air carrier and we are suing you in state and federal courts.
>
> *So, Mr. Icahn, if you thought we'd just stand aside and do nothing while you try to take over our company—think again!*
>
> Running one of the world's most respected airlines is a heavy responsibility. We think it's a commitment you just can't handle.[19]

TWA solicited help from their employees to fend off Icahn, asking them to testify to his unfitness to run an airline and engaging them in such public actions as wearing "Stop Carl Icahn" buttons when on duty.[20] IFFA testified both before the Aviation Subcommittee of the House Committee on Public Works and Transportation regarding a bill that would give the DOT more time to rule on Icahn's fitness and before the Senate Committee on Commerce, Science and Transportation on a bill "which is designed to discourage airline takeovers by buyers who plan to sell off assets instead of maintaining service."[21]

THE DEVIL YOU KNOW v. THE DEVIL YOU DON'T

And most dramatically, in an effort to foil Icahn's takeover, the Board of Directors put TWA up for sale. When Icahn offered $18 per share for TWA in late May 1985, TWA's Board of Directors decided it was time to look for another buyer, a "white knight" to save them from Icahn. It was at this time that Meyer sought out Frank Lorenzo as an alternative to Icahn. Lorenzo, President and CEO of Texas Air Corporation had earlier merged Texas International Air with Continental Airlines and had also started up New York Air. TWA offered Lorenzo a number of inducements to buy TWA and he became a serious contender for ownership.

This was not the first time that Lorenzo had shown interest in TWA, and it would not be his last. In 1979 Lorenzo was said to have invited the head of TWA at that time, Edwin Smart, to breakfast at the Hotel Carlyle in New York City. He was intent on purchasing TWA. "Whereas most men in this situation might offer to buy breakfast, Lorenzo offered to buy TWA. Smart, stunned, walked out before the eggs arrived."[22]

The name Frank Lorenzo was well known to employees across the airlines. To labor, Lorenzo was anything but a white knight. Although these 1985 events at TWA predated the downing of Eastern airlines, Lorenzo was already infamous for having used chapter 11 bankruptcy law to eliminate union contracts and reorganize Continental as a nonunion carrier.[23] Frankovich's comment that "from our perspective, what happened there was a blood bath for the employees" was representative of organized labor's view of Lorenzo's actions.[24]

Finding out that TWA was courting Lorenzo as an owner was viewed as a serious threat to the viability of the labor unions at TWA. IFFA, ALPA, and IAM had already formed a coalition to deal with the pressing issues of ownership that surfaced with Icahn. The TWA Labor Coalition began with the goal in mind of finding an alternative buyer to Carl Icahn, possibly one that would be interested in some kind of equity arrangement with the employees, for example, an Employee Stock Ownership Plan (ESOP). When they found out that TWA had approached Frank Lorenzo their interunion coalition focused their efforts on ridding themselves of Lorenzo—the "anti-christ" of labor:

> [T]he TWA Unions have formed a unified coalition to oppose and otherwise deal with the proposed purchase of TWA by Texas Air and Frank Lorenzo. The coalition—consisting of IFFA President Vicki Frankovich, acting President and General Chair of IAM Bill O'Driscoll, and Captain Harry Hoglander, Chair of ALPA Master Executive Council at TWA—has retained the services of two well-known and respected investment bankers and will explore all avenues and options for preventing the Lorenzo purchase.[25]

Eugene Keilin is from the New York investment firm of Lazard; Freres would represent IFFA and later ALPA as well; and Brian Freeman from his own firm would represent IAM. It would be Keilin and Freeman who would make the initial contacts with Icahn. Only later would IFFA realize that there might be some disadvantages to using the same representative as the pilots.

The union coalition worked with their investment bankers to find an investor "with sufficient capital to top the Lorenzo bid and purchase the airlines in partnership with employees."[26] To keep their memberships updated on the activities of the coalition and the status of ownership, the coalition provided recorded message phone numbers throughout the system. While the three unions collaborated to identify someone other than Lorenzo to buy TWA, management made it clear that they were not interested in the unions' plans. According to IFFA, TWA stated in a management directive " . . . it cannot and will not support or encourage the ESOP effort." IFFA observed, "Something is wrong in a world where Lorenzo is considered 'friendly' and employees are considered hostile."[27]

The unusual cooperation between management and labor in the "Stop Icahn" campaign unraveled. Fuel was added to fire when labor discovered TWA was multiplying managerial golden parachutes while doing nothing to protect contract employees. According to IFFA:

> The five "golden Parachutes" in existence prior to Icahn's takeover efforts . . . providing up to three years of salary, stock options, and bonuses to corporate executives terminating for any reason other than conviction of a felony . . . *were increased by thirty (to be funded by, guess what, employee concessions).*
>
> When questioned by incredulous Members of the House of Representatives about these "Golden Parachutes" for executives and the lack of protection for employees in the event of a hostile takeover of the airline, Ed Meyer defended the Executive perks on the basis of necessity and cavalierly commented that employees are protected by their contracts . . . (do you see in our Contract severance pay, furlough protection, or benefits for us if a portion of the airline is sold?)[28]

On June 13, 1985, TWA Board of Directors agreed to sell TWA to Lorenzo at Texas Air Corporation. Presented as a "friendly merger," TWA would remain separate with their own management and board. With a selling price of $793.5 million for the largest transatlantic carrier, the deal was on track to be completed by December.[29] The merger would make Texas Air the second largest airline in the industry.[30]

Eclipsing this internal news, in the early morning of June 14, TWA Flight 847 from Athens to Rome was hijacked by Shi'ite terrorists demanding the release of prisoners held by Israel.[31] For the next seventeen days, TWA and the nation, were focused on the resolution and safe return of the hostages, in all 145 passengers and eight crew members. After a forced landing in Beirut and then flying back and forth to Algiers, one Navy diver was killed, hostages were physically and mentally terrorized, released sporadically, with the final thirty-nine men released on June 30, 1985. The calm and commanding demeanor of Pilot John Testrake, and the equally calm and creative abilities of flight attendant, Purser Uli Derickson, made the crew heroes upon conclusion of the crisis.[32]

Both sides of this international crisis were punctuated by the takeover of TWA and ensuing battle between Lorenzo and Icahn. According to Frankovich in court testimony, their investment banker Freeman:

> called me and informed me that it would be necessary for us to consider dealing with Carl Icahn because we were looking at the devil we knew (Lorenzo) as opposed to the devil we didn't know (Icahn), and if the goal was to insure that Frank Lorenzo did not succeed in the takeover of TWA there were only two people who were the real players in this game.
>
> One was Frank Lorenzo because of the stock he had been given by TWA, and the other was Carl Icahn, because of his continuing acquisition of stock which meant he could not be ignored as a primary controlling influence in the outcome of who the owner of the corporation would be.[33]

Acknowledging their anxiety and doubt about Icahn, the union coalition turned their attention to forging a workable solution with him to displace the impending sale by Lorenzo. Labor assessed a collaboration with a known raider:

> *IFFA:* "He contends he wants to be an airline operator—that may or may not be true . . . We don't want to run from a deal with Lorenzo if that means running from the frying pan into the fire . . . These guys are all sharks and are all trying to get a piece of our hides."
>
> *IAM:* "The machinists acknowledged that working with Icahn might be the only way they could avoid a similar fate to Continental Airlines where Lorenzo voided union contracts and dropped wages by half. Hell will freeze over before labor does business with Lorenzo . . . The last option is Carl. It's a question of lesser evils."
>
> *ALPA:* Even the pilots who will enter into an agreement with Icahn in early July 1985 are apprehensive. "Do we think he's absolutely committed to do this deal? No . . . It was one of those things where the prime minister had a knife at the king's throat and the rioters were at the palace gate . . . Who do you go with?"[34]

Icahn's continued purchasing of TWA stock made him the only real contender to Lorenzo. Particularly to the pilots, over time, Icahn appeared as the white knight who would save the airline, save their jobs, and topple Lorenzo.

They entered into an agreement with him that initiated the turnaround that made it possible for Icahn to defeat Lorenzo. With the concessions offered to Icahn by the pilots, and later the machinists—approximately $150 million per year for three years—Icahn was in a financially preferred position over Lorenzo. The Icahn-pilot takeover, as it was known, was the first such known collaboration. Icahn assured the pilots and machinists that he was a changed man—that he intended to run the airline and to use their concessions and any profits made to reinvest in the airline. He rejected the notion that he was in it for greenmail or to liquidate and sell off TWA assets. Icahn, with the millions he had garnered through takeover attempts that resulted in sizable greenmail profits, consistently argued that his intentions had always been to take control of companies, but, when he could not, he would withdraw with the consolation of greenmail. He backed up his assurances to the pilots and machinists with an oft quoted, "I am a man of my word."[35]

When TWA management realized that they were not going to be able to come to a workable agreement with Lorenzo and Icahn would succeed in his takeover attempt, they made a reversal. On Friday the 13th, September 1985, Lorenzo and Texas Air Corporation agreed to pull out of the battle for TWA. In exchange, TWA agreed to pay $43 million to Lorenzo for canceling the merger agreement.[36] This turned out not to be the last of Lorenzo, and he would make one more appearance in his attempt to purchase TWA.

Even though Icahn anticipated finishing the deal quickly, it would drag out through the Fall and into the Winter. On September 26, he reached agreement with TWA Board of Directors and through resignations took control of the board.[37] Meyer had officially resigned days earlier to become president of Hilton International, part of Trans World Corporation that had spun TWA off in 1984. Pearson became President.[38] "After completing the agreement on September 26 a jubilant Mr. Icahn donned the pilot's coat of Harry Hoglander, the head of the pilots union, which had spearheaded the drive against Mr. Lorenzo for Mr. Icahn, and he ran around his office shouting: 'We've got ourselves an airline! We've got ourselves an airline!' "[39]

Icahn's originally stated plan was to buy the stock of all minority shareholders at $19.50 in cash and $4.50 in preferred stock, thereby taking it private. Paine Webber, however, had trouble getting the financing together. Icahn had typically used Drexel Burnham Lambert, "the dominant player in junk bonds," but they had been unavailable because they were working for Lorenzo. When Paine Webber was unable to meet its deadline for financing, Icahn turned to Drexel Burnham Lambert to complete the transaction.[40] The major reason given for the failure to secure financing was the unexpectedly high airline losses; TWA lost money in the third quarter of 1985, a quarter that was typically TWA's strongest one. An additional reason cited was the potential of a strike with the flight attendants.[41]

Icahn in collaboration with Drexel Burnham Lambert began to restructure the financing. Citing the heavy losses in the industry, Icahn began negotiating with the TWA Board of Directors to lower the cash amount on stocks and increasing the no-cash preferred stock. He offered something in the vicinity of $15 in cash, and the rest in preferred stock.

Seeing an opening, Lorenzo reentered the fray and put forward a $22 share in cash bid, and offered to negotiate with the unions.[42] TWA brought Lorenzo's bid up at a meeting with the unions and it was "bitterly turned aside" by ALPA and IAM. "They said that their members might take steps to disrupt the operations of the airline during the six months it would take to complete a merger."[43] IFFA, having not been successful negotiating with Icahn, said they would study *any* offers. In the absence of overall union support which could translate into major difficulties for the airline, with no other viable buyer coming forward, and a board now leaning toward Icahn support, a lower bid from Icahn was accepted. TWA and Icahn first agreed to lower the bid to $11 in cash with $13 being given in preferred stock. As the losses continued to grow, in the end, the offer would be no cash and $24 in preferred stock. And, Icahn would only purchase half of the remaining stock available.[44] By not giving out any money to the purchase of the stock of minority shareholders, Icahn anticipated having $750 million. Drexel Burnham Lambert came up "short" citing the bad financial shape of the airline for the lower $660 million.[45] In allegations denied by Icahn, the charge was that Icahn asked Drexel Burnham Lambert to come up short so that he could change the deal. Icahn said that he would use the available money to "help the carrier ride out its losses, withstand a threatened strike by flight attendants and buy planes." Another possibility was to merge TWA with another airline, such as Northwest or American.[46]

On January 3, 1986, Icahn owned an airline. By a combination of strategies, in collaboration with segments of organized labor, he had defeated TWA and Lorenzo, and stepped into his first real test as an owner versus liquidator.

NOTES

1. William A. Jolley, *Plaintiff IFFA's Suggestions in Opposition to Defendant TWA's Motion to Dismiss* (Kansas City, MO: 1986), 109.
2. IFFA, *Hotline*, May 20, 1985.
3. Ibid., May 24, 1985.
4. Ibid., May 31, 1985.
5. "Carl Icahn would Oust TWA President if Takeover Successful," *Aviation Daily*, May 30, 1985.
6. Eric Schmidt and Kenneth N. Gilpin, "Consultant Guided Icahn's T.W.A. Bid," *New York Times*, April 1, 1986.

7. Drexel Burnham Lambert known for junk bonds, often managed by Michael Milken, filed for bankruptcy 1990.

8. IFFA v. TWA (W. D. Missouri, Bad Faith Bargaining 1988), Exhibit 511.

9. Mark Stevens, *King Icahn: The Biography of a Renegade Capitalist* (NY: Dutton, Penguin Books, 1993).

10. Fred R. Bleakley, "T.W.A.'s Brief, Futile Battle," *New York Times*, June 24, 1985.

11. TWA, *TWA Skyliner*, Special Issue, "TWA vs. Icahn," May 20, 1985.

12. IFFA v. TWA (W. D. Missouri, Bad Faith Bargaining 1988), R. Pearson Deposition, 116.

13. TWA, *TWA Skyliner*, Special Issue, "TWA vs. Icahn," May 20, 1985.

14. Ibid., quote from TWA's Petition to DOT. They were specifically opposed to his voiced plans for the airline but generally opposed to his reputation for not running companies but for selling them off in bits and pieces.

15. John S. DeMott, Madeleine J. Nash, and Adam Zagorin, "Three Who Watch, Wait and Strike," *Time*, March 4, 1985.

16. Colin Leinster, "Carl Icahn's Calculated Bets," *Fortune*, March 18, 1985, 142–48.

17. John S. DeMott, Madeleine J. Nash, and Adam Zagorin, "Three Who Watch, Wait and Strike," *Time*, March 4, 1985.

18. John S. DeMott, Lee Griggs, and Frederick Ungeheuer, "The High Price of Freedom," *Time*, March 18, 1985. Prior to this, "Icahn's most controversial takeover before his current fight with Phillips came in 1982, when he went after Dan River, a Virginia textile company. Residents of Danville rose up in protest against the aggressor from the North, and more than 100 of them began buying Dan River stock as a sign of local support. After 6 months of struggle, company officers bought up the public stock and turned Dan River into a private firm. Icahn, who had started buying shares at $12 sold out for $22.50, for a total profit of $8.5 million. After his victory, Icahn named his new German shepherd attack dog Shiloh in honor of the Civil War battle in which the North defeated the South." John S. DeMott, Madeleine J. Nash, and Adam Zagorin, "Three Who Watch, Wait and Strike," *Time*, March 4, 1985.

19. May 20, 1985, advertisement appearing in *New York Times* and *Wall Street Journal*.

20. William A. Jolley, *Plaintiff IFFA's Suggestions in Opposition to Defendant TWA's Motion to Dismiss* (Kansas City, MO: 1986), 109.

21. IFFA, *Hotline*, June 7, 1985.

22. Thomas Petzinger, Jr, *Hard Landing: The Epic Contest for Power and Profits that Plunged the Airlines into Chaos* (Armonk, NY: M.E. Sharp, 1995), 102.

23. Aaron Bernstein, *Grounded: Frank Lorenzo and the Destruction of Eastern Airlines* (New York: Simon and Schuster, 1990).

24. IFFA v. TWA (W. D. Missouri, Bad Faith Bargaining 1988), Transcripts, 3881.

25. IFFA, *Hotline*, June 19, 1985.

26. Ibid., June 28, 1985.

27. IFFA, *The 630 News: The Official Publication*, Summer 1985, 12.

28. Ibid., 16.

29. John Crudele, "23-a-Share T.W.A. Bid is Reported," *New York Times*, June 14, 1985; "TWA Deal," *Telegraph*, June 14, 1985.

30. Mark Potts, "Texas Air to Acquire TWA Inc.," *Washington Post*, June 14, 1985.
31. Rodney A. Snyder, *Negotiating with Terrorists: TWA Flight 847* (Washington, DC: Georgetown University, 1988).
32. Robert Thomas, Jr., "John Testrake, 68, T.W.A. Pilot Who Became Hero in Hijacking," *New York Times*, February 7, 1996; "She (Purser Uli Derickson) Deserves the Congressional Medal of Honor," *TWA Skyliner*, July 1, 1985; "Chronology of Hostage Crisis," washingtonpost.com, Sunday, June 30, 1985; "T.W.A. Purser is Hailed as Courageous," *New York Times*, July 1, 1985.
33. IFFA v. TWA (W. D. Missouri, Bad Faith Bargaining 1988), Transcripts, 3878–88.
34. Bryan Burrough, "Union Officials Question Icahn Pact on TWA," *Wall Street Journal*, July 5, 1985.
35. William A. Jolley, *Plaintiff IFFA's Suggestions in Opposition to Defendant TWA's Motion to Dismiss* (Kansas City, MO: 1986), 137–138; IFFA v. TWA (W. D. Missouri, Bad Faith Bargaining 1988), Transcripts, 3957–59. Icahn defended the importance of being a man of his word on Capitol Hill when refuting TWA management's assertion to the contrary. John Weir Close, *A Giant Cow-Tipping by Savages: The Boom, Bust, and Boom Culture of M&A* (New York: Palgrave Macmillan, 2013), 81.
36. Jonathan Hicks, "Texas Air Halts Pact with T.W.A.," *New York Times*, September 14, 1985.
37. Associated Press, "Icahn Acquires Rest of T.W.A.," *New York Times*, September 27, 1985.
38. "Executive Changes," *New York Times*, September 24, 1985. Icahn had already made it clear in May that he would remove Meyer from presidency once he owned the airline, and the transition to Pearson had been announced after the earlier agreement with Texas Air, with the planned departure being at the conclusion of the Texas Air merger.
39. "T.W.A. Deal: Losses Shaped Tactics," *New York Times*, January 6, 1986. This story was often repeated, always with slightly varying in details. "By August 20, he had a victory. On that day, hearing by phone that the TWA board had rebuffed a Lorenzo bid that topped his own, Icahn donned the jacket and cap of a TWA pilot and marched around his office proclaiming, We got ourselves an airline." Carol Loomis, "The Comeuppance of Carl Icahn," *Fortune*, February 1986.
40. Agis Salpukas, "Icahn Said to Ask for New Funds," *New York Times*, November 28, 1985.
41. Agis Salpukas, "Icahn Said to Weigh Shift in Bid," *New York Times*, December 9, 1985.
42. "T.W.A. Studies New Icahn Bid," *New York Times*, December 18, 1985.
43. "T.W.A. Deal: Losses Shaped Tactics," *New York Times*, January 6, 1986.
44. Agis Salpukas, "Icahn Gets Control of T.W.A.," *New York Times*, January 4, 1986.
45. Connie Bruck, *The Predators' Ball: The Junk-Bond Raiders and the Man Who Staked Them* (New York: Simon and Schuster, 1988).
46. Agis Salpukas, "Icahn is Closing in on T.W.A.," *New York Times*, January 3, 1986; Agis Salpukas, "Icahn Gets Control of T.W.A.," *New York Times*, January 4, 1986.

Chapter 4

Labor Deals with Icahn

White Knight or Predator?

The deal struck between ALPA and IAM with Icahn, heralded at the time as an innovative template for labor and management relations, a deal that both unions would sorely regret later, was forged without IFFA. Negotiations with Icahn never looked positive for the flight attendants. Despite being a part of a coalition, it became difficult to see which side the pilots and machinists were on. The pilots took center stage in these negotiations, Icahn is impressed with IAM and seemingly somewhat intimidated, and Icahn and IFFA were at odds from their very first meeting.

Representing the labor coalition, Freeman and Keilin had approached Icahn on their behalf and set up a meeting between the coalition and Icahn on June 27, 1985, three days before the final conclusion of the hostage crisis. This would be the very first meeting between Icahn and Frankovich, but ALPA's Hoglander had met Icahn at his home earlier in the month and there was some indication that Icahn met someone from the machinists as well. As detailed later in court, Icahn was unclear whether he had also met with anyone from IAM. What everyone was clear on was that this was the first meeting with Icahn and Frankovich, and she believed that both ALPA and IAM had met with Icahn before and she raised that issue at the meeting. She clearly felt that she was coming into the meeting at a disadvantage with both unions farther ahead in their dealings with Icahn.

Prior to their meeting with Icahn, the coalition met with Freeman and Keilin at the IFFA offices. The investment bankers pointed out that Lorenzo was offering a financial inducement to Icahn to refrain from voting against the merger, and the dual goals of the meeting should be to convince Icahn not to take the offer from Lorenzo, and to consider a bid for the ownership of TWA with some kind of employee equity arrangement.[1] The investment bankers gave the coalition a heads up that Icahn was probably going to be talking in the range of 20 percent reductions.[2]

According to Frankovich in court testimony, when they met that evening, Icahn set the tenor by telling them:

> [H]e was here at our request, and, as he understood it, we needed him, and he wanted it to be very clear from the outset that he could make his money by taking his deal with Lorenzo and going, but if there was something we could work out here, it was fine.
>
> He wanted to do it fast. He did not have a lot of time to spend on this deal. He had other deals pending. "If we don't work out a deal, that is fine. We could shake hands and leave and be friends." He wanted to know upfront were we going to be able to do it or not, because it had to be done fast.[3]

Icahn said he needed 20 percent, or approximately a $300 million reduction in the labor costs at TWA in order to consider purchasing the airline. Frankovich described the meeting:

> Mr. Icahn asked each of the groups to tell him what they thought about his offer. We started with ALPA, who was at the far end of the table, and Harry Hoglander said that he thought they could agree to a 20 percent concessions, and he had a few little details that he talked about.
>
> It went on to the IAM. Brian Freeman and Tim Conley did the talking for the IAM . . . Basically, Tim Conley was saying, "The IAM does not make concessions. We are not going to start now. It is sure not going to be 20 percent. No way." After some discussion and debate back and forth between Mr. Icahn and Mr. Conley, Mr. Conley conceded as how possibly the IAM could agree to a ten percent equity investment, and that was it. There was not going to be any more than that. That was all they could do.
>
> For my part, I told Mr. Icahn that I had not been party to any of the discussions they had had before and I really was not in a position tonight to make the kind of commitment that he was talking about. I would have to talk to my negotiating committee and my executive board, but that I thought preliminarily I could tell him that 20 percent was an enormous cut for flight attendants, and I did not know that we would be able to do that.
>
> I thought that I could probably persuade the board that what we would have to do would be a ten percent cut and maybe we could deal with something in the vicinity of [an additional] five percent in productivity.[4]

According to Frankovich, Icahn replied, "Everybody else knows what is going on here. How come you don't know what is going on? Everybody knew what this deal was." And she responded, "Hey, I had no other meetings than this, and you have to take me at my word. . . . You are going to have to give me a couple days to get back to you."[5]

After separate caucuses and group discussions, the three unions agreed that, since the pilots were ready to make an agreement that night, they should proceed forward. IAM and IFFA left late that night, and Icahn and ALPA stayed until around 4 AM and entered into a tentative agreement which they would sign on July 2, 1985. The pilots offered 20 percent to snap back in 1988, and in exchange, they would gain equity and profit sharing. Seen as a protection from Icahn's past raiding maneuvers, they connected the concessions to a requirement that Icahn restrict the selling of TWA assets and maintain capital spending.[6]

Part of the agreement listed the schedule of future negotiations where Icahn would seek concessions first from IAM and then shortly after from IFFA: one week to negotiate with IAM with ten days to ratify and 1 week to negotiate with IFFA, with thirty days to ratify. ALPA also agreed that they would cross other employee picket lines in the event of a strike.[7]

This timetable never got off the ground. Frankovich did not meet with Icahn again until the first week in August. There was a lot of negotiating going on in July between Icahn and ALPA and IAM, phone conversations with IFFA, but Icahn's goal to complete agreement quickly was not met.

Icahn met several times with representatives of IAM, but the one—short—meeting with John Peterpaul, General Vice President of IAM convinced him that they would not go over 15 percent. Icahn summed up his impression of him: "Peterpaul struck me as a very shrewd negotiator. He knew what he wanted, he knew what he would give." Icahn then turned back to ALPA and said, "You guys have to decide to give more or there is going to be no deal. They aren't going to give any more. It is amazing they are giving anything."[8] ALPA pushed back but Icahn did not budge. He said, "You can never get this guy (Peterpaul) on the phone. He appeared from nowhere at this one meeting, maybe on the phone one other time. Then he disappeared. . . . I told them that was it. I told the pilots you have to give more to compensate. Otherwise forget it."[9] Peterpaul's seeming unavailability worked to IAM's benefit, and Icahn never really changed his opinion of Peterpaul and accepted that IAM would not go higher.

Negotiations in the month of July are complex: Peterpaul was shrewd and unavailable; the pilots were telling him he could get more from IAM; Drexel Burnham Lambert was telling Icahn to make a deal with Lorenzo because he was "not going to ever get a deal with the IAM"; and, Icahn was telling the pilots that they had to give more.[10] Plus, Lorenzo had sweetened "his offer to Mr. Icahn to $50 million not to oppose" his merger plans with TWA.[11]

Icahn's dealings with the flight attendants were very different. While Icahn was going back and forth with IAM and ALPA, IFFA was on hold. Frankovich, who resided in California but as President worked in New York City, remained in New York over weekends in the month of July because

Icahn "kept telling me, you know, the deal is going to happen right away. We are going to get it done."[12] Conversations that they did have revolved around the status of the negotiations with IAM and when IFFA was going to be able to start. In the latter part of July, Freeman told Frankovich that IAM would probably do a 15 percent reduction with a snap-back. Based on this information and because it looked like the negotiations with IAM and ALPA were finalizing, Frankovich told Keilin that she thought it was time for her to meet with Icahn.[13] Icahn, however, "is just not ready to meet yet." Shortly thereafter, Frankovich called Icahn to set up a meeting and, according to her, he expressed his busyness and "did not know at that point when he would be available." Icahn did confirm that it looked as if IAM was giving 15 percent and that ALPA would increase their original 20 percent offer.[14]

THE WEEKEND: "YOU SHOULD HAVE BEEN THERE"

The first weekend in August turned out to be a critical one in the negotiations that led to Icahn's ownership of TWA. The outcome of this long weekend reverberated throughout all of the negotiations going forward and characterized the major parties in the eventual labor conflict.

Icahn called Frankovich on Friday morning, August 2, and said he thought the deal would happen this weekend. Frankovich, who had remained in town over multiple weekends when the deal was supposed to happen said to Icahn, "This is an old song now. I keep hearing from you as the weekends draw close that the deal is going to happen. Why do you think this weekend is any different than the other weekends so far?" Icahn replied, "No, I really think it is going to happen this weekend." Icahn told Frankovich, "I think you ought to be sure to be here."

Frankovich explained that she could meet with him on that day, Friday, or on Sunday but she had a family commitment on Saturday in California. She and her husband were hosting his grammar school reunion and guests were flying in for the event. According to IFFA counsel, "Once Frankovich identified the one day that was a problem, Icahn said, 'Well, Saturday is the day you got to be here.'" IFFA counsel further argued that Icahn had a "penchant" for insisting "on specific meeting times after ascertaining Frankovich's problem with or unavailability on a particular date"[15]

After more discussion in which Frankovich suggested meeting right away, Icahn rejected it and reiterated "It is going to have to be . . . this weekend . . . you are going to have to be here Saturday."[16] Frankovich pointed out that a deal could be made on Friday or Sunday and that she "saw no reason to specifically have to be present on Saturday." In the end, Icahn set a meeting with her for that afternoon. Frankovich and Jolley met with Icahn in his office. According to Frankovich:

> Icahn began by saying that he had to get the deal taken care of, that time was slipping away, that he had to have the $300 million. He said that it looked like the pilots were going to go more than twenty, but that he did not know by how much. He said that the mechanics were going to go fifteen "and it looked like the stewardesses were going to have to go twenty."[17]

According to Frankovich, he used "stewardesses, and girls" to refer to flight attendants throughout this meeting.[18] Frankovich made numerous arguments explaining why flight attendants should not be asked to cover more than IAM, but Icahn did not move away from the 20 percent. In court testimony, she said that what IFFA was offering:

> was already more than he was getting from the IAM, because, as I understood the terms that they were discussing, the $2 an hour wage cut was going to be like somewhere—13 percent or so in wages or 11 percent if you were talking about taking it from wages and benefits [aggregate], so he was getting a far better deal already at a 15 percent offer from us.
>
> We had to have a snapback, and we would give him a "B" scale, and I told him that, in my opinion, the "B" scale over the long term would do what he needed to do in terms of the composition of the work force, would lower the unit cost, and he said, "Listen, my deal is 20 percent, and if you want a 20 percent deal, you better stay this weekend."
>
> The way the meeting ended, as I recall, is that I told him I had plans on Saturday, as I had told him. If there was a possibility that we could have a deal that was comparable to the IAM, not his 20, but comparable to the IAM, that I would stay on Saturday. If that was not possible, then I was leaving, that I would give him my home phone number. The committee would be available in New York. We could meet again as soon as I got back, Sunday if he wanted.
>
> He told me the deal was 20 percent, and he thought I ought to stay for the weekend. I left, and I think that is about it.[19]

Before leaving, they agreed to meet again on Monday, August 5, 1985. Meetings did take place throughout that weekend, concluding around noon on Monday, August 5. ALPA renegotiated its earlier offer and agreed to a 26 percent wage and benefit concession, with 4 percent coming from a deferred wage increase and 4 percent which could be traded for productivity improvements. IAM would make an agreement along the lines previously discussed, a $2.00 an hour pay reduction with the elimination of a 2 percent employer contribution to retirement, subject to ratification by members within fifteen days. Both agreements included five-year "b-scales" for new hires.

Both agreements also included snap-backs; ALPA's was an optional snap-back that "allowed them not to snap-back if they chose instead to continue an agreement that would ward off Mr. Lorenzo coming back in."[20] In return, they each received stock ownership and profit sharing, proportionate to their contribution to the overall concessionary request of $300 million from employees. Based on these agreements and on the same day, Icahn purchased "over 2 million" more shares of TWA stock.[21]

The meeting between Icahn and Frankovich, with their respective advisors, would be moved to Tuesday, August 6. In that meeting, Icahn explained the deals with ALPA and IAM each carrying a snap-back. As IFFA counsel described the meeting:

> Icahn told Frankovich that she *should have been there for the weekend.* And told her that, *"Your deal is 20 percent"* (tr. 3955). Icahn then told Frankovich that *he had entered into an agreement with the pilots that specified that the Flight Attendant portion would be between 20 and 22 percent of the aggregate* (tr. 3958).[22]

There is nothing in this information from Icahn that set well with Frankovich. From this time on, Icahn would repeatedly bring up the fact that Frankovich had not been at the meeting, and as he depicted it, she had gone to a "party" instead. There is substantial disagreement as to whether Icahn told Frankovich to be *at* the meeting or to be *in* New York available in case the other deals were made. IFFA counsel argued that "Frankovich was never asked to *attend a meeting* that weekend, nor has Icahn ever accused her of not attending *a meeting*. She was simply told by Icahn to *remain* available (so that they could meet *after* he concluded his deals with ALPA and IAM—which did not occur, in fact, until Monday)."[23] And, again, according to IFFA counsel, when Frankovich and Icahn met on August 6, and Icahn told Frankovich that:

> she should have been there for the weekend meeting, and Frankovich reminded Icahn that there had been no specific meeting set up for the weekend but that, rather, Icahn had wanted her to be *available* during the weekend.[24]

TWA's counsel and Icahn in deposition argued that Icahn wanted her to be "at" the meeting, not merely "available." According to TWA counsel, "Mr. Icahn told Ms. Frankovich that he would be meeting with the other two unions over the weekend of August 3 to make a final deal, and urged her to attend."[25]

Icahn recalled:

> This was how I remember thinking about it from a negotiating posture. It is very important she come to the August 3rd meeting because in my mind I felt that it was possible at that meeting and at that meeting only to close this deal, that you might get them—you might get the IAM up a couple percent to close it.

> I figured if I get them up to 2 percent in keeping with what you are saying that IFFA would also go up 2 percent, and that was the 2 percent we needed to make the deal.[26]

Icahn reported being annoyed, angry, and stalemated that Frankovich did not attend the meeting, and that she was insane, acting with sheer stupidity, "it was like I was talking to a child . . ." "I was amazed. I couldn't believe how somebody would not come to a meeting that was so important."[27]

IAM's Peterpaul who had brokered the original figure of 15 percent for the machinists, was not at the meeting, and according to Icahn, "we were on the phone to him but he wasn't there."[28] Nor was Icahn. He had left the negotiating with IAM and ALPA up to his advisors until Sunday afternoon. Frankovich had told him that the negotiating team was available to meet and that she could be there physically on Sunday, and on the phone all weekend. As it turned out, ALPA and IAM did not conclude their separate agreements until Monday August 5. None of which mattered in the depiction of Frankovich by Icahn in the months and years that followed.[29]

When Icahn and Frankovich met that Tuesday, and Icahn began his refrain, you should have been there, Frankovich thought he was joking. Frankovich had stayed in town for three weekends in a row in July and when he told her to stay for this weekend, she saw it just like the weekends before. She spoke with her negotiating committee and the executive board and they both said—don't bother. When Icahn further said "you could have had a deal," she laughed because she couldn't believe it.[30]

On Wednesday, August 7, IFFA offered to go up to 17 percent (15% wage cut plus productivity at 2%), but Icahn said it was "too late." According to him, he could not go back and ask for more from IAM playing one union off the other, although he had renegotiated with ALPA. Now that he had shored up two of the three major unions, he did not need to negotiate with the flight attendants.[31] In deposition, in questioning by IFFA counsel:

> *Jolley:* Seven months went by after that weekend in August and March 6 when the strike started, roughly, from August the 2nd to March 6th?
>
> *Icahn:* Yes.
>
> *Jolley:* Are you saying that there was a deal that could have been made, then, that couldn't be made later?
>
> *Icahn:* Absolutely correct.[32]

Frankovich was skeptical about what *would have* taken place at that meeting, and doubted that there was a deal to be made:

> Nonsense. If the 15 percent deal was available on Saturday, why wasn't it available on Monday? This is typical Icahn. He creates diversionary tactics, finding a way to shift responsibility for his stubborn position from himself to those he is negotiating with. But the truth is, if I had camped out in Icahn's office all of June and July it wouldn't have made any difference. He'd never made us a 15 percent or even a 17 percent offer, and he wasn't going to.[33]

Reaching agreements with IAM and ALPA, Icahn began purchasing more TWA stock. Going forward, he showed no interest in negotiating with the flight attendants below 20–22 percent, and as Icahn stated, he "wasn't in the mood to compromise."[34]

Based on his alliance with the pilots, he had a further inducement to resist IFFA's increased offer (15% plus 2). ALPA agreed to cross employee picket lines in the event of a strike, and although IAM did not enter into such an agreement, their existing contract with TWA already had a no-strike clause.

Even though pilots across the airlines were becoming more "union like" in the tumultuous climate of the eighties, there had been no indication that TWA pilots would support other employee strikes, and in the case of the flight attendants, they had demonstrated open hostility. Prior to the 1980s, ALPA which is a member of AFL-CIO, had been known as a conservative union:

> For the past 20 years, ALPA's 47 Locals have amounted to a loose confederation of individualists who practically ignored the Union Headquarters in Washington and usually crossed picket lines of other Unions. But after absorbing 52 concession contracts since 1981, the pilots have made good on their pledge by giving ALPA leaders much stronger control over bargaining.[35]

IFFA positively acknowledged these changes in ALPA's union identity, and hoped for such changes at the local TWA level. "A good start would be the cessation of its juvenile attitude towards Flight Attendants." One such example was the pilots' attitude about XCAP. According to IFFA:

> Ever since IFFA won the XCAP Arbitration Award giving us priority to First Class seating over pilots, ALPA has been on a warpath. Not only has it filed suit in Federal District Court, but many pilots are removing Flight Attendants from First Class because of 'aircraft weight,' Flight Attendant appearance, and the like. A better alternative would be, we think, for ALPA to act like a Union . . . and to recognize the job that our Union did in *securing* this benefit in *our* contract with TWA. Our benefits, in comparison to those received by pilots, are slim. It is unbecoming and certainly unlike a 'real Union' to react so pettily when we manage to obtain a better benefit.

This statement in IFFA publication, *630 News*, came after IFFA reprinted a pilot's letter to the editor of TWA ALPA's newsletter, *Lancet*, that read in part, "Firstly, the XCAP situation. It is degrading, even in its conception, to compare the status of professional airline pilots to that of cabin service employees." IFFA responded:

> If anything is degrading, it is the publication of such a comment . . . designed solely to further inflame the unwarranted and hostile attitude of pilots towards Flight Attendants. We have News for those in ALPA fostering this attitude. We are professionals, and every bit as professional as pilots. Yes, pilots have the skill of flying a sophisticated aircraft. But we perform service, we react in safety and emergency situations and we . . . more than any single workforce within this Company . . . are responsible for repeat passenger business.[36]

IFFA concluded with an acknowledgment to those pilots at TWA who do respect the flight attendants and ended by saying that "Our quarrel is with ALPA itself and with the many pilots who demean us and undermine our Union efforts to enhance our careers."[37]

When Frankovich met with Icahn on that Tuesday following the weekend negotiations, she found out that he had promised the pilots that he would get 20–22 percent from the flight attendants. According to Icahn, part of the ALPA agreement was that he would use his "best efforts" to get 20–22 percent from the flight attendants.[38] He later explained that Hoglander did not want to be "embarrassed" by "an agreement with IFFA that was so much lower than his." Icahn did not take too seriously his agreement, later explaining, "My understanding of this was cosmetics, and that I was pretty free to do what I wanted . . . "[39] When Icahn met with Frankovich on that Tuesday, he was steadfast in demanding 20 percent and used his agreement with ALPA as justification. According to her:

> I said, "You have made your good faith effort. You say that is what you want. I am telling you that you are not going to get it so you have complied with your ALPA agreement. Let's go on and make whatever best agreement we can here."
>
> He responded, "No, I am a man of my word. I have made a promise and I am not going to do anything that is going to adversely affect their possibilities of ratification . . . . The deal is twenty."[40]

Frankovich was furious that he had dealt with another union over the fate of IFFA. According to court documents, "Frankovich told Icahn it was a mistake for him to enter into [an agreement with] some other work force that controlled what he had to do with Flight attendants.." and Frankovich said, "It looks as though the pilots have signed our agreement for us."[41] In a Friday, August 9, 1985 Hotline, IFFA reported to its members:

> IFFA has not reached agreement with Mr. Icahn . . . because of hurdles and obstacles unnecessarily placed in our way by the Pilot Union, ALPA. The ALPA agreement with Icahn specifically requires Icahn to seek concession reductions from IFFA between 20 percent and 22 percent of our salary and benefits. This would represent reductions in our salary alone to between $7,000 and $7,700 per year. IFFA met with Icahn on Friday, August 2 and Wednesday, August 7 and offered concessions of 15 percent . . . the same percentage accepted by the IAM. Icahn rejected IFFA's offer because he promised ALPA that he would seek 20 percent to 22 percent reductions from Flight Attendants. ALPA has made it clear to Mr. Icahn that its ratification of its agreement depends on Mr. Icahn fulfilling his commitment.[42]

This weekend was a critical one in Icahn's bid for ownership and a difficult one for IFFA. First, IFFA's position was always one of comparability with IAM, the labor force that they saw themselves as parallel to, and that Pearson treated as parallel. For example, the average salary and benefits for IAM and IFFA employees were $44,000 and $39,000, respectively. The issue of comparability formed the basis of IFFA's negotiating position. There was no indication that Icahn ever saw, and definitely never treated them, as comparable.

FLIGHT ATTENDANTS ARE NOT BREADWINNERS

There would be no face-to-face meetings between Icahn and Frankovich from their August 6 meeting until December 9, 1985. From the very first meeting between them on that first weekend in August, the situation for the flight attendants went from bad to worse. It was in the first meeting on that Friday afternoon, August 2, that Icahn explained why he was asking more from the flight attendants than any other group. His explanation galvanized the flight attendants over unequal treatment and reverberated throughout the labor conflict and its aftermath. Frankovich, in court testimony, recounted:

> I told him I did not understand why he would be concluding an agreement with the IAM at 15 and saying that he had to have 20 percent from us. His initial explanation was that the mechanics were skilled work force, to which I responded by saying, "Flight attendants likewise are a skilled work force."
>
> . . . I listed a number of items of difficulties about the job . . . different things that I thought were indications of the skill level of the work force.
>
> His response was that the IAM was able to show that the mechanics were competitive with the industry, and I told him that we were likewise competitive with the industry. I told him that our salaries leapfrogged in contracts because people had three-year contracts that overlapped.
>
> . . . He said, "No, you are missing it. You are missing it. You don't understand what I am talking about is the marketplace. You don't understand the

marketplace. I can hire a mechanic for the same thing I am going to pay him for, but you, you are different." He said—this is a much shortened version of a long conversation. It was heated. He was saying, "You got a glamorous job. You lay around in hotels in Paris. Lots of people would like to do your job. I can get people to do your job for a lot less than you want." He said, "See that woman? See that girl? See that girl on the street out there? That is a stewardess."

. . . In any event, we went back and forth about skill levels and qualifications, and I was attempting to say that flight attendants were likewise skilled and we were competitive in the marketplace, we were competitive with other groups. That was not working, so I switched arguments, and I said, "The IAM does not only represent skilled employees. Assume that, in fact, flight attendants are not as skilled as mechanics. There are other work groups within this group who you are agreeing to a 15 percent cut who are not as skilled as flight attendants, either comparably skilled or lesser skilled," and I made an analogy, and I specifically asked him, "Why would you agree to a 15 percent cut for a janitor and demand more from a flight attendant when we are paid about the same." His response was, "A janitor is a breadwinner. He probably has got a family at home to support." He said, either, "You girls or stewardesses," and I don't remember which term he used in that context, because he used those terms interchangeably throughout the conversation, "you are second incomes, and you don't need the money."

We argued rather vehemently about the question of whether or not it was true that women were second incomes. I was irate at his comment, and I told him so. The conversation continued, and at some point, I told him, "Listen, the flight attendants are not going to accept this kind of disproportionate treatment," and I don't recall the exact words I used, but I was sticking with the IAM argument, you know.

"They are at 15 percent. You are demanding more from us." I believe what I told him was that they would not accept this kind of disproportionate, disparate, discriminatory—I am not sure which one of those words I used—treatment. "They are not going to accept this kind of difference."

His response was, "Well, what are you going to do about it? Are you going to blow up the airplanes? Are you going to burn down the airline?" About that time, I think we took a break, because we were heated . . . [43]

Icahn's description in his court deposition of this meeting affirmed that there was a discussion of breadwinners, but he related that he was sticking up for janitors and their financial needs while Frankovich was dismissing them:

I said, Look, I said, This business, I said, some of these people are giving up more than 15 percent because they are giving $2 an hour, and if you are a porter and you are giving up—you are a janitor giving up $2 an hour on 11, 12, 14, you are giving up more. You are giving up 20 percent.

She said, well they are just janitors. I said, well, and they are breadwinners, too. That is how the whole thing came up.

> That is how I was putting it. They are breadwinners, too. You have to think of them, too, I said.[44]

U.S. District Court Judge Sachs later in his opinion in the bad faith bargaining case accepted "for this ruling the firm trial testimony of Frankovich, insofar as it departs from the deposition testimony of Icahn, which seems somewhat unsure as to exact dates and statements, and at one point in phrasing seems calculated"[45] Judge Sachs, accepting Frankovich's testimony, referred to Icahn's breadwinner comment as a "debating point that boomeranged."[46] There were other statements, however, that raised whether this was merely a debating point or a viewpoint that influenced his disparate treatment of the flight attendants. Again from his deposition, IFFA counsel asked him "Did you ever tell Vicki Frankovich that flight attendants were stewardesses were second incomes" to which Icahn replied:

> I might have said in many cases they are second incomes. I don't think I categorized the whole thing as second incomes.
>
> . . . I don't think I said it as a general thing. I might have said it, that in certain cases or in a number of cases they don't.
>
> . . . I don't believe that. I believe a lot of them have to—need the income. I never believed they don't.
>
> Question from IFFA counsel: Do you believe that a lot of them don't?
>
> Answer: I believe there is a number of them that don't.[47]

When Icahn acknowledged that there might be flight attendants who were breadwinners, he did not change his argument to bring them up to parity with other breadwinners, but rather to bring them down to the reality of women's secondary position in the labor market. Talking about a Kansas City woman who was supporting two kids, he was reported as having said, "Now, I can see she is going to have a tough time, but, you know, people got to accept the realities here."[48]

Icahn's breadwinner comment angered the flight attendants about what they saw as his discrimination against women workers. There would be more comments and more actions that pointed to a differential evaluation of women workers, and in particular, Icahn and TWA's adherence to stereotypes of flight attendants as a basis for unequal treatment.

"WE'VE GOT OURSELVES AN AIRLINE!"

Once Icahn completed agreements with IAM and ALPA, the flight attendants who had been marginalized in the coalition's early dealings with Icahn, were now alone. Frankovich knew that Peterpaul was going to sign with Icahn and asked him to wait, but he said he could not wait.[49] The IAM agreement which was determined to be around 15 percent, was 15 percent of payroll only ($336 million). If aggregate labor costs had been the measure ($465 million), which includes expenses, taxes, benefits, etc., the total concessionary amount would be 11 percent. When Icahn met with Frankovich on Tuesday, August 6, his requirement was 20 percent of the *aggregate* which translated into $57 million versus $38.2 million if he had applied the same payroll only formula he had used to calculate IAM concessions. Thus the disparity between IAM and IFFA was 11 percent versus 20 percent. IFFA counsel showed that the ALPA deal was about $100 million, and the IAM deal $49 million.[50]

With agreements from ALPA and IAM, Icahn escalated purchase of stock, raising his stock to 13.9 million shares or 40.6 percent, and tendering a new offer for TWA. Discarding his original $18 offer, and surpassing Lorenzo's offer of $23, Icahn came in with a $24 a share offer, $19.50 in cash and another $4.50 in new issue preferred stock.[51] The agreement with the pilots and machinists proved to be the deciding factor in his ability to wrestle control out of the hands of Lorenzo. Lorenzo, who by all accounts was the primary player in his own loss, was referred to as having snatched loss out of the jaws of victory. There had been a "standstill" agreement that had been negotiated between Icahn and Leon Black representing Lorenzo, at $16 million plus the money Icahn stood to gain from the profit of stock, but when Black presented the package to Lorenzo, he refused to sign it; he would later offer much more just to be a player in the takeover game at TWA.[52]

The higher stake, combined with the promise of major concessions from two of the carrier's three major unions, positioned the Icahn group to win control of the airline. "Icahn has got all the cards."[53] Icahn's success was tied to his successful agreements with labor. He got agreements that Lorenzo would not have been able to get from labor. Having these agreements with labor increased his ability to get the financing. And, Icahn effectively "dispelled the fear of the workers and T.W.A.'s board that he would liquidate the airline as he has done with some of his past acquisitions." He agreed to maintain capital spending, to use revenue instead of distributing it to stockholders if the airline had no income, and to restrict investments and the sale of assets.[54]

The collaboration between the male unions and Icahn was the first example of such a coalition between labor and a takeover/white knight working together, and it proved to be the turning point in what had been an all-out battle for the airline. "The union concessions are what primarily undercut Mr. Lorenzo's bid."[55]

On September 26, 1985 TWA and Icahn entered into a merger agreement. The story of acquisition would actually not be over, the terms of the agreement would be dramatically altered, Lorenzo would make a reappearance, and all before the final conclusion of ownership in January 1986. But own an airline, he would.

NOTES

1. IFFA v. TWA (W. D. Missouri, Bad Faith Bargaining 1988), Transcripts, 3895.
2. Ibid., 3897.
3. Ibid., 3903.
4. Ibid., 3906–3908.
5. Ibid.
6. Agis Salpukas, "Pilot Pact Puts Curbs on Icahn," *New York Times*, July 4, 1985,
7. IFFA and ALPA were using the same investment banker and Frankovich was angry when she found out that they had signed a no-strike clause and that they made a timetable with them as third. IFFA quit using these investment bankers and made a strategic mistake, used IAM's.
8. IFFA v. TWA (W. D. Missouri, Bad Faith Bargaining 1988), C. Icahn Deposition, 88–91.
9. Ibid., 103.
10. William A. Jolley, *Plaintiff IFFA's Suggestions in Opposition to Defendant TWA's Motion to Dismiss* (Kansas City, MO: 1986), 119.
11. Murray Gartner, *Defendant TWA's Suggestions in Support of Its Motion to Dismiss* (NY: 1987), 60.
12. IFFA v. TWA (W. D. Missouri, Bad Faith Bargaining 1988), Transcripts, 3930.
13. Ibid., 3936.
14. William A. Jolley, *Plaintiff IFFA's Suggestions in Opposition to Defendant TWA's Motion to Dismiss* (Kansas City, MO: 1986), 120.
15. Ibid., 121.
16. Ibid., 122.
17. William A. Jolley, *Plaintiff IFFA's Suggestions in Opposition to Defendant TWA's Motion to Dismiss* (Kansas City, MO: 1986), 123; IFFA v. TWA (W. D. Missouri, Bad Faith Bargaining 1988), Transcripts, 3942–43.
18. IFFA v. TWA (W. D. Missouri, Bad Faith Bargaining 1988), Transcripts, 3947.
19. Ibid., 3948–49.
20. Ibid., 3955.
21. Murray Gartner, *Defendant TWA's Suggestions in Support of Its Motion to Dismiss* (NY: 1987), 64. TWA would also say that "Because he had not also reached an agreement with IFFA, however, he was eventually forced to obtain his financing on more expensive terms than he originally had anticipated." See Exhibit LLLL.
22. William A. Jolley, *Plaintiff IFFA's Suggestions in Opposition to Defendant TWA's Motion to Dismiss* (Kansas City, MO: 1986), 136.
23. Ibid., 127.
24. Ibid., 139.
25. Murray Gartner, *Defandant TWA's Suggestions in Support of Its Motion to Dismiss (NY: 1987)*, 61–62.
26. IFFA v. TWA (W. D. Missouri, Bad Faith Bargaining 1988), C. Icahn Deposition, 127–29.
27. Ibid.
28. Ibid., 88.

29. Ibid., 88–91. Peterpaul's seeming unavailability in July had actually worked to IAM's advantage. The differential characterization and treatment of Peterpaul, as "a shrewd negotiator," and Frankovich, as "a child," is emphasized by IFFA counsel and will later become part of IFFA's charges against Icahn. As IFFA counsel explained:

"Icahn described his frustration with his inability to get ahold of Peterpaul during July; he met with Peterpaul once only; he described Peterpaul as "disappearing" (supra) he described Peterpaul as knowing what he wanted and what he would give (Icahn Deep. 88) who took a position that "they (the IAM) aren't going to be giving any more" (Icahn Deposition., 91). Icahn characterized Peterpaul as a shrewd negotiator. Frankovich took a firm position, had offered to be and was available to meet, and "annoyed" Icahn. Icahn characterizes discussions with Frankovich, inter alia, "like talking to a child." IFFA believes that these characterizations are still more evidence of Icahn's sexually discriminatory attitudes." See Jolley, 131.

30. Vicki Frankovich, interview, St. Louis, MO, July 1989.

31. Ibid.

32. IFFA v. TWA (W. D. Missouri, Bad Faith Bargaining 1988), C. Icahn Deposition, 211.

33. Mark Stevens, *King Icahn: The Biography of a Renegade Capitalist* (NY: Dutton, Penguin Books, 1993), 204–5.

34. William A. Jolley, *Plaintiff IFFA's Suggestions in Opposition to Defendant TWA's Motion to Dismiss* (Kansas City, MO: 1986), 147.

35. IFFA, *The 630 News: The Official Publication*, 1985, from an article in *Business Week* reported by IFFA.

36. IFFA, *The 630 News: The Official Publication*, 1985.

37. Ibid.

38. The agreement was really 20–22 percent from all other employees. Interestingly, the agreement spoke of getting 20–22 percent from *employees* not represented by ALPA and IAM, but Icahn in his deposition only remembers that "I agreed to I thought was my best efforts to get 20 to 22 percent from IFFA." His rendering of the discussion with Hoglander revolves only around IFFA. In contrast, press reports at this time all refer to 20–22 percent for *all* other employees.

39. William A. Jolley, *Plaintiff IFFA's Suggestions in Opposition to Defendant TWA's Motion to Dismiss* (Kansas City, MO: 1986), 138.

40. William A. Jolley, *Plaintiff IFFA's Suggestions in Opposition to Defendant TWA's Motion to Dismiss* (Kansas City, MO: 1986), 137–138; IFFA v. TWA (W. D. Missouri, Bad Faith Bargaining 1988), Transcripts, 3957–59.

41. William A. Jolley, *Plaintiff IFFA's Suggestions in Opposition to Defendant TWA's Motion to Dismiss* (Kansas City, MO: 1986), 137–38.

42. IFFA, *Hotline*, August 9, 1985.

43. IFFA v. TWA (W. D. Missouri, Bad Faith Bargaining 1988), Transcripts, 3943–3948.

44. William A. Jolley, *Plaintiff IFFA's Suggestions in Opposition to Defendant TWA's Motion to Dismiss* (Kansas City, MO: 1986), 128.

45. IFFA v. TWA (W. D. Missouri, Bad Faith Bargaining 1988), Judge H. Sachs, 1988, 14.

46. Ibid.

47. William A. Jolley, *Plaintiff IFFA's Suggestions in Opposition to Defendant TWA's Motion to Dismiss* (Kansas City, MO: 1986), 129–30.

48. IFFA v. TWA (W. D. Missouri, Bad Faith Bargaining 1988), Transcripts, 4013.

49. Vicki Frankovich, interview, St. Louis, MO, July 1989.

50. William A. Jolley, *Plaintiff IFFA's Suggestions in Opposition to Defendant TWA's Motion to Dismiss* (Kansas City, MO: 1986), 133–34.

51. Agis Salpukas, "Icahn Back in T.W.A. Bidding," *New York Times*, August 6, 1985,

52. Connie Bruck, "Kamikaze: How Texas Air's Frank Lorenzo Wrecked His Own Chance to Acquire TWA—and Carl Icahn Picked up the Pieces," *American Lawyer*, December 1985

53. Agis Salpukas, "Icahn Raises T.W.A. Stake to 40.6%," *New York Times*, August 7, 1985.

54. Ibid.

55. Agis Salpukas, "Icahn Closes in on Control of T.W.A.," *New York Times*, August 8, 1985.

Source: Image provided courtesy of The Independent Federation of Flight Attendants Archives, held by Mary Ellen Miller, Kansas City, Missouri.

Source: Image provided courtesy of The Independent Federation of Flight Attendants Archives, held by Mary Ellen Miller, Kansas City, Missouri.

Picket team from Chicago. Source: Image provided courtesy of The Independent Federation of Flight Attendants Archives, held by Mary Ellen Miller, Kansas City, Missouri.

Flight attendants block traffic in a sit-down demonstration at TWA's overhaul base. Source: Image provided courtesy of The Independent Federation of Flight Attendants Archives, held by Mary Ellen Miller, Kansas City, Missouri.

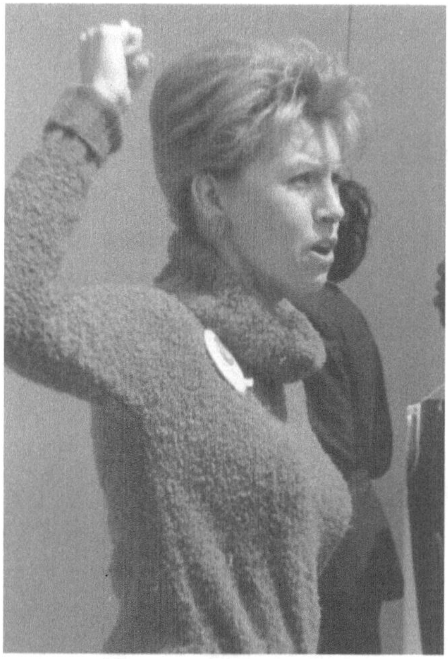

Mary Ellen Miller, IFFA Safety, Legislation and Communication Director. Source: Image provided courtesy of The Independent Federation of Flight Attendants Archives, held by Mary Ellen Miller, Kansas City, Missouri.

Image provided courtesy of The Independent Federation of Flight Attendants Archives, held by Mary Ellen Miller, Kansas City, Missouri.

Image provided courtesy of The Independent Federation of Flight Attendants Archives, held by Mary Ellen Miller, Kansas City, Missouri.

Cesar Chavez, President of the United Farm Workers, with Vicki Frankovich. Source: Image provided courtesy of The Independent Federation of Flight Attendants Archives, held by Mary Ellen Miller, Kansas City, Missouri.

Cesar Chavez

La Paz, Keene, CA 93570

May 1987

Dear Flight Attendant,

As someone who has spent most of my life fighting against what seemed to be impossible odds I am writing to tell you how moved I am by the courageous stand that you have taken.

Several months ago while I was in New York to launch the United Farm Workers' "Wrath of Grapes" boycott campaign, I took the opportunity to stop by your National Headquarters to visit your President, Vicki Frankovich. Although I arrived late in the evening I found the offices filled with your leaders and volunteers who were hard at work on a number of projects that you now know as the "Boycott of Conscience." I was impressed with their individual and collective ability and dedication. When I left that night I was convinced that you <u>can</u> win if you are willing to fight.

I speak from experience. I have spent most of the past 25 years fighting against major corporations whose political and financial resources were far greater than those of the group now known as the United Farm Workers. Like you, we were considered the underdogs with not a chance of success. Our only assets were faith in justice and the determination to win . . . and we did win. That night that I spent at your headquarters watching your leaders and volunteers I knew that you could win too. I saw it in their eyes and read it in their faces. The determination was there.

These are few of the many reasons why I am proud to join your Boycott of Conscience. This is not just a fight against Carl Icahn. It is a fight against those who, like Carl Icahn, choose to exploit workers for personal gain. You must stop him for your own sake as well as for the sake of workers throughout this country. You must help reaffirm the basic right of every U.S. laborer, to earn a decent wage by doing a job under decent conditions with dignity. You must help stop the slow erosion of workers' rights. You have an obligation to help prevent our children and grandchildren from inheriting Icahn's legacy. You MUST AND CAN WIN!!

In solidarity,

Cesar E. Chavez
President

Image provided courtesy of The Independent Federation of Flight Attendants Archives, held by Mary Ellen Miller, Kansas City, Missouri.

Local P-9 on strike at Hormel sharing support with IFFA. Barney Allis Plaza, Kansas City, Missouri. Source: Image provided courtesy of The Independent Federation of Flight Attendants Archives, held by Mary Ellen Miller, Kansas City, Missouri.

Image provided courtesy of The Independent Federation of Flight Attendants Archives, held by Mary Ellen Miller, Kansas City, Missouri.

Karen Lantz, IFFA Vice President, with Eastern Airlines flight attendant Nancy Currier, united in their appeal to "Stop Worker Abuse" by their owners Icahn and Lorenzo. Source: Image provided courtesy of The Independent Federation of Flight Attendants Archives, held by Mary Ellen Miller, Kansas City, Missouri.

IFFA and union supporters picketing outside TWA's Jack Frye Training Center. Source: Image provided courtesy of The Independent Federation of Flight Attendants Archives, held by Mary Ellen Miller, Kansas City, Missouri.

International support from Paris workers. Source: Image provided courtesy of The Independent Federation of Flight Attendants Archives, held by Mary Ellen Miller, Kansas City, Missouri.

Image provided courtesy of The Independent Federation of Flight Attendants Archives, held by Mary Ellen Millen, Kansas City, Missouri.

Vicki Frankovich and Congresswoman Barbara Boxer announce the Boycott of Conscience on the steps of the Capitol. Source: Image provided courtesy of The Independent Federation of Flight Attendants Archives, held by Mary Ellen Miller, Kansas City, Missouri.

Image provided courtesy of The Independent Federation of Flight Attendants Archives, held by Mary Ellen Miller, Kansas City, Missouri.

Image provided courtesy of The Independent Federation of Flight Attendants Archives, held by Mary Ellen Miller, Kansas City, Missouri.

Minneapolis picketers. Source: Image provided courtesy of The Independent Federation of Flight Attendants Archives, held by Mary Ellen Miller, Kansas City, Missouri.

William A. Jolley, IFFA general counsel. Source: Image provided courtesy of The Independent Federation of Flight Attendants Archives, held by Mary Ellen Miller, Kansas City, Missouri.

Flight Attendants in front of the Federal Courthouse in Kansas City, Missouri, during the Bad Faith Bargaining trial. Source: Image provided courtesy of The Independent Federation of Flight Attendants Archives, held by Mary Ellen Miller, Kansas City, Missouri.

Flight attendants and legal counsel at the Supreme Court for the union security case. Source: Image provided courtesy of The Independent Federation of Flight Attendants Archives, held by Mary Ellen Miller, Kansas City, Missouri.

Image provided courtesy of The Independent Federation of Flight Attendants Archives, held by Mary Ellen Miller, Kansas City, Missouri.

Flight attendant Sally Gibson delivers checks from recalled full-term strikers to IFFA Treasurer Bill Hoffman for their Special Assistance Fund to help flight attendants still out of work. Source: Image provided courtesy of The Independent Federation of Flight Attendants Archives, held by Mary Ellen Miller, Kansas City, Missouri.

Image provided courtesy of The Independent Federation of Flight Attendants Archives, held by Mary Ellen Millen, Kansas City, Missouri.

Chapter 5

Off the Line

Strike!

Icahn does not formally take control of TWA until January 1986 but began managerial decision making in the Fall 1985. In October, he withdrew the comprehensive package that had been on the table since NMB recessed negotiations May 21, 1985. When he realized that this offer was still on the table, and *lower* than his offer to IFFA in August, he "raised hell." He recounted:

> I said how the hell can you leave an offer out there when I know I turned down something that was better than that offer?
>
> Everybody sort of got nervous, nobody could give me the answer.
>
> I said get that damn thing off.[1]

TWA informed IFFA that they would be sending them a new comprehensive package. Although much was happening in terms of TWA, its future, and the unresolved flight attendant agreement, there had been almost no contact between the two parties. There had been no NMB negotiating meetings; and, Frankovich had had limited phone calls with Icahn in August, none in September, none in October. What phone conversations they did have ended in deadlock, always, according to Frankovich, punctuated with the refrain "you should have been there."[2] Icahn argued that IAM was competitive in the industry and Frankovich asked for comparison airlines and countered that she could "match it." According to IFFA counsel in court documents, "Frankovich called Icahn to tell him that she had done comparative studies on Flight Attendants and all of the IAM-represented classifications with salaries at Continental Airlines. She give him the information, which Icahn dismissed."[3]

Icahn once claimed that IFFA had received "a lot more" increases than IAM. "Frankovich offered to 'buy' Icahn's deal if she could prove him wrong. (tr. 3966). Icahn was in fact wrong, as TWA would subsequently acknowledge to IFFA."[4] It was also during these conversations that Icahn further characterized the flight attendants in less than positive ways:

> In the post-August telephone conversations with Frankovich—and prior to December—Icahn continued to reveal his perception of Flight Attendants. Thus he told Frankovich that:
>
> > ". . . *stewardesses can't even type*"
> > (tr. 4039, emphasis supplied).
>
> Referring to those Flight Attendants who were either sole wage earners or important family incomes, Icahn retorted:
>
> > ". . . *they should have married a pilot, should have married a rich husband*"
> > (tr. 4039–4040).
>
> And, discounting any value to experience, he told Frankovich:
>
> > "There are *thousands of 19-year Olds* who will do this job" (tr. 4040–4041, emphasis supplied).[5]

Late November, Icahn called Frankovich and said that he was finishing up the acquisition and getting ready to sign the other union deals, and that it was "time to make a deal." He confirmed that they would be sending IFFA a new package.

Just as contract negotiations are heating up, TWA flight attendants celebrated the 50th anniversary of flight attendants at TWA. TWA hired its first "hostesses" in 1935 and flight attendants had their first union contract in 1947. This anniversary only heightened flight attendants' awareness of their historical struggle and its comparison to the struggle they were now in. Frankovich, in her president's report in the Fall of 1985, commented on those parallels:

> 1985 sees us in a new collective bargaining environment. Instead of a set of federal laws allowing sex, age, and race discrimination, we labor under a pro-business political climate where governmental officials routinely turn their backs when it comes to the rights of workers. Instead of dealing with an employer that would have us work underpaid because of the "glamour" of the job, we face an employer insistent on underpaying us because there may be others to take our place. And in many respects our quest for liveable salaries and for dignity in the workplace faces the same hurdles faced by our predecessors over the years.[6]

IFFA told their membership that they anticipated that the new package would be "at least" a 20–22 percent combination of salary and work rule changes.[7] The new package was a staggering twice that. It was a combination of the very first comprehensive package presented to IFFA that incorporated high demands in terms of work rule changes coupled with the elevated wage concessions demanded by Icahn. TWA priced the total concessions between $80 and $110 million. According to IFFA, this December 2, 1985 package represented a 44 percent reduction in their contract—22 percent from wage reductions and 22 percent in increased productivity. This proposal, which would be the basis of the strike to come, would take IFFA from having the best flight attendant contract in the industry and drop it second only to Lorenzo's Continental enforcement of below industry standards.[8] Icahn had originally said he needed a total of $300 million in concessions, but with the pilots, machinists, and noncontract employees he would have $250–275 million. Rather than requesting the remainder from the flight attendants, the package he required from IFFA outreached his original demand to the labor coalition and required massive cuts from the predominantly female labor force.

The flight attendants viewed the combination of wage cuts and work rule changes as a total reversal of all the gains they had made over the years and turned the occupation back to the 1950s and 1960s. The issue of equity had a practical as well as ideological side. The package was so large, many of the flight attendants could not imagine being able to continue in the job under the new conditions. Many of IFFA members could personally give testimonials to what it was like before their independent union and the impression was that they had never got anything free, and in fact, had hurdles put in their way. Their successes, in terms of salary and working conditions that made family life and retirement possible, and the fact they had come by these changes only in the recent past, made them potent forces of solidarity. It may have been one thing to have a "temporary setback," but to go back permanently was too much. To add insult to injury, for the flight attendants, these were to be permanent changes with no snap-back which had been given to machinists and pilots. Their message, often repeated in their publications, it was time "to draw the line."[9]

IFFA received the December 2 comprehensive package from TWA, but Icahn was not at the meeting. IFFA counsel described how it was "indeed comprehensive" and how it put back, with one exception, "virtually every proposal originally submitted to IFFA." IFFA's response was to seek specific costs and implications of each proposal particularly in terms of head count. They also wanted to be able to see which ones could do the most, give the "biggest bang." According to IFFA counsel, "Hoar told the IFFA Committee that TWA needed the entire package . . . and indeed, as subsequent events would show, this was not idle talk."[10]

In a message to its membership, Frankovich and the negotiating team communicated that they were "dismayed that Carl Icahn was not present. In the November 4, 1985 *Skyliner* Icahn spoke of how he does his own negotiating. He said, and we quote, 'I think if the head of the airline sat down with the head of the union, something could be done.'"[11]

Frankovich called Icahn and they met on the evening of December 9. She explained the purpose of the meeting:

> I wanted some indication as to what he seriously thought was possible out of this package. He told me the company was bleeding to death, that the employees had been sucking the life blood out of the company for years, that he had to turn this thing around, that what he asked for was what he needed and that is what he had to have.
>
> I asked him what the value of the package was, because I knew at the table they said it was $88 million, but there were people at 605 [TWA] who had told me it was actually $100 million to $110 million. He said that it is $110 million . . .
>
> I once again brought up the fact that I felt that it was wrong for him to have made a deal with the IAM at 15 percent, and now not only demanding 20 percent, or whatever the percent represented by this new proposal, was onerous and unacceptable and I didn't think he understood the full impact of what he was asking.
>
> He told me it was only two hours a week. "Where did that come from: I have never heard this: What are you talking about?" "Two hours a week is all it is." And his people were telling him that it is really the same as in the industry and the people like it and will be willing to do it.
>
> As to the other work groups, don't talk to me about the IAM. "The IAM is a done deal. If you want the IAM deal, you should have been there in August. You should not have gone off to a party. You are irresponsible. If you had wanted to take care of your people, you should have been there. You shouldn't rely on me to take care of your people."[12]

In December, Frankovich also met with Pearson in an attempt to make a deal. Icahn was not officially the owner yet, and so there was a possibility, though probably slim, that TWA management under Pearson could make a deal with the flight attendants. Frankovich met with Pearson both prior to her December 9 meeting with Icahn and then about a week after that meeting. Pearson said that IFFA was going to have do 20 percent, and Frankovich wanted to know whether he could do the deal, and he responded, "Yeah, I am still president, but, you know, I could be gone any day."[13]

Frankovich met with Pearson again, at his request, after an important TWA Board of Directors meeting on December 17, 1985. There was a resurgence of doubt about Icahn's bid for ownership. Either because he was having difficulty getting the financing because of the worsening economic situation at TWA or he wanted the appearance of difficulty, doubt surfaced about Icahn's merger agreement, and Lorenzo reappeared with a new offer. By this time, the board—half of which were now Icahn appointments—favored Icahn and Frankovich believed that the board wanted the unions to provide an out for them to decline Lorenzo's bid. According to her, the pilots said "there would probably be a wildcat strike . . ." and they "were very supportive of the Icahn agreement . . . and the board of directors would be best advised to not entertain the Lorenzo offer." The machinists concurred and "anticipated that you would not be able to control the IAM membership because they would be so irate about the possibility of Mr. Lorenzo coming in and destroying the lives of the average IAM member." Frankovich, unable to come to agreement with Icahn, conjectured that an agreement with Lorenzo "might be better than no agreement at all." She described her position:

> We did not see many white knights at this point. I suggested to Mr. Pearson and to the board members present that what I really thought would be in the best interests of flight attendants is if the corporation agreed to enter into an agreement with us now, that I thought an agreement was possible.[14]

When Pearson met with Frankovich and Jolley, he said "So you really think a deal is possible" and there was a discussion back and forth. "I think Mr. Jolley suggested to Mr. Pearson that he was the president, he could sit here, sign the deal with us right now and he could go back into the board of directors and say, 'here is the deal. I have got the deal.' I think Mr. Pearson indicated, 'Yeah, I have half a mind to do that. I might be able to do that.' " Pearson asked her if they would do 20 percent, and she said, "I am not going to like it. I think that there may be a way that we can deal with this, but I am not going to like it."[15]

No progress and no follow-up came out of these discussions. Icahn renegotiated his earlier offer for TWA several times in December, dropping the cash offer from $19.50 to $15 to $11 and in the final—no cash, $24 a share in preferred stock, and reduced the amount of minority stocks he would purchase. The agreement also stipulated that he would "raise $750 million in cash for TWA's budget by issuing debt securities through the investment banking firm Drexel Burnham Lambert Inc."[16] Icahn took control of TWA in early January 1986.

Pearson, with a twenty-year tenure at TWA, would remain on but would be forced to resign six months later. The return to the original TWA comprehensive proposal, plus inflated wage cuts, reflected an ascendancy of members of the TWA negotiating team by Icahn, most notably Hoar. He, though supported by members of the negotiating team, had objected to the reduced comprehensive package of February 1985 engineered by Pearson. Hoar had spoken of the need for a contract that changed flight attendant lifestyles. He would later be promoted by Icahn, first to Senior Vice President of Labor Relations, and then head of TWA as Chief Operating Officer, a position that he would hold until TWA's first bankruptcy in 1992.[17]

The adversarial climate at TWA which would soon end in a strike mirrored the difficulties workers were facing in other industries. Similar to other workers, TWA was asking for heavy concessions in wages and work rules. TWA dismissed any of IFFA's proposals, and did not budge on its own take it or leave it package. TWA started training new flight attendants and made it clear they would be hired as permanent replacements. And, for workers, the demands were perceived as so extreme that they meant giving up much of what they had worked for in the last decades.

GEARING UP FOR CONFRONTATION

With no agreement in sight, both sides step up their preparations for a strike. TWA had made it clear that they planned to use permanent replacements in the event of a strike. In a letter to Flight Service Managers, IFFA reported:

> While we cannot get acknowledgement from TWA, inside sources confirm that Icahn has directed TWA management to begin Flight Attendant strike replacement training. We need to dramatically notify Icahn that he should be negotiating with us, not trying to fight with us. It is infuriating, that in spite of the fact that we have offered a 15 percent concession we still have to be confronted with these negotiating tactics. We don't believe for a minute that 1,000 partially trained scabs can replace 7,000 professional Flight Attendants but we intend to do everything we can to make sure this attempt does not succeed. We will be picketing, communicating with potential scabs and taking our message to the public.[18]

Similar to the letter published by TWA management when they first encountered Icahn, IFFA elevated their conflict to the national level by publishing, "An Open Letter to Carl Icahn from the TWA Flight Attendants" in such major newspapers as the *New York Times* and *the Washington Post*, December 16, 1985:

> Dear Mr. Icahn:
> In recent days, considerable attention has been focused on your efforts to complete your acquisition of TWA. We are IFFA, the Flight Attendant Union at TWA, and we are concerned about the future of our company.
>
> Our 7,000 members have invested an average of 14 years of service to TWA, and all of us are doing everything within our power to see that TWA flourishes. That's why, since this past August, we've been offering you a concession equivalent to 15 percent of our salaries. Our offer matches or exceeds the reductions obtained by you from all other comparably paid employees. If we were not concerned about the future of our airline, we would not be offering you over $30 MILLION per year from our own pockets. Why haven't you accepted our offer?[19]

This open letter went on to say that he was asking TRIPLE of what he had asked from comparably paid employees, mentioned the 96 percent strike vote of its labor force, and cautioned Icahn about the cost of the most recent strikes in the airline industry.

IFFA also launched an aggressive campaign to thwart TWA's recruitment and training of replacement flight attendants. Members did informational picketing at the Jack Frye Training Center in Kansas City, the primary location for flight attendant training. Members and their supporters attended recruitment seminars that were conducted throughout the United States, both in domicile and non-domicile cities. Flight Attendants were instructed to listen to the radio and check the newspaper to find TWA recruitment announcements. They were to go in uniform and talk to the recruits, distribute materials, and keep the domicile representatives informed.

IFFA members were the union's best defense. They came out in large numbers and they responded to calls for action from the leadership.

URGENT MESSAGE:

> I just left meetings with Carl Icahn. He continues to reject our offer and is confident that you'll give up more and that he can break our spirit of unity.
>
> One of his tactics is active recruitment and training of new Flight Attendants to cross our picket line if we are forced to strike. In response, we have declared war on his tactics.
>
> And it's working. Icahn has reached only 25 percent of his recruitment goal.
>
> He's now escalating his program. We need to move quickly—*every one of us*—to undermine his plans to replace us.
>
> Let's make Icahn's greatest strength his greatest vulnerability![20]

IFFA's strategy to attend recruitment seminars and picket the training center met with success—some potentially interested people left when they encountered the flight attendants at the recruitment seminars, some would later join the flight attendant strike when called to work for the first time—but, there were plenty of job seekers. And, the cost to the new recruit was not insignificant. As IFFA summarized it, these recruits were paying $2,500 for what would be reduced to a $1,000 a month entry-level job. They were also being trained with no guarantee of a job, in a clearly confrontational environment. "The purpose of this picketing is to advise the prospective flight attendant trainee that the Company has no intent to hire at this time and that the training they would receive for their $2,500 is to be completed in eighteen days as compared to the previous training period of five weeks. We want to impress upon these recruits that they should be aware that TWA intends to use them as replacements in the event of a strike."[21] IFFA did their best to let these recruits know that this was serious business, in an industry where much of the turmoil of deregulation had rested on the heads of its employees.

One of the issues that became salient as they neared the possibility of a strike was the rights of new hires coming out of the training center. Trained with the intent that they would be permanent replacements for strikers, once they were offered employment, they become employees with guaranteed labor rights. New hires went through a probationary period where the airline had a fairly wide jurisdiction for firing without grievance or arbitration rights. The question arose as to what rights probationary employees had in terms of a labor conflict. IFFA made clear their position that probationary employees had a federally guaranteed right to participate in union activities, including strikes and sympathy strikes, and may not be terminated for such activities.[22] Their position was backed up by court decisions stemming from the recent United Pilots' Strike. In that strike, 500 trainee/new hire pilots refused to cross the picket line to replace striking pilots, and in turn, United refused to reinstate them. United had also offered what they called "super seniority" to all pilots who did cross (which could actually move a pilot up twenty-nine years, 5,000 places, with an annual gain of $66,000). In a lawsuit brought by ALPA, the Chicago District Court found both of these a violation in the RLA.[23]

Flight Attendants distributed a letter from IFFA to the new recruits explaining to them the current contract dispute between IFFA and Icahn/TWA and the rights that new flight attendants have if called to work. If a new recruit who had gone through training would be called to work, "you have the right to join us on the picket line. When the contract dispute is settled you will have seniority from the day you are asked to report to work. Then as vacancies occur you will take your place alongside other IFFA members as a TWA Flight Attendant."[24]

IFFA sent out a cassette tape and booklet to the membership outlining TWA's concession proposals, and included a tear-out card to send directly to Icahn, and encouraged everyone to send a note to Icahn.[25]

TWA continued to train a replacement workforce, preferably heavily female concentrated. In a TWA "Recruiting Newsletter," they anticipated having enough replacements ready by the end of the year, and further added about their recruitment of replacements, "One thing that is evident is that our acceptance rate among men is about 6 percent higher than what would be ideal. Keep that in mind while doing prelims."[26]

RELEASE AND COUNTDOWN

The next meeting Frankovich had with Icahn was on January 22, 1986, after he was owner. The negotiating committees were not making headway and Helen Witt, Chair of the NMB, wanted this negotiation completed and suggested a meeting of the "principals": Witt and the fourth mediator, Ralph Coleander; Frankovich and Jolley; and, Icahn, Hoar, and Jacoby.[27] Meeting at the Roosevelt Hotel in New York City, Frankovich recounted, "I presented a written proposal to the Mediation Board and to Mr. Icahn, which included a 15 percent pay cut, a snapback, B Scale, and other details." After some discussion, "Mr. Icahn rejected the proposal. He said it was unacceptable. He said he had rejected it before and he didn't know why he was wasting his time here." The next day, January 23, Icahn left "before IFFA portion of meeting" but Hoar stated again their rejection.[28]

IFFA continued to offer concessions, unacceptable to TWA, and argued against what they saw as the unfair level required of them vis-à-vis other comparable employees. On January 23, Hoar requested the NMB to "terminate its services in this dispute and initiate a proffer of arbitration to the parties forthwith." On January 31, the NMB offered, and TWA refused, arbitration. And, on February 4, 1986 the NMB released TWA and IFFA into a thirty-day countdown, expiring at 2400 hour, Eastern Standard Time, Thursday, March 6, 1986.[29]

The month of February was continued stalemate—with both parties' meeting for negotiating, and, preparing for release and the possibility of a strike. IFFA sent out a cassette with booklet to each member and encouraged them to tear out the card in the booklet and send directly to Icahn. "If you have not already done so, please make sure you mail your Icahn card today. We want him to know that we are all breadwinners and will strike, if necessary, to retain pride, dignity, and professionalism in our work."[30] Strike headquarters were set up in each domicile, seeking volunteers, and Frankovich began membership meetings in the seven domicile cities.[31] "Membership turnout for these meetings has been overwhelming. There has been capacity crowds ready to lend their support for the challenge ahead."[32] Rallies were scheduled throughout the United States for March 3 as they geared up for the last days of negotiations:[33]

> IFFA Flight Attendants demonstrated their solidarity and resolve in opposing TWA demands by attending rallys (*sic*) in New York, Boston, Chicago, St. Louis, Kansas City, San Francisco, Los Angeles and Phoenix. Nearly 1,000 Flight Attendants and supporters from other unions demonstrated in front of TWA Headquarters in New York. Carl Icahn had best take note—- IFFA members today sent a strong message to him that they will stand together and fight.[34]

On March 6, 1986, IFFA met with TWA for the final day of the thirty-day countdown. Frankovich had believed to the very end that some kind of compromise would be possible, combining wage and work rule changes.[35] But, despite some movement in the final period, agreement would not be reached and IFFA would later argue in a bad faith bargaining court case that "TWA negotiated toward unilateral implementation rather than toward an agreement."[36] Court transcripts that reflect those final hours, as reported by IFFA witnesses, provided a picture of the state of negotiations on the eve of the strike. One of IFFA's negotiating team members related how she remembered Icahn's presentation of his final offer:

> Mr. Icahn launched into a statement, and I recall Mr. Icahn said, "I don't know why I am down here, but I got a call, and here I am, and I got to tell you, you are going to have to take my deal. I am in a win-win situation. I cannot lose. You cannot win. All the other employees agree with me. Even if you could win, I am going to—you cannot win, I win, because what I do is I am going to take the company and I am going to liquidate and put it under Chapter 11, and you got to take my deal. You are leading your people over a cliff. I am the only guy who could have put this deal together. I called in all my friends. I brought in all my markers. I put $600 million together. Only I could have done it. You are leading your people over a cliff. I tell you what. I am going to change the deal. Here it is. This is the deal. This is my deal. I will give you 17 percent, not the 22 (wage reduction) . . . .you can keep your $1.75, and you can keep your stewards, your stewards. I don't have to take away the stewards.
>
> You can keep those. But that is my deal. You cannot win. All I need is 3,500 people to operate this airline. If you leave, you are never coming back. I am not going to negotiate on this deal. It is my deal. I don't need your deal."[37]

Icahn in his own deposition confirmed this offer, and said that IFFA's counter–proposals during this last day were in the millions, but "pretty meaningless."[38] He stated that the package TWA had on the table was worth $90–100 million and that IFFA never went above $50 million. Fifty million, it was later argued, represented about 20 percent of aggregate flight attendant costs, and gave TWA the $300 million labor costs Icahn had requested earlier.[39]

IFFA's last proposal came in after midnight and was rejected. TWA's chief negotiator Hoar was quoted as saying, "midnight had come and gone and so had their proposal" and it was "off the table." Mediator Brown asked how much time they still had before a flight went out and a decision had to be made. Frankovich responded one and a half hours, but Icahn was reported to have said, "No, we are implementing now. Things are set in motion. It is now."[40] The mediator had the parties separate and Frankovich explained their private meeting:

> It was an emotional time. We discussed what, if anything, was possible at that point to try to reach agreement. Mike M. (IFFA negotiating team) asked whether or not adding a point or two to our wage offer to bring it up to 17 percent would possibly make any difference. We discussed the fact that there had been a direct question on my part as to what was needed. It had not been answered or had been answered by Mr. Icahn, by Mr. Hoar and by Mr. J. (TWA negotiating team) with an answer that, 'It will take all.'

> I suggested to the committee that I thought it was very clear that the decision at this point was not whether or not we tried to dig up another item to see if it would make a difference. The decision was whether or not we would accept this package.
>
> The mediator came in and out of the room. He talked to us. We talked about the fact that it was clear they were implementing the package. That was mentioned several times. We talked about whether or not we should consider putting it out for a vote, even though they were implementing the package.
>
> Bob L. (IFFA negotiating team) became angry at that discussion and said that he could not understand why we were even discussing that, because people in his seniority would be gone the minute there was implementation. We discussed the Eastern situation where 1,000 flight attendants were furloughed when the company implemented the package while the union voted on it, and Bob's comment was, "I am going to be gone. People like me are going to be gone the minute this thing is implemented [because of the increased work rules would decrease need for employees]. Now, if we strike, I may be gone, too, but at least I have a chance to fight it."[41]

On the final day of the thirty-day countdown, in the final hours, Icahn made some final changes: he said that he would reduce the pay cut from 22 percent to 17 percent, he would give them back their union representatives, and they could keep their hourly expenses as is. This offer retained a higher reduced wage than offered to other employees and extensive work rule changes. When IFFA met privately to discuss the final offer, the issue of job loss stemming from changed work rules was a pivotal one. Icahn, however, had said in the final evening, he would not "slash anyone."[42] Frankovich's reporting of it was:

> At some point in here, he said, "I am not going to replace anybody that is here." I said, "Are you talking about a no-furlough agreement?" He said, not the kind you mean. We went on. That was never further explored.[43]

Later, TWA referred to their comprehensive packages as a "priceless deal," but it was clearly not perceived that way by IFFA.[44] There appeared to be two paths, what Icahn would actually call Case 1 and Case 2, on the table that night. Case 1 was a deal that retained all the work rules that TWA wanted with movement on wage cuts from 22 to 17 percent, restoring payment of full-time representatives, and withdrawal of the hourly expense reduction. The apparent expectation on the part of Icahn and TWA was that these work rules would induce flight attendants to leave through a buyout, opening positions on the b-scale. "If the company's work rules are onerous, we will pay them to leave."[45] The second path, Case 2, was that the offer would be unacceptable and would lead to a strike. In this case flight attendants would be replaced by new hires at substantially reduced wages. Icahn was reported to have said:

> I am paying you 35,000, and I can replace you with 12,000. We will ask you for work rules. If you go on strike, I will replace all of you with $12,000 flight attendants. In Case 1 and Case 2 . . . it is my deal.[46]

For IFFA, both options resulted in the loss of the occupation for its incumbents. It was not necessarily assumed by IFFA that it would be the most senior flight attendants who took a buyout, though no buyout was actually on the table. The view at the end was that it would be the less senior flight attendants who would be out of a job because TWA and Icahn had estimated that, with the work rule changes, they could run the airline with only 3,500 flight attendants. According to Frankovich, IFFA had estimated that the work rules changes would result in a furlough of some 2,000 of its most junior workers. "We had started with 6,500 jobs and had faced an initial threat that somewhere in the vicinity of 2,000 of our members would be furloughed if we accepted the proposals."[47]

Shortly thereafter, the strike began. Some 6,000 flight attendants, with an average seniority of fourteen years, went out on strike as soon as the announcement was made. Because of the nature of the airline industry—this meant that flight attendants had to be prepared not to board any TWA airline after 12:01 March 7, 1986. Domestic flight attendants had been advised to make advanced ticket purchases on other airlines, and IFFA supplied charter airlines as "sweepers" to pick up 400 internationally stranded flight attendants.[48] In a letter dated March 7, 1986, IFFA's negotiating committee announced the beginning of the strike and shared the details of TWA's final offer and the reasons for their rejection. The negotiating committee attached a lengthy description of both IFFA's proposed offers to TWA as well as the extensive concessionary proposals that would now be unilaterally implemented by TWA. The letter conveyed both critical information and the gravity of the situation:

***

Dear Flight Attendant:

WE ARE ON STRIKE!

It is regrettable and unfortunate. We want you to know that we went beyond all reasonable limits in our efforts to reach an agreement.

The *total dollar value* of our offer far exceeded the amount accepted by Carl Icahn from the IAM—with 3,000 more members than the IFFA. We made this offer, knowing that it was more than you had authorized us to do, in order to avoid what may be a long strike.

Icahn's final offer . . . after all this time spent in negotiation . . . consisted of a 17 percent salary cut (which alone exceeds the total concessions of all other comparably paid employees), leaving our hourly expenses intact, and insistence on each and every work rule change proposed by TWA on December 2 which was explained to you on the last IFFA tape.

We negotiated beyond the midnight hour. Icahn insisted that we, the Negotiating Committee, do not speak for you. He demanded that we put his "Final Offer" out to you for a vote. We even considered stopping the clock and putting his demands to a vote . . . but he refused to stop the clock and insisted on *immediate* implementation of all TWA demands.

What was TWA's final offer? And how far did we go? TWA's demands and our offer are set out on the following pages.

This fight is not of our making. We went far beyond what any other comparably-paid employee at TWA has been required to do. For whatever reason, Icahn has chosen to treat Flight Attendants as second class employees. The battle lines have been drawn . . and now, we have no choice but to WIN!

Thank you for your support and your understanding. In the days to come, we will need it more than ever. We will keep you informed of any and all developments.

Sincerely,
The IFFA Negotiating Committee

IFFA PROPOSALS

We made the following offer:

- 15 percent wage cut with snap-back
- Code 92 (707/747 differential)
- Purser jacket cleaning allowance
- Abolition of last trip protection
- Extend recovery balance on International by one day beyond same calendar day
- Abolition of 8 in 24 Domestic scheduling limitations
- Downgrade of International rest seats from First Class seats to Ambassador Class seats
- Downtown hotels on Domestic layovers of twenty-four hours or more
- Share ground transportation with pilots
- Increase trip rig to one hour for every four hours (1:4)

- Average credit for multiple duty periods on Domestic
- Extension of Domestic on-duty limits from 12:30 to 13:00 for turn-arounds
- Combine Flight Service Manager and Purser reserve categories
- Provide a single bid package at locations having both Domestic and International
    - (Note: This is not cross utilization)
- Reduce reserve spread by 1 day to 11 days
- Domestic reserves to call in twice daily
- Reduce vacation accrual by 20 percent with snap-back
- Increase Domestic monthly limitations to eighty credit hours
- Increase International quarterly limitations to 250.5 credit

In return we asked for retirement improvements and other items of dignity having no cost.

COMPANY'S PROPOSAL

#1 COMPENSATION

- Reduce all elements of pay currently in effect by 22 percent for incumbent Flight Attendants.
- Reserve Incentive guarantee would be reduced from ten hours to five hours per month.
- Abolish 707/747 pay differential (Code 92)—Letter of Agreement V.
- Abolish FSM/PUR cleaning jacket allowance.
- Abolish the Purser/FSM override in Art. 3(D).

#2 EXPENSES

- Reduce non-taxable $1.75 hourly expense payment by $.25 per hour.
- Provide domestic downtown hotel for layovers of twenty-four hours or more instead of current sixteen hours.
- Share ground transportation with pilots.
- Abolish the $7.00 payment Flight Attendants receive when Company fails to provide crew meals.

#3 SATELLITES

- Establish Flight Attendant Satellite Stations for both Domestic and International operations.

- #4 FLEXIBLE MONTHLY CREDIT CAP

- Establish an adjustable (month-to-month) flight credit limitation for both the Domestic and International operations.
- Company proposes that April through September be considered as normal calendar months.

#5 SCHEDULING OF FLIGHT ATTENDANTS
- Eliminate last trip guarantee.
- Eliminate inversal and move-up protection.
- Eliminate same calendar day balance and permit the Company to balance Flight Attendants on other than their Guaranteed Days Off.

#6 BIDDING PROCEDURES
- Combined bidding and Cross-Utilization.
- Delete International quarterly limitations of 235.5 credit/255 pay.
- Eliminate Sembower Arbitration Award and International Letter of Agreement IX.
- Eliminate current 6-B (T) rest.
- Combined reserves.
- Change standby, call-out, and holding time from rated items to credit/ pay items.

#7 TRIP AND DUTY FORMULAS
- Amend trip rig formula to one (1) hours of credit/pay for every four trip hours (1:4).
- Reduce minimum credit for each on-duty period from current 4½ hours to 4 hours. This means for every duty period.

#8 ON-DUTY LIMITS
- Reduce International report time from current 1½ hours to 1 hour; reduce International release time from current 1 hour to 30 minutes.
- Increase Domestic scheduling on-duty limitation from current 12½ hours to 13 hours.
- Company proposes to average on-duty credit within a trip.

#9 MINIMUM REST
- Reduce International rest at domicile and layover stations.
- Reduce Domestic rest at domicile and layover stations.

#10 VACATIONS
- Reduce vacation accrual by 20 percent (e.g., thirty-day vacation would be reduced to twenty-four days).

- Eliminate trips missed payment for vacation.
- Delete Article 9(K).

#11 RESERVES
- Combine Domestic and International reserves work rules and create one reserve pool.
- Reduce the minimum notice of assignment.

#12 CREW COMPLEMENT
- Eliminate/Reduce Understaffing penalty payment.
- Would eliminate requirement that the Company additionally staff aircraft based upon passenger loads, serve, length of segment, etc.
- Reduce International basic crew complement.
- Eliminate the Purser position; reduce International basic crew complement.
- Provide Service Managers on all narrow body equipment.
- Greatly reduce basic staffing on charter flights.
- Reduce to two years the minimum requirement for becoming a Domestic Flight Service Manager.

#13 NEW HIRE WAGES
- New Hire wage reductions.
- Increase new hire probationary period to twelve months instead of current 5 months.

#14 MANAGEMENT SENIORITY AND XCAP USE
- Management seniority.
- Management use of XCAP seat.
- Priority seating.

#15 ARTICLES 16 AND 24
- Abolish full-time Union Representatives and close the local domicile IFFA offices.
- Stop Union dues check-off procedures in the event of job action.

#16 INSURANCE
- Restructure medical insurance to reduce medical coverage and institute mandatory hospital pre-admission certification.
- The Company has offered first dollar (100%) coverage, without deductible, of the following: Outpatient surgery, accident benefit, outpatient

X-ray and laboratory benefit, second opinion for surgery, pre-admission testing.
- Restructure dental insurance to reclassify dental services into four classes, from today's three classes and reduce coverage on certain dental procedures.

#17 RETIREMENT
- Further reduce benefits for early retirement by increasing the current 4 percent per year reduction factor to 5 percent per year.
- Increase current contractual interest assumption from 7 percent to 2 percent over prevailing Pension Benefit Guarantee Corporation rates for lump sum distributions from the retirement plan.

#18 DURATION
- Amend Article 28 so that the Agreement becomes effective not later than 1/1/86 and becomes amendable 12/31/88.

#19 GENERAL
- Company proposes to prohibit IFFA from authorizing, encouraging, or participating in any work stoppages, strike or job action of any kind during the term of a new agreement.

#20 REOPENERS
- The Company has withdrawn this proposal.

#21 CREW REST SEATS
- The Company wants to change the type of seat and where it is located.

#22 BOARDING ASSIST/COUPON LIFT
- Amend Article 2(A) and (C) to allow Company to require Flight Attendants to assist ground personnel in the board process of each flight departure. This shall include but not be limited to the lifting of flight coupons in the gate area (off the aircraft).
- Stock and Profit Sharing.
- "Early-Out" proposal.[49]

***

NOTES

1. IFFA v. TWA (W. D. Missouri, Bad Faith Bargaining 1988), C. Icahn Deposition, 259–60.

2. IFFA v. TWA (W. D. Missouri, Bad Faith Bargaining 1988), Transcripts, 3969; William Jolley, *Plaintiff IFFA's Suggestions in Opposition to Defendant TWA's Motion to Dismiss* (Kansas City, MO: 1986), 142.

3. William A. Jolley, *Plaintiff IFFA's Suggestions in Opposition to Defendant TWA's Motion to Dismiss* (Kansas City, MO: 1986), 142.

4. Ibid.

5. Ibid., 142–43.

6. IFFA, *The 630 News: The Official Publication*, Fall 1985.

7. IFFA, *Hotline*, October 18, 1985.

8. William A. Jolley, *Plaintiff IFFA's Suggestions in Opposition to Defendant TWA's Motion to Dismiss* Kansas City, MO: 1986), 196.

9. *Draw the Line*, narrated by Vicki Frankovich, by IFFA, audiocassette, recorded Spring 1985.

10. William A. Jolley, *Plaintiff IFFA's Suggestions in Opposition to Defendant TWA's Motion to Dismiss* (Kansas City, MO: 1986), 150–57.

11. IFFA, *Hotline*, December 3, 1985.

12. IFFA v. TWA (W. D. Missouri, Bad Faith Bargaining 1988), Transcripts, 3985–87.

13. Ibid., 3994–96.

14. Ibid., 3998. TWA counsel, M. Gartner, objects to Frankovich's definition of the purpose of the meeting being to get the unions to back the Icahn bid. See also, Mark Tran, "TWA Drifts as Icahn Dithers," *Guardian* (London), December 20, 1985, "It was a table banging meeting,' said a union leader.' Lorenzo, because of his anti-union tactics, was called every name in the book. Some labour leaders said they couldn't control their members, that their members would burn the airline before going along with any deal with Lorenzo."

15. IFFA v. TWA (W. D. Missouri, Bad Faith Bargaining 1988), Transcripts, 4003–5. While Frankovich was meeting in New York City, there were NMB negotiating meetings going on in Kansas City.

16. "Icahn, TWA Modify Takeover Deal," *Washington Post*, January 4, 1986; "Proposal to T.W.A.," *New York Times*, December 10, 1985; Agis Salpukas, "Icahn's T.W.A. Bid Reportedly Revised," *New York Times*, December 21, 1985.

17. Daniel F. Cuff, "President is Out at T.W.A.," *New York Times*, June 12, 1986; Robert Dallos, "Former TWA President Named Chief at Continental," *Los Angeles Times*, December 7, 1988; Paul Stephen Dempsey and Andrew R. Goetz, *Airline Deregulation and Laissez-Faire Mythology* (Westport, CT: Quorum Books, 1992), 33; Chuck Thibaudeau, "Sweat Inside the Boardroom with Icahn," http://www.twaseniorsclub.org; "2 T.W.A. Appointments," *New York Times*, September 25, 1992.

Pearson was out by June 1986, but Icahn had already changed the organizational structure such that he was subordinated to Joseph Corr, an executive brought over by Icahn earlier from another of his takeovers, ACF Industries. Corr and Pearson did not share similar visions of the management of TWA, and Corr asked for his resignation and replaced him as CEO. Corr left in 1988 for Continental Airlines, named by Texas Air's Lorenzo as Chairman and CEO. Icahn had been looking for another airline to purchase and the speculation, denied by Corr, was that Icahn had his sights on Continental and that was Corr's reason for moving. But Corr gave a different reason. "TWA President Joseph Corr resigned when he became convinced that Icahn would not buy the planes the airline needed." Corr was replaced by veteran TWA executive Jerry Nichols as Chief Operating Officer. But, according to another TWA executive, "Jerry did his best to keep Icahn in line but it was a short one year later that a frustrated Jerry threw in the towel and retired ending a thirty-plus year TWA career." Nichols was then replaced by Hoar.

18. November 7, 1985 Letter to Flight Service Managers, IFFA.

19. December 16, 1985 advertisement, *New York Times*.

20. IFFA, Urgent Message, January 1986.

21. IFFA, *Hotline*, November 15, 1985.

22. IFFA, *The 630 News: The Official Publication*, Summer 1985, 8.

23. Ibid., Fall 1985, 16.

24. IFFA to TWA Flight Attendant Recruits, January 24, 1986.

25. IFFA, *Hotline*, January 31, 1986.

26. William A. Jolley, *Plaintiff IFFA's Suggestions in Opposition to Defendant TWA's Motion to Dismiss* (Kansas City, MO: 1986), 189.

27. Ibid., 177.

28. IFFA v. TWA (W. D. Missouri, Bad Faith Bargaining 1988), Transcripts, 4014, 4020.

29. William A. Jolley, *Plaintiff IFFA's Suggestions in Opposition to Defendant TWA's Motion to Dismiss* (Kansas City, MO: 1986), 189.

30. IFFA, *Hotline*, February 21, 1986.

31. Ibid., February 7, 1986.

32. Ibid., February 14, 1986.

33. Ibid., February 21, 1986.

34. Ibid., March 3, 1986.

35. Murray Gartner, *Defendant TWA's Suggestions in Support of Its Motion to Dismiss* (NY: 1987), 93–94.

36. William A. Jolley, *Plaintiff IFFA's Suggestions in Opposition to Defendant TWA's Motion to Dismiss* (Kansas City, MO: 1986), 255.

37. IFFA v. TWA (W. D. Missouri, Bad Faith Bargaining 1988), Transcripts, 3156–57.

38. Ibid., C. Icahn Deposition, 359.

39. William A. Jolley, *Plaintiff IFFA's Suggestions in Opposition to Defendant TWA's Motion to Dismiss* (Kansas City, MO: 1986), 254.

40. Ibid., 251.

41. Ibid., 252.

42. IFFA v. TWA (W. D. Missouri, Bad Faith Bargaining 1988), Transcripts, 2079.

43. Ibid., Transcripts, 4030.

44. Ibid., Exhibit 269.

45. Ibid., Transcripts, 2086.

46. Ibid, Transcripts, 2089.

47. IFFA, *The 630 News: The Official Publication*, Summer 1987, 15. In this interview, Frankovich also noted the irony that "many of the people we were fighting to protect had decided to cross the lines and take the jobs of more senior Flight Attendants."

48. IFFA, *Hotline*, March 10, 1986.

49. IFFA v. TWA (W. D. Missouri, Bad Faith Bargaining 1988), Exhibit, 523.

Chapter 6

Strike Solidarity and Labor Discord

Throughout the strike, membership support remained strong, both contrary to the early expectations of TWA and in a climate of increasingly worsened conditions. Icahn, apparently advised by TWA management, assumed that at least 20 percent of IFFA members would cross on the first day, with greater numbers to follow.[1] This did not occur. Virtually the entire labor force of 6,500 went out on strike after midnight, Friday, March 7, 1986. TWA had expected that flight attendants on international flights would fly home before striking, but IFFA had prepared for sweeper flights to pick up these now stranded flight attendants; and, domestic flight attendants had been prepared as well by procuring flights on other airlines in the event of a strike.

In the first six days of the strike, only forty people crossed and returned to work.[2] The number rises slowly over the next several weeks, but even by the last days of March, only 351 out of 6,500 had crossed. "To put this in proper perspective, the Company expected 20 percent or roughly 1,300 of us to cross on the first day of the strike."[3] In their system-wide Teleconference, on April 1, 1986, IFFA counsel Jolley told them, "A lot of traditional unions would give their eye teeth to have 95 percent on day one, and you have it on day 26."[4]

In the early days of the strike, Frankovich and Icahn squared off on a number of national news programs, including *McNeil-Lehrer Newshour*, *Larry King Live*, and *ABC Nightline*. Icahn used this forum to convey his sense of the flight attendants as "girls" that worked little and were unwilling to add any time to their work schedules. He explained on *Larry King Live* that TWA was only asking for two more hours of work from the flight attendants, a theme that he repeatedly voiced. Frankovich and other flight attendants tried to refute his statements, but his characterization made for good TV bites, versus the complex explanation of flight attendant rules. Frankovich argued that Icahn "doesn't understand that every added hour of work means six hours away from home."[5] Icahn took these media opportunities to portray flight attendants as lacking the ability to understand economic realities, and portrayed the work rules in a simplified manner that worked in his behalf. It was Icahn who never understood the details of the flight attendant work rules, and openly articulated that, but he was effective in drawing on cultural stereotypes of women in general, and flight attendants in particular, that denigrated their competency and trivialized their concerns. On *Larry King Live* Icahn likened Frankovich to a "spoiled daughter" who couldn't understand that her whims were less important than economic necessity.[6]

The theme of denigrating women's ability to understand economics was woven into the conflict, and not only from Icahn and TWA.[7] IFFA did not see it that way, and saw themselves in the same place other workers repeatedly found themselves in the 1980s: no real choice.[8] If they had accepted TWA's offer, a significant percent of the labor force would be gone. TWA said that the work rule changes would mean that TWA could fly with 3,500 flight attendants.[9] Such a large labor force reduction certainly contradicted the press worthy "only two hours" evaluation of the work rule changes facing the flight attendants. The flight attendants were facing massive furloughs. Barring any expansion, furloughed attendants would over time be dropped from employment.

At the time of the strike, TWA had seven domicile cities: New York, Boston, Chicago, St. Louis, Kansas City, Los Angeles, and San Francisco. With flight attendants spread throughout the country, the strike took place on a national level, and involved multiple forms of picketing, rallies, media events, and fund raisers. Several days before the strike deadline, the flight attendants organized large noon rallies in Boston, Chicago, Kansas City, St. Louis, Los Angeles, San Francisco, Phoenix, and New York. "Nearly 1,000 Flight Attendants and their supporters from other unions demonstrated in front of TWA Headquarters in New York."[10] The activism of the flight attendants was varied, intense, and dispersed. Seemingly, no action was too small, nor too large to be undertaken. Primary strategies employed by IFFA targeted two groups: keep recruitments *out* of training, and keep passengers *off* the airline.[11]

TWA made it clear from the very beginning that they were treating new hires as permanent replacements. Even prior to the strike, TWA had been advertising across the United States for flight attendants. In an effort to stop replacement hiring, recruitment seminars were targeted places of engagement. Typically set up in hotels at various locations, IFFA had started attending these recruitment meetings to convince interested job seekers—mostly young women—that they were walking into a potential strike situation and to discourage their participation.

Once the strike began, this strategy intensified. Flight attendants, in uniform, picketed these seminars and tried to persuade attendees to turn away;

sometimes they would try to convince them to apply for jobs elsewhere.[12] IFFA described the encounters:

> IFFA's Scab Recruitment Seminar raiders struck again. In Atlantic City 29 people showed up, 15 were ours. We arranged media coverage and are told the police outnumbered the entire turnout. There were no takers for the scab jobs. Seminar reports from around the country report that recruits are easily persuaded to apply for jobs at American or United (where no strike is taking place and they are not required to pay $2,500 for training). In response to our success in the Seminars TWA is now attempting to hold Recruitment Seminars in locations as far away as possible from domicile cities. Undaunted we even ruined the Company recruitment in Dover, Delaware and Rapid City, South Dakota. Please keep an eye out for advertisements, keep up the good work. Now's the time for maximum pressure."[13]

Family members would help out as well, and when TWA put on a recruitment seminar in the small town of Post Falls, Idaho a father of a Chicago, based flight attendant passed out information and tried to convince attendees to reject TWA.[14] In an attempt to stop the picketing of these seminars by IFFA, "Scab hotels" in Los Angeles and New York filed charges with the National Labor Relations Board (NLRB), later dismissed.[15] As the strike heated up, there were countless clashes both at recruitment seminars and at the central location for training new recruits, the Jack Frye Training Center in Kansas City, Missouri. Once new recruits started the training process, flight attendants would picket the center, trying to get recruits to drop out of the training. Kansas City flight attendants tried to get the city to stop renting space at the municipal auditorium to TWA for training. They thought they had succeeded but overnight the decision was overturned. When the Labor Industry Trade Show took place next door to the auditorium, IFFA picketers announced with placards "Scabs in Union Land" and "Scabin Attendants in Union Land."[16] Clashes at seminars and training centers turned into wars of words, and sometimes, physical clashes, with arrests made on both sides.

One of the most contentious encounters was on April 24, when Kansas City flight attendants organized a demonstration at the overhaul base in Kansas City, a confrontation that became the bases of attempted lawsuits against the participating flight attendants. Members had picketed at the overhaul base before, at first with IAM supporters, but on April 24, they intensified the picketing and blocked traffic and prevented machinists from getting to work at shift time. While making it clear that this was not a union-driven event, IFFA noted its effectiveness:

> we tip our hats to the many Kansas City flight attendants who today successfully put together a massive demonstration—with nearly 1000 strikers and

> supporters—delaying the overhaul base shift start and tying up highway traffic to the airport for nearly two hours.
>
> Acting on their own, our Kansas City members dramatically demonstrated their ongoing and increasing resistance to TWA's demands. Now is the time for each of us to reach back for more energy and creative, but lawful ways to demonstrate our resistance.[17]

There was no place the flight attendants would not picket. Los Angeles flight attendants picketed the Drexel Burnham Lambert conference in Beverly Hills; and, flight attendants picketed the homes and businesses of Icahn's investors.[18] They even picketed a TV station that was giving TWA tickets as a part of a prize package. On Saturdays, flight attendants would picket outside Icahn's residence in Bedford, New York, and Icahn would come out and talk with the picketers trying to persuade them to end the conflict and remove their leadership.[19]

Strike-related demonstrations and mass rallies would often raise funds as well for flight attendants in financial need. IFFA did not have a strike fund available to distribute money to striking flight attendants. Through contributions, they set up a "Special Assistance Fund" at IFFA Strike Control in New York City. Mindful of the need for a quick financial help, their promise was to respond fast. In a rally of 500 flight attendants and supporters from the United Auto Workers, Communication Workers of America, Coalition of Labor Women, and National Organization of Women in Los Angeles, they raised $4,500; in Kansas City, $1,100 was raised from the Labor Convention; and, in Chicago, $500 from flea market and bake sales.[20] Add to this potlucks, dances, car washes, sale of strike-related items from clothing to posters, to the Grounded Gourmet cookbook. Raising funds was ever present. With such a large strike force, the funds available were fairly limited and the financial burden became oppressive over time. To help disseminate information during the strike and publicize all the activities generated to support the flight attendants, IFFA started a new publication, "Off the Line: The Newsletter of Unflight Attendants," a reversal of their old on-the-line publication.[21]

Strike-related activities were directed as well at keeping passengers *off* the airline. Their primary strategy involved targeting issues of safety. The safety responsibilities of flight attendants are often fairly invisible to passengers, to the point where passengers may actually think that it is the, almost always, male cockpit crew who will intervene in the case of a safety emergency. Partly due to the "voice" that is heard after turbulence or a long wait, and partly because of our generalized perception of males as stepping in as protectors in times of crises, passengers may assume that the pilot is in charge of safety. There is a contradiction in the image of flight attendant as "service" worker and "safety" steward. The "coffee, tea, or me" image does not square well with someone focusing effectively on a safety crisis. As the flight attendants moved into their strike, one of their main strategies was to give primacy to their safety position and they focused on both their training and their experience. They fought the flip side as well, emphasizing the lack of training that the "18 day wonders" had and the fact that the Federal Aviation Administration (FAA) had helped TWA compromise safety by approving an abbreviated training process. They took their battle to Congress in testimony, to travel agents, and to the public. In their battle, IFFA articulated their safety role. As they explained in court:

> The primary duty of Flight Attendants on commercial aircraft is that of a safety officer and a secondary function is that of passenger service (Tr. 64). Prior to March, 1986, TWA Flight Attendants received five weeks of initial training, the majority of which was devoted to safety; in addition Flight Attendants are required to maintain annual emergency qualifications through annual tests known as Emergency Reviews (AERs). Flight Attendant training is mandated by the Federal Air Regulations (P. 2) which require, *inter alia*, that Flight Attendants be able to evacuate a full passenger load in *ninety seconds or less* (Tr. 532–536). The Flight Attendant is required to maintain an updated emergency handbook and to be familiar with all provisions therein (Tr. 65–66). The Flight Attendant's safety responsibilities begin pre-flight and continue through the boarding and actual flight including takeoff and landing.[22]

IFFA used the strategy of safety quickly in their public stance. They revealed that they had received a number of reported FAA violations by the "scab" flight attendants. Examples of "drinking before flights, fewer than FFA minimum on board the aircraft, unqualified personnel on board the aircraft, insufficient training—no recurrent training, no security (Rambo) training, etc." Striking flight attendants were given an 800 number for the FAA and the number of IFFA's own safety director to report any known violations.[23]

In an effort to apply pressure on TWA, IFFA publicized both their successes as experienced safety stewards and the cost of inexperienced ones. In a flyer requesting support for their strike, they reminded the public of how they had effectively managed the attack by terrorists on TWA Flight 847, Athens to Rome, on June 17, 1985. They evoked the scene:

> The fear of dying was real. By all accounts, the control and sense of order maintained by the five flight attendants had a calming influence on the hijackers and passengers alike and was directly responsible for replacing panic and insanity with a sense of reason. The direct intervention by flight attendants on behalf of individually threatened passengers has since been acclaimed and credited as lifesaving.[24]

As IFFA was pointing out their role as safety "professionals," they also took the opportunity to point out the way that an inexperienced crew responded to a potential crisis. On a March 26, 1986, TWA Flight 184 from Boston, smoke filled the aircraft and, according to passengers and airport personnel, the new hire and/or contingent flight attendants failed to respond to the crisis. According to IFFA, "The passengers crawled to emergency exits and evacuated themselves!" They reported passenger responses: "I'm sure the Flight Attendants didn't know what to do . . . there was no leadership . . . they should have responded . . . why didn't they do something;" and, "We had to get ourselves out over the wings . . . the smoke was too bad . . . you couldn't see or breathe . . . we thought we were going to die"[25]

The day after this incident, IFFA met with the Congressional Subcommittee on Government Operations and Transportation. Later in April, the House Affairs and Transportation Subcommittee held hearings on the incident. IFFA reported to its members some of the substance of that hearing:

> Yesterday in Washington, D.C., the House Affairs and Transportation Subcommittee held Investigatory Hearings to look into the many reported safety violations on TWA during the last weeks of our strike. Testimony was presented by Mary Ellen Miller, IFFA Director of Safety and Legislation. Testimony was also given by passengers who witnessed safety infractions by the inexperienced Cabin Attendants/Strike Replacements. The passengers testified that TWA has been using unqualified Flight Attendants who are unable to deal properly with emergencies. Passenger Tom Morin, U.S. Airforce/Aircraft Mechanic on board Flight #184 said "TWA said everything went smoothly but the only reason things went smoothly is because the passengers took it upon themselves to exit the plane the best way they could." Congressman Tom Lantos questioned whether TWA was acting responsibly, particularly in view of recent terrorist acts, to attempt to operate flights with no experienced crew members. He criticized TWA for taking Flight Attendants who had not flown for 25 years, training them for 5 days and then putting them on as training supervisors for new hire Flight Attendants. Of course he was referring to the Clipped Wing contingent employees. One of the two new hires who testified stated that she decided to join the strike after her first flight when she saw everyone reading their manuals on the jump seat during take off. Two of her fellow first flight new hires were air sick for take off. One of the air sick Flight Attendants laid down in the first class cabin and a deadheading crew member took her place on the jump seat for take off. She said it was clear there was no one with experience upon whom she could rely. . . . Bill Borden testified on behalf of TWA and admitted that there were flights operated with all new hire Flight Attendants. Testimony on behalf of the Federal Aviation Administration was that FAA inspectors had found only 10 violations on the cabin spot checks that they had conducted. They have not however concluded the investigation on the 100 incidents filed by IFFA nor on the hundreds of other incidents filed by passengers and other sources.[26]

These hearings came shortly after another terrorist bombing on TWA Flight 840 on April 2, 1986. On a flight from Rome to Athens, a bomb which had been planted under a cabin seat, exploded creating a wind tunnel hole in the side of the plane. Although the pilot was able to land the plane, four Americans died.[27] Two of the four flight attendants working Flight 840 were new hires, one with three weeks experience and one with only eighteen days.[28] While acknowledging the difficulty of a terrorist attack for even trained employees, IFFA condemned the abbreviated training that FAA allowed TWA to conduct during the strike period with its "neglect of the terrorist security requirements." "With inexperienced, untrained new hires, having no prior experience with these high risk routes and pressed into service without adequate terrorist training, detection is impossible."[29]

Another group that IFFA targeted in their campaign to call attention to their safety skills and the lack of such skills in the new flight attendants was travel agents. At this time, travel agents were the highest revenue producers for TWA.[30] According to IFFA, travel agents accounted for between 70 and 75 percent of all bookings for TWA flights, which at the time of the strike was about $2.8 billion of the $4 billion in annual revenue.[31] To target these agents, IFFA sent out letters to travel agents, informing them of their strike and the fact that TWA was now an unsafe airline and that the travel agents ran the possibility of a liability case if they knowingly booked someone on an unsafe airplane. It was a bold move that was followed up with direct contact by individual members of IFFA. And TWA responded quickly. In a Western Union Mailgram to travel agents:

> You may have recently received a flyer from the Independent Federation of Flight Attendants in regard to their current strike against TWA. In testimony today in Washington before the aviation subcommittee of the House Committee on Government operations, an official of the Federal Aviation Administration said the FAA has seen no compromise of safety at TWA during the current strike of its Flight Attendants. John Kern, the FAA's director of Flight Standards, told the committee that "based on our close surveillance of TWA, we have confirmed that safety is not being compromised by the flight attendants' strike. Our overall assessment is essentially that the flight attendants currently serving aboard TWA aircraft are adequately trained and performing their duties competently."
>
> Obviously, there is no basis for IFFA's claims and thus there is no legal duty on your part to warn your clients about the safety of TWA's operations. In fact, we feel sufficiently comfortable about this that TWA hereby agrees to defend, indemnify and hold harmless any travel agent against any claims by clients alleging damages sustained on account or as a result of failure by the travel agent to warn them of alleged unsafe conditions on TWA flights due to the use of allegedly untrained and/or inexperienced flight attendants during the current contract dispute. Once again, let me emphasize that our flight attendants now working are fully safety qualified and are eager to serve your clients.[32]

Safety was one of the main arguments of IFFA when they took their fight to the federal level as well. In a press release, IFFA charged that the U.S. Executive Branch interfered in their labor dispute with specific agencies favoring TWA. Specifically, their claims were against the FAA, the former Immigration and Naturalization Service (INS), and the NMB. According to IFFA they "have all taken actions which unfairly advantage TWA in its attempt to break the Union and replace the striking Flight Attendants."[33]

The primary complaint against the FAA had to do with the abbreviated training that FAA allowed TWA in its training of new flight attendants. FAA approved a modification in the training period from five to six week training to 18 days. To IFFA, these "eighteen day wonders" represented inexperienced, poorly trained employees who were filling their positions and undermining their strength. By cutting the training period, TWA was able to get new hire flight attendants out on the line much quicker filling flight attendant positions with permanent strike replacements, and clearly upping the stakes of the confrontation. IFFA argued that this shortened training was a violation of the FAA's mandate to insure safety. IFFA also charged FAA with allowing a reduction in the in-air operating experience and with failing to investigate reported safety violations "thoroughly and impartially."

The INS was implicated by IFFA for approving TWA's request for D-1 Crewman visas which then allowed them to bring in foreign nationals to fly as flight attendants. IFFA was able to get the Congressional Chair of the Committee on Education and Labor, Representative William Clay, to look into whether the INS had any regulations that barred them from granting visas in this manner. Representative Clay is quoted as saying "that such actions, if true, are equivalent to government interference in a private labor dispute and unfairly protecting TWA from resolution of its labor dispute."[34]

The arguments against the NMB centered on what they interpreted as preferential treatment given to TWA during the negotiation process. They charged that the NMB responded swiftly to the requests made by TWA, and in doing so, favored TWA and hampered the process of negotiations. TWA's request for a mediator early in the negotiating process was granted even before IFFA had finished their presentation of opening proposals. The NMB had denied IFFA's request for a release into the thirty-day countdown in May 1985, but granted such a release quickly when requested by TWA in January 1986.

Once the press release went out, the network of flight attendants in the trenches was activated and offered a good example of the way that IFFA operated effectively during the strike. The goal was to reach members of Congress, as well as other government personnel, by mail and by phone with their message of their "concern over the White House unfairly advantaging TWA in our dispute." The packet was sent to Strike Coordinators and Phone Tree Coordinators that relayed the message across the membership. Though a sample letter was included in the packet, instructions on writing members of Congress reminded them that it was important to "use your own words." Among standard instruction for writing to a member of Congress (e.g., let them know you are a constituent) was also "Keep the letter polite and brief. Avoid sarcasm."[35]

INTERUNION SUPPORT

No matter how creative the flight attendants were in the strategies they employed, and no matter how much support they received from other labor organizations and women's groups, and it was extensive, the support they most needed was from within. IFFA knew that their strike would be critically enhanced if they were able to obtain interunion support. Both the 1985 strikes—Pan Am machinists and ground personnel (TWU) and the United pilots (ALPA)—had shown increased interunion support, and the flight attendant unions were an important part of that solidarity. The United pilots overcame the traditionally difficult relationship between pilots and flight attendants and recognized the benefit of flight attendant support.[36] These examples of interunion support, however, were strikes by male unions that obtained the support of female unions. The IFFA strike was one that tested the reverse premise: would a male union support a female union. And, whereas there are moments of hope and individual acts of support, in the final analysis they stood alone. Miller, Director of Safety and Legislation, articulated IFFA's belief that airline management learned from the United strike that flight attendants (female union) will come to the support of machimists and pilots (male unions); but, if management targets flight attendants first, no one will be there.[37] IFFA knew that, despite the encouraging signs of ALPA's sense of themselves as a union and their strike experiences at Continental in 1983 and United in 1985, the ALPA pilots at TWA would not support them. And, in fact, their relations were at an all-time low. Still stinging from IFFA's garnering of XCAP, the pilots clearly pursued strategies that hindered the flight attendants. Signing the only no-strike clause in an ALPA contract, they had further sought from Icahn a written assurance that he would get 20–22 percent from the flight attendants.[38] As Frankovich said, "it appears that the pilots have made an agreement for us."[39] There were some indications that other ALPA groups wanted to expel TWA ALPA who had not developed a labor identity similar to other ALPA groups as they confronted airline demands for concessions.

The pilots had a special meeting shortly before TWA/IFFA final countdown, and one of the primary discussions was about the impending strike. According to the minutes, there had not been any contact between the pilots and the flight attendants, although they had met with Icahn to discuss "not breaking unions," and had a phone conversation with Hoar who told them that the talks with IFFA in Washington, DC, were not "going anywhere." Pearson, who had been invited to the special meeting, confirmed Hoar's interpretation and said that they anticipated a strike.

A question about TWA's position on pilots doing the "struck work" of flight attendants was raised. Pearson began by saying that TWA does not expect pilots to do "any such thing," and referenced a meeting where Hoglander had repeatedly told Hoar that pilots would not do "struck work." But, Pearson then introduced a scenario—airline ready to go, unmanned door, available pilot—where a pilot might be asked to assist. Hoglander spoke up, "*For the record, pilots will not do struck work.*" Pearson responded that in "recognition of the pilots' feelings" the only person who would ask would be "Pearson, and, not a Chief Pilot." It is unclear whether the adamancy of not performing "struck work" reflected labor solidarity, which there had been no indication of in connection with the flight attendants, or men's feelings about doing stereotypically defined women's work.[40] As it turned out, about a month into the strike, Pearson noted that "Pilot support for the airline has been terrific . . . Some pilots deadheading home have even helped serve drinks to the passengers."[41]

There was the possibility that some *individual* pilots would honor the strike, but according to Pearson there was no "position of conscience" in the ALPA/Icahn agreement and when this question was raised at a TWA/ALPA meeting days before the strike, Pearson said that it would be a matter for the courts.[42] The flight attendants did receive support from other pilots, in particular, the pilots from United and Eastern walked the IFFA picket line. In some places, notably Phoenix, United pilots refused to allow TWA pilots to deadhead on their flights.[43] United flight attendants, who had supported their own pilots' strike, held fundraisers to financially help the TWA flight attendants.[44]

It was to TWA's IAM that IFFA looked for their greatest support, and initially received it. Frankovich had been invited two consecutive years to IAM conventions and she told IFFA members that their General Vice President Peterpaul had given his union's support and that they would not cross the picket line. However, in an article for the *St. Louis Post-Dispatch*, which appeared shortly before the strike deadline and stated that IAM support was "essential" for the success of the strike, Peterpaul denied it and went on to further criticize Frankovich in the article:

> At a combined press conference and flight attendants' meeting here Thursday, Frankovich told reporters that she had received several assurances from Peterpaul that IAM wouldn't cross a picket line set up by her union.
>
> But Peterpaul, in a telephone interview Monday from his office in Washington, said he had never given Frankovich such assurances, "To the contrary," he said, "she asked and we said, No way."

> At a dinner meeting a week or two ago in Washington, Peterpaul said, IAM officers told Frankovich that the IAM doesn't want a strike and wants to keep the pressure on both sides to settle. If a strike does take place, the IAM will decide then whether to support it, he said the IAM officers told her.
>
> Peterpaul said he was angry to have learned that Frankovich had represented the IAM's position differently in St. Louis. "In fact, I'm going to call her up now and chew her out."
>
> If the flight attendants do strike, Peterpaul added, individual IAM members will be entitled to honor or break the picket lines as they see fit, he said.[45]

President William W. Winpisinger, International President of IAM, did not issue an official support of the strike but left it up to individual members.[46] Rather than lend support, "there is reason to believe that it sought to make any pledge of support contingent upon IFFA formally affiliating with the IAM."[47] However, for the most part, IAM workers honored the flight attendant picket lines. In Kansas City, where about one-third of the 10,000 machinists worked, virtually all of workers refused to cross the picket lines (99%), with equally high numbers in the hub city of St. Louis and New York City. IAM said that about 90 percent of its workers were out in the combined cities of Kansas City, St. Louis, and New York City.[48] Nationwide estimates ran about 80–85 percent of the machinists did not cross.[49]

TWA fought IAM workers right to a sympathy strike from the inception of the IFFA strike. Before 8:00 AM on the first full day of the strike, Friday, March 7, 1986, TWA applied for injunctive relief, and a temporary restraining order on IAM's participation in the strike.[50] Judge Sachs, who played a prominent role in many of the court cases that were to come, denied the TRO but set a hearing on the preliminary injunction for the following Monday afternoon.[51] IAM argued that their no-strike provision did not preclude a sympathy strike for another union group, and TWA countered that the provision covered *all* strikes. Judge Sachs believed that the no-strike clause that had been in IAM contract for forty years, and was affirmed in the agreement with Icahn, was ambiguous. He ruled, however, that TWA had met the standards for injunctive relief, one of which was the likelihood that TWA would be successful in winning its grievance in arbitration.[52] Judge Sachs ordered IAM:

> to use union and airline bulletin boards, the union's telephone "hot lines" and other means to tell members that it was not authorizing a sympathy strike.
>
> Union members are to be told that they are free to cross the picket lines and to perform their customary work for TWA without disciplinary action by the union.
>
> Any member of the union who honors the flight attendants' picket line or who refuses to work or who engages in picketing could be disciplined by TWA, according to the injunction.[53]

IFFA announced the District Court decision to return IAM workers back to work while waiting for an arbitrated decision.[54] Judge Sachs requested a quick judgment and arbitration was set for latter March. The fact that Judge Sachs granted a preliminary injunction signaled a high chance of success for TWA, and IFFA told its membership that "While we are hopeful that this will result in the IAM winning the case and being able, once again, to honor our picket lines, we shold [*sic*] not rely on that. Much to the surprise of Carl Icahn and TWA we are today managing to hold our own without the support of the pilots and with the IAM forced back-to-work."[55] Just about a month into the strike, April 7, 1986, IAM lost the arbitration and the right to honor IFFA's picket line.[56] By this time, IFFA had been on strike for thirty-two days, and they reasoned, "We are disappointed but we haven't lost anything because we haven't had picket line support of the IAM since the injunction was granted March 12th." The five days that locals and workers supported the strike was both "greatly appreciated," and also showed what their sympathy strike could have done.[57] Individual workers and locals continued to provide support to IFFA—halls for strike headquarters, financial assistance—but a significant potential weapon had been lost.

INTRA-UNION STRENGTH

"We are holding our own on our own."[58] The unification of this flight attendant population is one of the most distinguishing characteristics of this strike, and for the vast majority of strikers, ran from the beginning to the conclusion of the labor conflict. As an independent union, IFFA had developed a structure that worked effectively with disseminating information, getting workers involved, and keeping action going. They had IFFA Information Representatives that got information to workers, phone trees, multiple mailings, hotline messages almost daily and sometimes even more, publications, and meetings across the domicile locations. They were located in large urban areas making access to media more possible, and spread their activities across the United States.

As an occupation, they were experienced in working with the public. As workers, they were experienced unionists, and had been on strike previously. TWA flight attendants had successfully struck in 1973, and effectively closed down the airline for forty-three days; because of the mutual aid pact that existed between airlines prior to deregulation, airlines were able to weather a strike.[59] In a deregulated environment, with industry-wide concessionary bargaining under the threat of permanent replacement, the strike was different in every way, and increased the need for a unified labor force.

One of the reasons for such solidarity was the similarities in terms of age and life experience. At the time of the strike, the age distribution was highly concentrated with much of the flight attendant labor force being roughly the same age. Over half of all flight attendants were between the ages of 35 and 42; and, 70 percent of the labor force fell between the ages of 35 and 50. Despite this fairly high age concentration, these figures somewhat understated the historical concentration of the flight attendants by age at TWA. In 1985, TWA began hiring again and in that year, hired 700 flight attendants which had the primary age effect of bringing in younger workers.

This age distribution had a significant impact on the strike itself. As workers in the 35–50 age category, they were a fairly stable workforce—neither new employees nor employees with their eyes set on retirement. They had a history at TWA and a history within the union.

The age of the flight attendants was reflected in their seniority. The average seniority of a flight attendant on March 7, 1986, was fourteen years which meant that many of them were at the top of the pay scale which leveled at twelve years. Reaching the top pay scale, with the best contract in the industry, made them aware of what they were losing and strengthened their resolve to fight. It would be difficult to make a parallel move, in terms of both finances and skill acquisition. And in particular, based on their history of working to make it a career, they were heavily invested in their jobs. They had overseen the changes in an occupation that took it from an eighteen-month average length of service when they came in, to one that reflected the financial and benefit needs of long-term participants in the labor force. These strikers were experienced workers and equally important, loyal unionists.

One of the ways that the flight attendants showed their support for the strike was through the wearing of their IFFA pins, and over time, the pin becomes a source of controversy with TWA. During the strike, they also wore a "Pride and Dignity" pin—the term pride and dignity became their watchwords for the strike. Those on strike also turned their TWA wings upside down, mirroring their *Off the Line* publication's masthead. Some of the San Francisco flight attendants also wore a "golden foot" similar to what other unions had done, indicating that they had walked.

IFFAs historical struggles over the definition of women as workers and what they saw as their unfair treatment, mobilized this labor force and shaped their labor militancy. From the very beginning of this conflict over a new contract, IFFA framed the struggle in terms of their history. Individual flight attendants, as well as IFFA leadership and their publications, referred to this contract as a backward step in their historical struggle to transform this occupation from a temporary one for young, unmarried women to a career that allowed a person the ability to accrue seniority, combine their job with family, and plan for retirement. They had a sense of themselves as historical actors who would determine whether or not the gains in the past decades would be replicated in the future or diminished by their actions. They were very much aware that the work rule changes, combined with salary reductions, would be like "turning the clock back. It would be like flying in the 1950s and 1960s."[60]

The flight attendants saw the demands placed on them as unfair treatment relative to other employees, in particular to IAM who they saw themselves as most parallel. And, they defined this unfair treatment in terms of gender, i.e., that more was required of them because they were a primarily female labor force. In a speech made by Frankovich where she talks about Icahn's 44 percent demand package of wage and work rule concessions, she was clear in her interpretation of sex-based inequality:

> Today, I want to dispel the myth that equality exists and that sex discrimination has been eliminated.
>
> TWA is a microcosm of the failure of our system. Our Flight Attendants are victims of inequality and sex discrimination by a powerful corporation . . .
>
> Let's place this sex based discrimination into perspective. Nine thousand predominantly male employees gave back $49 million and they were only temporary give backs. Everything is restored at the end of a three year period. Six thousand predominantly female employees were expected to give back $110 million with no snap back. They were expected to settle for a permanent salary, benefit and work rule concession of $16,000. This represents a give back of three times more than the male employees. NOW, I ASK YOU IS THIS DISCRIMINATION?[61]

This was a message often repeated. "The IFFA negotiating team continues to stress that Flight Attendants are willing to do their fair share but no more."[62] As one of their picketing signs read "We won't go away, Carl. Justice will be done;" and, in reference to the extremely high demands, "Carl What Next? My first born child?"[63]

The flight attendants felt the demands were unjustly high, and that they had been singled out by a primarily male management determined to change their "lifestyles." Though other groups met with concessionary demands, there was no such highly publicized reference to the desire to change their lifestyles. Flight attendants definition of themselves as workers flew in the face of airline management's tenacious hold on their image of flight attendants. "We faced the 'Coffee, tea or me,' 'We really move our tails for you,' mini-skirt, paper dress and other such sex stereotype advertising schemes which minimized and belittled the serious safety responsibilities which are the primary function of our jobs." Such an image justified monetary devaluation. Frankovich reminded members of their former foe:

> We all remember the infamous Frank Lorenzo quote made during the takeover of Continental Airlines and the bankruptcy chaos which followed the takeover. When a Continental Flight Attendant asked how Lorenzo expected a Flight Attendant to

be able to make a mortgage payment at the substantially reduced wages he was seeking, he responded, "A Flight Attendant shouldn't own a home."[64]

There was no issue related to unfair treatment that mobilized the workforce more than Icahn's definition of flight attendants as secondary participants in the labor force. Comments and actions that delivered the message that women workers were not equal to men in the labor force, thereby justifying inequity, ignited a collective anger in the flight attendants. This anger began with the August 1985 meeting between Frankovich and Icahn where the issue of breadwinners first came up. According to Frankovich, Icahn explained the reason he was asking more from IFFA than IAM was because, "you are second incomes, and you don't need the money."[65]

Breadwinner comments struck a chord with the flight attendants, resonating throughout the strike and its aftermath. And, other such comments attributed to Icahn such as flight attendants "should have married a pilot, should have married a rich husband," only added fuel to their fury.[66] "We too are breadwinners" became probably the most often recited refrain in their rallies and appeared on pickets everywhere: "My Parent *is* a breadwinner," "Flight Attendants Offered TWA 15 percent Concessions—TWA Wants Blood—We too are Breadwinners."[67]

The one thing that posed the greatest threat to union solidarity was a break in the ranks. As critical as it was to keep recruits out and passengers off, it was equally important to keep striking flight attendants from crossing over to return to work. In TWA's Strike Operation Plan, they counted on over 1,000 flight attendants crossing on the first day, and then a cascading increase in the days to follow. That this did not happen reflected a misunderstanding by TWA of the flight attendants' resolve as well as strategies by IFFA and its members to maintain solidarity and discourage workers from crossing the line.

IFFA made it clear by example how they would handle resignations. One flight attendant's resignation was received on the first day of the strike, and IFFA announced the flight attendant name in their Hotline and explained, "Because our membership solidarity is so critical and because of the importance to each of us from knowing who we can count on, IFFA will continue to advise you if any other Flight Attendant members of IFFA submit resignations from Union membership."[68] The next day, IFFA announced that the flight attendant had withdrawn the resignation, and had not crossed the picket line. Announcing names would be replaced over time by lists kept in each Domicile. Flight Attendants were asked to check the list and persuade any one they knew to return to the strike.[69]

At the six-week point, 90% of the flight attendants were still honoring the picket lines, and IFFA moved from "an open invitation to those few who have weakened and crossed the picket line, to rejoin the strike effort" to an adopt-a-scab program and an offer of amnesty.[70] "Teams of strikers will each be assigned a specific Flight Attendant SCAB in your area . . . and you will work together to contact that SCAB in person, at home and by telephone . . . to persuade him or her to rejoin the strike. We want constant and legal contact—and if we're successful, the impact on TWA will be devastating."[71]

One TWA flight attendant had been internationally profiled less than a year earlier for her heroism during the terrorist attack on Flight 847 from Athens to Rome, June 17, 1985. Uli Derickson became well known for her protection of hostages and her dealings with the terrorists and is credited with saving lives. No one person epitomized the potential value of an experienced flight attendant in a crisis more than her, so having her support during the strike was important. Derickson had said that she would not cross the picket line, but later did cross, raising the ire of the strikers.[72] One incident, and its reaction, was particularly intense. IFFA claimed that Derickson had intentionally tried to run down a striker as she drove into Hangar 12 at Kennedy International Airport. A picketer was crossing the driveway and recounted "All of a sudden, I looked up and saw her turning the wheel right in my direction. She made no attempt to stop. When I came down in front of the car, I could read her lips. She was saying, 'get out of my way.'" A Port Authority spokesperson reported, "He and her vehicle came into contact. As far as we're concerned this was an accident." The Queens District Attorney's Office said no charges would be filed. TWA's spokesperson went further, "I dispute that there even was a collision."

The union interpreted all of this as a "total coverup . . . If a striker had done this to a scab, we would have been arrested and charged." Karen Lantz, Vice President of IFFA was further joined by IFFA's counsel Jolley, "I find it very improbable that under circumstances where a pedestrian has been struck and, as I understand it, ended upon the hood of a car, there is no cause for an investigation."

When Derickson returned from her trip, IFFA retaliated. Playing off of the fact that Derickson had been named an outstanding mother by the National Mother's Day Committee, the picketing flight attendants waited for her with banners, Uli: Driver Scab of the year; Uli: Scab Mom. Children of the strikers presented her with bouquets of dead flowers and "Happy Mother's Day, scab." TWA's spokesperson commented, "I think it's sick . . . what kind of people would get their children involved in this?"[73] This strike action reflected the sense of betrayal striking flight attendants felt when a person who could have so helped their case, had chosen to cross. It was not unusual for children to walk the picket lines with their parents, carry signs, and participate in strike-related activities. When parents are on strike, children are by definition involved whether visible or not.

The issue of the number of flight attendants crossing went on throughout the strike and was a constant source of mixed messages put forward by TWA and refuted by IFFA. “Contrary to rumor, believed to be started by the Company, there was *NO* massive crossing of the picket lines this weekend.”[74] These forecasted “stampedes” of flight attendants seemed to surface around weekends, and served the purpose of trying to undermine the strength of the strikers’ resolve. Sometimes these rumors painted the strikers as crossing not to return to the fold, but to destroy it. “There is internal company concern that a predicted May 1 mass crossing will be for the express purpose of sabotaging aircraft and disrupting service.”[75] Rumors put to rest also included ones proclaiming the crossing of high-profile flight attendants who were strong advocates and leaders in the strike, and even, the resignation of Frankovich.[76]

Combined with maintaining tallies and managing rumors about crossovers, was the constant attempt to monitor how many new hires, or permanent replacements, were being brought on. IFFA differentiated between new hires and crossovers in terms of the labels they used. They were all referred to as scabs, but the new hires, mostly young women in their late teens or early twenties were referred to by their shortened training, the “18 day wonders,” a diminutive, “scabbette” and a hostess “twinkie.” Gendered age and experience stereotypes flew both ways, and the strikers were called “dinosaurs” implying their extinction, and combined with “over the hill,” their age. Over time, the striking flight attendants expropriated the dinosaur as their own, and used it as at meetings and get togethers.

Garnering less attention, were the contingent workers, temporary replacements who would return to their company jobs when the strike was over. The contingent labor force was also made up of members of the TWA Clipped Wings, former flight attendants who were recruited back to TWA to fly during the strike. IFFA had only limited success in getting Clipped Wing members not to fly during their strike. Full-term strikers found it such a betrayal by these former flight attendants, that they would later create a new retirement organization for strikers, Silver Wings International. As the strike wore on, IFFA would relay to its members that the contingency workforce was wearing down, and that even with all the various groups helping out, it was looking like supervisors were going to have to join in as well.

THE NUMBERS WAR

The number of crossovers, new hires, and contingent workers at any given time was part of the overall numbers war that went on between IFFA and TWA throughout the strike; as well, the number of flights and passenger load factors were constantly in contention. TWA publicly reported the number of flights taking off from the very beginning. They had anticipated 50 percent within the first week, and, assuming that they could get IAM back to work, getting to 100 percent within weeks. Even TWA and Icahn gave different numbers of flights taking off in the first weeks of the strike. Although IFFA disputed and deflated TWA numbers, they also conceded a fairly steady and high number of flights taking off. By their April 1 Teleconference, IFFA said that TWA was operating around 85 percent "not the 100 percent that Icahn has been telling you."[77] When TWA reported on April 8 that TWA had attained 100 percent of all flights in the air, IFFA calculated flights at 90 percent.[78] Sporadically, IFFA would announce problems TWA was having with short staffing of Flight Attendants and canceled flights, and in late April, reported that the machinists and pilots were worried that there would be furloughs in the coming months.[79]

Passenger load factors were down as well, and the anticipation was that the timing of the strike would put increased pressure on TWA. The strike started right before the Easter buildup as well as the major buildup of travel, particularly overseas travel, in the summer months. Throughout the strike, IFFA's main position was that if they remained strong, there would not be enough flight attendants available for the coming months. The tally of new hires coming out of training, contingents from nonunion employees at TWA and former flight attendants from Clipped Wings was not adding up to the number they anticipated TWA needed even under the new imposed work rule changes. They monitored the number of new hires, and estimated by April 1 that TWA had about 1,500 new hires, though TWA put the number at 1,800.[80] By either account, and even with the increasing numbers of new hires, IFFA believed it was not going to be enough to cover the seasonal buildup for the summer months.[81] In a Hotline message in April, "As May and June buildups approach, the gap between the number of Flight Attendants that TWA has and the number of Flight Attendants that it needs is widening. Today, TWA scabs have no vacation, no sick leave and are flying eighty-five hours CAPS with FAA minimum staffing. That's why they need you to return to work."[82]

To bolster their argument, they provided examples of how management had to step in to cover positions and how Icahn demanded management to come up with 1,000 more flight attendants:

> [W]e have learned that if we do not reach an agreement. . . . TWA supervisors will be required to fly as F/A's the schedule change at the end of the month. To relieve the shortage of office staffing that will result from this redeployment of personnel, supervisors have been contacting F/As who were on Maternity Leave of Absence at the commencement of the strike, offering them flight pay

> for crossing the picket line and working in the hangar offices. This is another indication that TWA doesn't have the replacements that it would like you to believe it has."[83]

To IFFA's claim that TWA needed them, TWA countered that they were overpaid, and even with their offered concessions, they were still not in line with TWA demands. One of the single most persistent debates between IFFA and TWA was whether or not IFFA was competitive within the industry. It worked to IFFA's disadvantage that they had been able to secure the best contract in the industry in their last negotiations, concluding with the 1983 Red Book agreement. It also worked to their disadvantage that their gains had been quick. Despite the fact that the flight attendants were the lowest paid of all three unionized groups, their rise in pay had been recent and collapsed into a fairly short period of time.

TWA reported the average pay of a flight attendant at TWA in 1984 was $34,722.[84] As one flight attendant explained, this was an inflated picture of TWA flight attendant salaries. He argued in Letters to the Editor, *Kansas City Times*, that the salary reflected increased pay due to overtime that TWA, as a cost savings measure in order to furlough flight attendants, had added to the labor force. This salary also reflected the fact that it was a senior labor force and that the salary was a close approximation to comparable workers at TWA with that seniority. He also put salaries in perspective, by pointing out that he only made $22,000 in 1985.[85]

TWA did acknowledge that the strike was having an effect on their bottom line. Combined with terrorism and high oil prices, TWA had significant financial loss in 1986. In the first and second quarter, respectively they lost $169.6 million, and $84 million. In comparison, these quarters in 1985 had been lower losses of $74.3 million and $18.1 million.[86] By the third, however, TWA showed its first profit of the year, $65.2 million.[87]

NEGOTIATIONS

The negotiations throughout the strike were unsuccessful, and even though there were hopeful moments on the part of IFFA, even that optimism was tempered. The first negotiations called by NMB's Helen Witt, with mediator Bob Brown attending, occurred about a week into the strike, March 12, 1986, in Philadelphia. There was no progress in negotiations, and they ended without any further meetings scheduled.[88] Icahn was absent from this negotiation, and will not be present for the handful of meetings that took place. On one occasion when flight attendants were picketing outside his home in Bedford, New York, a flight attendant asked him why he would not negotiate with them, and he responded that he was willing and that it was IFFA who was at fault. He said that flight attendants would accept the contract *if* IFFA would let them vote on it. When one flight attendant disputed a statement he had made about how many days they worked, he said he did not understand their rules and that was why he should not be at the negotiations. In a Hotline message summarizing this encounter, Frankovich said that the negotiating committee has been "constantly available" and she would call him on Monday morning and schedule a meeting.[89]

There was a private meeting with Icahn on Tuesday, March 25, attended by Frankovich, Jolley, and IFFA Treasurer and member of the negotiating team, Bill Hoffman. Despite a 6-hour meeting that ended after midnight, "TWA did not budge one inch again."[90] The next day, with federal mediator Brown in attendance, the full negotiating committees of both IFFA and TWA met in New York City but the parties remained "far apart."[91] That Friday, March 27, TWA upped the ante. According to IFFA:

> TWA rejected IFFA's New Compromise Proposal which was made in an attempt to resolve this dispute. Instead the Company demanded that we accept their 22 percent paycut and entirety of their concessionary demand package which has now been unilaterally implemented, without a back to work agreement, without snapback, without stock and without any concrete commitment on a buy-out. They also demanded this package be sent for a Flight Attendant vote without comment from the IFFA leadership.[92]

A teleconference that was in planning for April 1, the 9th birthday of IFFA, was given over to a discussion and vote of TWA's position. IFFA rejected what they saw as a gag order and put the offer up to the membership during the video conference. The vote, coming from flight attendants in good standing from thirty locations around the country, was transmitted by telephone and video tie ins. Ninety-seven percent of the 2,400 in attendance voted to remain on strike and rejected TWA's demand to put their offer up for a formal vote of the membership.[93]

Over the next week, there were no official meetings, but IFFA told its membership that there were off-the-record meetings between Icahn and Frankovich.[94] IFFA also contracted with two Washington, DC, financial analysts to price out their offer to TWA as of March 1986. When they got the results of that information, Frankovich requested resumption of negotiations and the NMB set up a meeting.[95] In preparation for this meeting, IFFA told members that they anticipated TWA would need time to review this information and not to expect anything to happen quickly. Where this might soften any disappointment of the membership, IFFA also set a hopeful tone that they were in the "final phase of this battle."[96]

IFFA and TWA met in New York City on Thursday, April 24, 1986. The nine-hour bargaining session was the longest meeting during the strike.[97] It was also to be the last. IFFA outlined the findings of the financial consultants. They calculated the package that IFFA presented to TWA at the end of the thirty-day countdown to be worth more than they had actually priced it. This value would have placed them sixth in flight attendant labor costs out of the twelve major carriers. In the Thursday meeting, IFFA added two more items that TWA had wanted. With these items, IFFA reported that the average flight attendant labor cost would make them 8th out of twelve, coming in even below Ozark with whom they were merging. IFFA priced the full package they were offering at $76.5 million, compared to the $88 million package TWA had implemented at midnight, March 7, 1986.[98] Part of the IFFA proposal was a severance settlement to buy out senior flight attendants.[99] IFFA reported, "TWA representatives were impressed by these reports and their preliminary review indicated no disagreement with the calculations." Once they have reviewed it internally, "We are hopeful . . . today's action might prove to be the opening of the door to agreement."[100]

When they heard word the next day that TWA had canceled any further recruitment of flight attendants, they saw this as a potentially positive sign, and were "guardedly optimistic." IFFA Vice President Lantz told Kansas City Times, "It could mean that they are ready to settle with us. . . . Or they could be using it as a scare tactic to get union workers back to work."[101] They gave credit for TWA's decision to halt recruitment to the striking flight attendants and all the work they had been doing, "The effects of all your individual efforts are beginning to take the toll on Icahn & TWA."[102]

The first sign from TWA, however, was not a positive one. In the days following the April 24 meeting, TWA told reporters that "no progress was made and no new talks are scheduled."[103] IFFA saw TWA as publicly implying that negotiations had been broken off and IFFA countered that talks were only recessed and that mediator Brown ended the session saying he would notify the parties for the next meeting.[104] Absent from TWA's response to the April 24 meeting was any sense that they were reviewing IFFA's new offer.

Several days after the meeting, IFFA told its members, "There have been no new developments today in our negotiation process. It will take some time for TWA to digest our information and for the National Mediation Board to set-up our next meeting. We are hopeful that we will be meeting again within the next two weeks, and that those meetings will finally be productive."[105] To be sure that Icahn had seen the results of their negotiating session, Frankovich said she would be calling him directly, and on April 30, 1986, IFFA reported, "Although we have been in telephone contact with Carl Icahn since our last contract negotiating meeting, there have not been any formal sessions scheduled as yet!"[106] In the first week of May, Frankovich told members in

New York that she was "in contact with Company Negotiators and we hope to be back in formal negotiations in the near future. With the end of the strike so close, it is essential we remain *united*!"[107]

The lack of movement in discussions began to weigh on the membership. In a May 8 message Lantz said:

> We have received a number of calls from Flight Attendants asking what is going on and when will it all be over? In the past two years, we tried our best to keep you all informed as to what was happening regarding every proposal. As a result of all the public airing of the issues, the Company was forced to take a public posture. They dug their heels in and refused to budge. This was of great concern to many, so we are trying to get around that problem.
>
> Vicki has been attempting to find a way to end this strike as soon as possible, but in order to protect these efforts, the parties with who [*sic*] she is speaking and the issues must be held in strict confidence. This will allow both parties to agree to what needs to done to end the strike. It is essential that you remain strong during this time to help facilitate the progress.[108]

Even though the state of negotiations were being kept confidential, Frankovich was meeting with flight attendants across the system and flight attendants were still actively pursuing strike goals. The silence on negotiations was paralleled with statements about the end of the strike coming soon. Anxiety was rising on the part of the strikers, not only from lack of bargaining information, but the increased reports by TWA that there would be few, if any, jobs left. In the second week of May, Icahn told picketers only 500 jobs remained, another source put it at 300, another that there were no jobs left and only a waiting list being generated for coming back.[109]

Throughout the first half of May, IFFA relayed to the membership that talks were continuing and that they were informal and off the record. They thought that the chances of agreement might be better in this format than the formal negotiations under the NMB. "We believe that TWA wants a settlement of this dispute as much as we do and we are doing everything we can to reach an agreement."[110]

Although, even on the final day, IFFA told the membership that these informal meetings were going on, the tone of the May 16 Hotline was not confident. Lantz reported, "TWA management continues its callous posture and unacceptable demands which discriminate against flight attendants in comparison to terms for other employees."[111]

Even though the cost of the strike is escalating for TWA, no negotiations between the two parties moved the situation closer to a hopeful resolution. During the strike, IFFA made two offers to TWA, and had financial studies done to show that they made IFFA competitive; TWA did not move, and in fact, in the final days added what IFFA saw as onerous and impossible new stipulations on agreement. For IFFA, the population of strikers held remarkably resolute, but growing concern was slowly damaging the ranks. The concern was that TWA would completely replace their entire labor force. Rumors surfaced that there would be no positions left, and with the mounting days and no resolution in sight, Frankovich called an end to the strike on the evening of May 17, 1986—ten weeks after it began. On May 18, 1986, IFFA sent a press release with further information about the unconditional offer to return to work:

> After ten weeks of strike, our members are still 82 percent strong on the picket line . . . proof that they will not accept demands that discriminate on the basis of sex and which seek to replace us with a younger, lower-paid work force. If the package is rejected, or if TWA locks us out and refuses to return us to work, our fight will go beyond the picket lines. This is a new-era fight with a Corporate Raider willing to risk the destruction of the airline . . . and we will make more aggressive uses of consumer, labor, political and community allies.

For IFFA, the unconditional offer to return to work while maintaining a contract dispute meant that they returned their services but "informational picketing and lawful economic action other than withholding of services will continue until we have a contract." The strike was over, but the battle continued to be waged. Membership meetings were set up in each of the domiciles to allow members to vote on TWA's package the following Wednesday, May 21.

TWA showed little incentive to negotiate, and there was no substantive change on the part of TWA, and new conditions were added that would make it virtually impossible for IFFA to agree. For all practical purposes, it appeared that Icahn's TWA had won it all: they had replaced virtually the entire labor force with an average seniority of fourteen years with cheap new hires, reduced significantly the salaries of crossovers, while at the same time increased work rules, deleted paid union representatives and closed union offices on the property. They were positioned to have a new labor force and a broken union. TWA had to have anticipated at that time, that which they had promised, that if you go out, you will never be back.

NOTES

1. IFFA, *Hotline,* March 24, 1986.
2. Ibid., March 12, 1986.
3. Ibid., March 31, 1986.
4. *Teleconference, April 1,* produced by IFFA, 1986.
5. Aaron Bernstein and Chuck Hawkins, "Icahn Ponders Dismembering His Airline," *Business Week*, March 17, 1986, 57.

6. Tony Kaye and Miriam Rozen, "Icahn's Words Come Back to Haunt Him," *American Lawyer*, March 1988, 21–22.

7. Robert W. Kaps, *Air Transport Labor Relations* (Carbondale, IL: Southern Illinois University Press, 1997), 95–96.

8. *Preventing Replacement of Economic Strikers: Hearings on S. S. 2112 Before the Subcommittee on Labor of the Committee on Labor and Human Resources, June 6*, 101st Cong., second (1990). After an opening address by Senator Howard M. Metzenbaum, three workers spoke of their experiences of being permanently replaced and articulated the belief that they had no choice but to strike. One of those strikers was from the TWA/IFFA strike, Norma Adams.

9. IFFA, *The 630 News: The Official Publication*, Summer 1987, 15.

10. IFFA, *Hotline*, March 3, 1986.

11. Ibid., April 2, 1986.

12. IFFA, *IFFAgrams to Flight Attendants*, April 8, 1986.

13. IFFA, *Hotline*, 900, April 19, 1986. In addition to their Hotlines, during the strike IFFA also established what they called the 900 Line to disseminate additional information to the membership.

14. Ibid., April 26, 1986.

15. Ibid., March 26, 1986.

16. Ibid., April 26, 1986.

17. Ibid., April 25, 1986.

18. Ibid., April 5, 1986.

19. Tony Kaye and Miriam Rozen, "Icahn's Words Come Back to Haunt Him," *American Lawyer*, March 1988, 21.

20. IFFA, *Hotline*, April 14, 1986; April 28, 1986.

21. Ibid., April 3, 1986.

22. William A. Jolley, *Plaintiff IFFA's Suggestions in Opposition to Defendant TWA's Motion to Dismiss* (Kansas City, MO: 1986), 5–6.

23. IFFA, *Hotline*, March 12, 1986.

24. IFFA *Flyer, n.d., 1986.*

25. *TWA Flight Attendants' Strike on Cabin Safety: Hearings before the Subcommittee of the Committee on Government Operations, April 10*, 99th Cong., second (1986).

26. IFFA, *Hotline*, April 11, 1986.

27. Karen De Young, "Blast on TWA Jet Kills 4," *Washington Post*, April 3, 1986,

28. Karen De Young, "Turmoil Hid Loss of Passengers," *Washington Post*, April 4, 1986.

29. IFFA, *Hotline*, April 2, 1986.

30. Ibid., April 14, 1986.

31. IFFA, *IFFAgrams to Flight Attendants*, April 8, 1986, 2.

32. IFFA, *Mailing*, April 10, 1986.

33. IFFA, *Press Release*, May 9, 1986.

34. Ibid.

35. IFFA, *Packet*, U.S. Govt. Interference in our Dispute with TWA. May 10, 1986.

36. David J. Walsh, "Strikes in the U.S. Airline Industry 1919–2004," in *The Encyclopedia of Strikes in American History*, ed. Aaron Brenner, Benjamin Day, and Immanuel Ness (Armonk, NY: M. E. Sharpe, 2009), 583.

37. Mary Ellen Miller, interview, Kansas City, MO, 1988.

38. David J. Walsh, *On Different Planes: An Organizational Analysis of Cooperation and Conflict among Airline Unions* (Ithaca: ILR Press, 1994), 60.

39. William A. Jolley, *Plaintiff IFFA's Suggestions in Opposition to Defendant TWA's Motion to Dismiss* (Kansas City, MO: 1986), 137–38.

40. ALPA, *MEC Special Meeting: Notes, March 5* (New York: ALPA/TWA, 1986).

41. "Flight Attendants Unions Are Losing Strength," *Wall Street Journal*, April 8, 1986.

42. ALPA, *MEC Special Meeting: Notes, March 5* (New York: ALPA/TWA, 1986).

43. Mary Ellen Miller, interview, Kansas City, MO, 2009.

44. IFFA, *Hotline*, March 10, 1986.

45. "TWA Attendants, Icahn Still Far Apart as Strike Looms," *St. Louis Post-Dispatch*, March 4, 1986.

46. Michael Norman, "T.W.A. Cancels Half of its Flights as Attendants Strike Over Wages," *New York Times*, March 8, 1986.

47. David J. Walsh, *On Different Planes: An Organizational Analysis of Cooperation and Conflict among Airline Unions* (Ithaca: ILR Press, 1994), 60. "In contrast to the encouraging signs of 1985, the 1986 strike by flight attendants at TWA showed that inter-union strike support is still very much an open question."

48. John Crudele, "Support for Strike Could Hurt T.W.A. Seriously," *New York Times*, March 9, 1986.

49. Robert W. Kaps, *Air Transport Labor Relations* (Carbondale, IL: Southern Illinois University Press, 1997), 91.

50. TWA v. IAM (W. D. Missouri Mar. 18, 1986).

51. Ibid.

52. Ibid.

53. Jim Davis and John T. Dauner, "TWA Machinists Report for Duty," *Kansas City Times*, March 12, 1986.

54. IFFA, *Hotline*, March 11; March 12, 1986.

55. Ibid., March 23, 1986.

56. Associated Press, "Arbitrator Rules that TWA Mechanics Cannot Honor Attendants' Picket Line," *News Archives*, April 7, 1986. The arbitration was held in Seattle on March 26, 1986 and over the first weekend in April, Arbitrator Edgar Jones ruled in favor of TWA.

57. IFFA, *Hotline*, April 7, 1986; March 12, 1986.

58. Ibid., April 7, 1986.

59. "Flight Attendants Unions Are Losing Strength," *Wall Street Journal*, April 8, 1986.

60. *Message to IFFA Membership*, by Arthur Teolis, 1984, audiocassette.

61. Vicki Frankovich, "IFFA Strike 1986" (speech, National Organization for Women Convention, Lawrence, KS, Spring 1987).

62. IFFA, *Hotline*, February 14, 1986.

63. IFFA, *Off the Line: The Newsletter of Un-Flight Services*, October 1987; May–June 1986, 11.

64. IFFA, *The 630 News: The Official Publication*, Summer 1987, 1–2.

65. IFFA v. TWA (W. D. Missouri, Bad Faith Bargaining 1988), Transcripts, 3943–48.

66. William A. Jolley, *Plaintiff IFFA's Suggestions in Opposition to Defendant TWA's Motion to Dismiss* (Kansas City, MO: 1986), 143.

67. IFFA, *Off the Line: The Newsletter of Un-Flight Services*, April 1986, 12; March 1986, 18.

68. IFFA, *Hotline*, March 7, 1986.

69. Ibid., March 25, 1986.

70. Ibid., March 31, 1986 and April 18, 1986.

71. Ibid., April 18, 1986.

72. Donald Kaul, "They're Stewing, and with Reason," *Philly.com*, March 12, 1986.

73. "Strikers Hassle TWA Hijack Heroine," *New York Post*, May 13, 1986; "Union Critical of TWA Hijack Heroine," *Asbury Park Press*, May 14, 1986.

74. IFFA, *Hotline*, April 15, 1986.

75. Ibid., no date, estimate April 26, 1986.

76. Ibid., May 5, 1986.

77. *Teleconference, April 1*, produced by IFFA, 1986.

78. "Flight Attendants Unions Are Losing Strength," *Wall Street Journal*, April 8, 1986.

79. IFFA, *Hotline*, April 9, 1986 and April 21, 1986.

80. *Teleconference, April 1*, produced by IFFA, 1986.

81. IFFA, *Hotline*, March 19, 1986; March 20, 1986.

82. Ibid., April 18, 1986.

83. IFFA, *Hotline*, April 19, 1986; *Teleconference, April 1*, produced by IFFA, 1986; 900, April 22, 1986.

84. "TWA Flight Attendants Resume Contract Talks," *Kansas City Times*, April 25, 1986.

85. "Letters to the Editor," *Kansas City Times*, April 16, 1986.

86. Agis Salpukas, "T.W.A. and Northwest Post Losses," *New York Times*, April 26, 1986; "T.W.A. has Loss; UAL Posts Profit," *New York Times*, July 22, 1986.

87. 1986; "T.W.A. has Loss; UAL Posts Profit," *New York Times*, July 22, 1986.

88. IFFA, *Hotline*, March 12, 1986; *Teleconference, April 1*, produced by IFFA, 1986.

89. IFFA, *Hotline*, March 22, 1986.

90. *Teleconference, April 1*, produced by IFFA, 1986.

91. IFFA, *Hotline*, March 26, 1986.

92. Ibid., March 29, 1986.

93. IFFA, *Hotline*, April 1, 1986; *Teleconference, April 1*, produced by IFFA, 1986. "TWA Union Votes to Continue Strike," *Washington Post*, April 3, 1986.

94. IFFA, *Hotline*, April 11, 1986.

95. Ibid., April 16, 1986; April 18, 1986.

96. Ibid., April 24, 1986.

97. "The Nation," *Los Angeles Times*, April 25, 1986.

98. Ibid.

99. "Union Offers TWA Deal," *Newsday*, April 25, 1986.
100. IFFA, *IFFAgrams to Flight Attendants,* April 29, 1986.
101. "TWA Says it's Quit Hiring Attendants," *Kansas City Times*, April 29, 1986.
102. IFFA, *Hotline*, April 26, 1986.
103. "TWA Says It's Quit Hiring Attendants," *Kansas City Times*, April 29, 1986
104. IFFA, *Hotline*, April 26, 1986.
105. Ibid., April 28, 1986.
106. Ibid., April 30, 1986.
107. Ibid., May 7, 1986.
108. Ibid., 900, May 8, 1986.
109. Ibid., 900, May 13, 1986.
110. Ibid., 900, May 15, 1986.
111. Ibid., 900, May 16, 1986.

Chapter 7

Permanently Replaced and the Long Struggle Back

IFFA's May 17 unconditional offer to return to work ended the strike and began an equally contentious, and much longer, fight to return to work. Despite the legal right of strikers to fill available jobs, TWA disputed that the offer was really "unconditional," and proceeded to act as if there was no union, no contract. Although many of their actions will be determined as violations of labor law, TWA effectively disrupted and delayed the right of full-term strikers to return to work.

When IFFA made an unconditional offer to return to work, they legally stopped the clock on the hiring of permanent replacements. The rumors that had been rampant in the last days of the strike about how many positions were available escalated, and numbers from 800 to 0 flew. Not only how many jobs, but how the available jobs would be distributed, became a source of continually changing rumor. TWA knew that they legally had to fill available positions with striking flight attendants, but they said they had not decided how they wanted to bring them back.[1] Initially, TWA told full-term strikers to come to their domicile and put their names on a preferential "rehire" list, implying that the process would be a first-come first-served. Another alternative voiced by a TWA representative was, "We'd like to have the recall by lottery."[2] TWA also implied that, even though they had stopped taking crossovers, they could resume if they needed a larger workforce.[3] Such a policy violated the legal procedures for reinstatement after an unconditional offer to return to work by strikers, but it was one of the many scenarios TWA put forward.

TWA argued that the contract no longer existed and they could rehire in any fashion they wanted. This set up a lot of confusion, a lot of concern on the part of individual workers as well as the union: it potentially pitted workers, who had maintained exceptional solidarity, against one another and it undermined the union's position on seniority. IFFA reassured members that they did not need to put their name on a list because the legal recall would be by seniority.[4]

This battle over whose jobs were these would be the first of many. The very word TWA used to refer to these available positions revealed the differential treatment by TWA and IFFA. TWA called available positions *rehire* positions. To IFFA, they had never been *unhired*. IFFA always maintained the use of the term *recall* to refer to positions that were available, and by law were to be filled first by full-term strikers.

As the first week wore on, the number of available positions began to stabilize around 200, and TWA released the number to the press before any formal announcement to IFFA. "They might have told the newspapers that, but they haven't told us about that yet."[5] And, in the end, it would be by seniority, but not before TWA created more anxiety and disruption by repeatedly claiming their right to "rehire" as they wished. After throwing out the idea of a first-come first-served, a lottery, after telling flight attendants to get their names on a list and then suspending that list, TWA agreed to seniority recall.[6] IFFA labeled all of this as "just another TWA panic strategy."[7] If nothing else, this first week turned out to be representative of the difficult road ahead.

On Friday, May 23, TWA hand delivered a letter to IFFA saying that they would recall in seniority order, and the following day, announced that they would be recalling 200 flight attendants.[8] Since IFFA did not have the names or exact number to be recalled, they requested each person who received a recall notice to inform the union and IFFA announced a running tally to its membership, "as of 8:00 p.m., May 27th, the most junior flight attendant to be recalled was #265, seniority May 5, 1961."[9]

The final figure was 198, but the overall numbers did not add up correctly. Under the new work rules, TWA needed 4,500 to 5,000 flight attendants during peak travel times, and summer travel was starting to ramp up.[10] According to TWA, they had 4,100 flight attendants—about 1,300 crossovers and 2,800 replacement workers. TWA referred to these permanent replacements as new "non-union attendants," building on their argument that the contract, and the requirement of union membership, was voided with the strike.[11] Only 198 available vacancies fell short of a full complement that TWA would need for summer travel. The discrepancy in numbers turned out to be due to the 463 trainees who were not on the line at the time of the unconditional offer to return to work. This last group began training shortly before the end of the strike, and would complete training in early June. TWA planned to put them on the line, and Icahn had promised that they would have jobs.[12]

TWA's calculation that there were 198 positions available meant that over 5,000 full strikers were left without jobs.[13] On May 23, TWA gave IFFA the names of these recalls.[14] As it turned out, this recall would be the only one in

1986. By the end of 1987, over nineteen months beyond the end of the strike, less than 1,000 of the full-term strikers had been recalled.

CALLING THE VOTE

Alongside their pursuit of recall, IFFA had to navigate the increasing demands TWA was putting on resolution of the dispute and the signing of a contract. On May 14, Hoar had met with Frankovich outside formal negotiations and presented her with a new TWA package.[15] Once IFFA ended the strike, this new package was presented to the membership for a vote. IFFA did not relay the specifics of the package prior to the system-wide discussion. "Due to the complexity of the present situation, future plans of action and the vote that will be taken it is imperative that everyone receive the same explanation at the same time to ensure accurate information."[16] They quickly set up meetings in all domiciles for flight attendants, in good standing and with identification, to vote on TWA's proposals.

The package that had been unilaterally imposed on March 7, 1986, now carried even further "onerous" provisions.[17] In addition to everything that had been imposed when IFFA struck, TWA now wanted IFFA to drop all lawsuits pertaining to bad faith bargaining and withdraw all age and sex discrimination charges from both IFFA and any individual member charges. Further TWA demands were aimed at provisions that would threaten seniority rights for the full-term strikers.[18]

The threat to seniority rights involved the merger between TWA and Ozark which was going on during the same timeframe as the strike. TWA wanted IFFA to agree that in the case of a furlough of flight attendants—a possibility with combining both flight attendant workforces and structural changes from the merger of two airlines—any future recall would be to the permanent replacements who had been furloughed, rather than by seniority which would bring back full-term strikers. TWA also wanted the deletion of section 11(d) of their contract which insured protections in a merger. They wanted the integration of TWA/Ozark flight attendants to only cover current "active" employees. As Frankovich explained, "As of May 14, the number of still-striking flight attendants was approximately 5,000. This is the number which, for all intents and purposes, would be permanently excluded from TWA employment by implementation of TWA's most recent demands."[19] If the membership rejected TWA's contract offer, IFFA would not go out on strike again. As Lantz explained, "If the membership rejects the offer, our offer of unconditional return remains and we will continue our attempts to settle our contractual dispute through any economic and lawful means except for the withdrawal of our services."[20] By law, both parties continue negotiations.[21]

The May 21 meetings took place in seven domiciles and almost 80 percent of the eligible members voted in the largest vote in the history of IFFA. The vote was 3,997 to 95, a 97.5 percent rejection of the offer.[22] It is hard to imagine that this came as a surprise to anyone, anywhere. The flight attendants had nothing to gain from supporting this agreement, and everything to lose. Frankovich had asked Hoar if they could put the package up without these new additions and he said they were "indispensable." As the *Labor Beacon* wrote, "To accept this offer, worse than the one that sent them on strike, would have rendered meaningless all the flight attendants' efforts."[23] According to Frankovich, "It was during this time that Mr. Icahn commented that he had no choice but to 'bust the union'."[24]

Icahn's response to the rejection was predictable as well, "I think it is a tragedy that this union's leadership fails to comprehend that the concessions we ask are necessary for the company's survival."[25] TWA management used the rejection to volley another attack on bringing workers back by seniority. When IFFA members overwhelmingly rejected TWA's package, TWA reasserted their right to bring back strikers, for the few jobs that were available, any way they wanted. According to TWA, "preferential rehiring" by seniority was part of the new package, "but that contract was turned down."[26]

SUSTAINING THE FIGHT

During the strike, IFFA had focused on minimizing the pool of new hire and crossover flight attendants, and at the same time, discouraging passengers from flying TWA. In the aftermath, IFFA developed strategies that would simultaneously keep their struggle in the public eye and put pressure on TWA to bring about contract resolution. IFFA announced that they would be working in three areas: political, judicial, and consumer; and, stressed the critical importance of their memberships' continued activism across the United States in terms of informational picketing, contacting politicians and drawing on community organizations.[27]

They transformed strike headquarters to a fight-back headquarters and established a Political Action Campaign, coordinating activities out of the New York office with local political coordinators working at the national, state, and local levels to get political support from incumbent office holders. They publicized through their hotlines, newsletters, and media the successful and creative ways that members got the message out. Their greatest triumphs and defeats would come in the legal battles that would in the process transform labor law.

The central mission was singular and seemingly unattainable: the return of all full-term strikers to work. Icahn believed, as did TWA management, that once the strike was over, these jobs were essentially lost to the strikers. As Icahn said the night of the strike, "if you leave you are never coming back."[28] Shortly after the strike, TWA's Public Relations Director, Larry Hilliard reported, "A substantial part of the flight attendants' work force has been permanently replaced."[29] There was no reason to believe that these flight attendants would be anything but permanently without jobs. As one flight attendant noted, "something about replacement and loss of job—there is very little distinction."

BOYCOTT OF CONSCIENCE

IFFA's consumer strategy was a continuation of the strike goal to keep people off TWA. To that end, and in combination with political, labor, and high-profile supporters, they launched the Boycott of Conscience. The first formal announcement of the Boycott of Conscience came in a press conference on June 18, 1986. Organized by Senator Barbara Boxer, then a Congresswoman for California, and taking place on the Capitol Steps, Boxer stated, "The actions and attitudes of TWA are completely undermining any progress women have fought so hard to make in the last few decades to gain some level of economic equity in the workplace."[30] And she went on, "We say to all Americans who share a sense of fairness, make a statement in support of these working women. Don't fly the unfriendly skies of TWA."[31] Riled by the sex and age discrimination she saw in the treatment of a predominantly female labor force with long service to TWA, Boxer put together a Coalition to Support Economic Equity for Women in the Workplace. The coalition was composed of members of the U.S. House Representatives, Americans for Democratic Action, the Project on Equal Education, and high-profile women's organizations.[32] Eleanor Smeal, President of the National Organization for Women (NOW) spoke, "We're not going to stand silently by when one of the only unions dominated by women is being busted."[33] Irene Natividad, head of the National Women's Political Caucus, spoke, "Carl Icahn, Chairman of TWA, reflects the archaic attitudes I thought we had dispelled many years ago."[34] President of the National Federation of Business and Professional Women, Anne Steinbeck, commented "When Mr. Icahn says that female flight attendants are not family 'breadwinners' and so they can 'afford' larger salary cuts, we realize that some myths die hard."[35]

In addition to supporting the boycott, Boxer introduced a House resolution to essentially fast track IFFA's, as well as similarly significant labor complaints, filing with the Equal Employment Opportunity Commission (EEOC). After the strike, IFFA sent forward to EEOC charges of both sex and age discrimination on the part TWA. At that time, current Supreme Court

Justice Clarence Thomas was just starting his second term as head of the EEOC, having been originally nominated by President Ronald Reagan. In the time that Thomas had been at the EEOC, there had been significant changes in the role that the EEOC played. Thomas was quoted as saying that the EEOC was a source of laughter among others and that he was set on making it more efficient, better managed. His changes were ideological and affirmed the Reagan era stance. In his tenure, litigations fell, class action suits were dropped, and focus turned to individual complaints. "Agency reduced its rate of litigation, abandoning class action suits and pattern and practice cases," and issues significant to women (sexual harassment, equal pay, comparable worth) "became low priorities."[36] On March 15, 1987, Kansas City Director of the EEOC dismissed IFFA's sex and age discrimination charges, reporting there was "no reasonable cause to believe that the allegations are true."[37]

The public announcement of the Boycott of Conscience was followed by a celebratory "gala" at the Cathedral of St. John the Divine in New York City, July 1, 1986. Hosted by film and TV critic Jeffrey Lyons, speakers included a wide variety of labor supporters, from nationally known activist Bella Abzug to industry support from Murray Warren from ALPA at United Airlines, as well as noted actors Fritz Weaver and Shelly Winters. The event was then followed on July 3, 1986, with a full page ad in the *New York Times*. The Statue of Liberty, celebrating the 100th anniversary of its opening, became the symbol for justice for working women. "The ad contained approximately 350 names of labor leaders, human rights advocates, political leaders, celebrities and others."[38]

Cesar Chavez, President of the United Farm Workers (UFW), was an active supporter of the flight attendants and had written them a long and sincere letter of encouragement. The UFW supported their 1987 film production, *Grounded*, and Chavez appeared in the video detailing their fight and linking it to the collective struggle of American workers. The flight attendants in turn supported the UFW; Frankovich was in Delano, California, grape fields when Chavez ended his hunger strike in 1988, and she and other IFFA representatives fasted in support of UFW.[39]

Farm workers and flight attendants share an interesting history. When the farm workers asked consumers to nationally boycott grapes, Reagan who was then governor of California made a public show of eating grapes and calling the striking farm workers "barbarians." He also "ordered state agencies to send welfare recipients and prison inmates to replace the strikers."[40] When TWA enlisted their reservation agents into a contingent labor force as temporary flight attendants, some of their phone reservation work was transferred to wards of the California Youth Authority (CYA). In January 1986, TWA started up a program at the Ventura School of the CYA and the workloads of the youth offenders had increased with the strike.[41] California Democratic

Assemblyman and Chair of the Labor Committee, Dick Floyd, had tried unsuccessfully to fast track a bill to stop TWA. "Using these young people as strike breakers is an unconscionable act and cannot be tolerated. Government at all levels must remain neutral in a labor dispute."[42] The Director of the school made the argument that the work they were doing is "so minuscule in the grand design of TWA" to be insignificant; flight attendants picketed the school.[43]

The flight attendants received support from many others as well. Flight attendants from other airlines walked side by side, joined by workers throughout the labor movement and workers who were drawn by the sex and age discrimination they saw unfolding. Actress Patty Duke, then President of the Screen Actors Guild, joined many other actors who publicly supported the strike and the Lady Liberty boycott. NOW members walked the picket line for the flight attendants. United pilots, who had been supported so strongly by their own flight attendants in their 1985 strike, walked the picket line on day one. Hundreds of unions across the United States either picketed or sent support and publicly joined with IFFA; between 300 and 400 high-profile union members, actors, leaders in the women's movement, and labor scholars became endorsers approving the use of their name in IFFA work; and, numerous city and state resolutions were drafted from New York to California in support of the Boycott of Conscience.[44] Ray Rogers and the Corporate Campaign, Inc. lent both financial and organizational network help to IFFA.[45] Poland's Solidarity Movement sent a letter of support.[46]

A review of all the forms of support the flight attendants received, coupled with the numerous and varied actions they carried out, highlights one of the most important aspects of this labor conflict. Flight attendants took ownership of this strike and took responsibility to do whatever they could in whatever ways they could. As individuals, in small groups and large, flight attendants worked to publicize their labor conflict and garner support. Being located in different domiciles across the country meant that they went to their local groups, their state representatives, and to the U.S. House and Senate getting the word out about their conflict and seeking resolutions in support of their boycott. They tapped their own connections, and the connections of spouses and friends. Although certain activities would be organized through IFFA offices, many times flight attendants would initiate actions on their own and, at times in protection of IFFA, would not reveal their actions until after the fact. To a remarkable degree, flight attendants got the message that what they did mattered. They fully embraced the call to action and felt empowered. In unison they rallied around, and dug in, to bring every full-term striker back.

A variety of supporters helped IFFA get out their message to the public and sustain their fight. In the early days of the strike, Phil Donahue had Frankovich and IFFA members on his popular talk show, *Donahue*, publicizing the strike. In addition to the help supplied by the UFW, the United Steel Workers, Local 4889, and the Amalgamated Transit Union, contributed to IFFA's production of their film, *Grounded*. Rev. Jesse Jackson, then President of the Rainbow Coalition, participated in the narration of the film and showed his support for flight attendants and their families. In the Fall 1987, Jane Fonda offered support and contributed her ranch for a week-long stay as a raffle fund raiser for IFFA.[47] In his book, *The Great Divide*, Studs Terkel profiled two flight attendants, and, he lent his encouragement to all members on their 1988 IFFA Teleconference.[48]

In turn, IFFA had a long history of supporting organized labor and they were very much in touch with other unions and solidarity within the labor movement. They came out in uniform to picket with the UFW and the grape boycott.[49] They had publicly supported the PATCO strike at a time when much of organized labor, particularly within the airline industry, had either openly opposed the strike or had given reluctant support.[50] Housed at IFFA Headquarters, the Coalition of Flight Attendants took out a national ad in the *New York Times* requesting President Reagan return to the bargaining table with PATCO, "The Public's Safety and our jobs are at stake."[51] When the former president of IAM, William Winpisinger, was asked why he had made the decision not to lend support to the PATCO strikers, he explained in part that there was no support from labor to build on—with some notable exceptions. "Two unions indicated support, he said, the Brotherhood of Railway, Airline and Steamship Clerks, and the flight attendants' union at Trans World Airlines. Only the attendants expressed unqualified support, he said."[52] In IFFA's strike, Winpisinger and the International Headquarters in Washington DC, were silent. IAM workers "received no official instructions . . . as to what course of action to take," leaving local unions and members to make their own decisions in the early days of the strike.[53] Later, as the struggle waged on for the flight attendants, Winpisinger, as well as the outspoken local leader of the Eastern machinists, Charles Bryan, would look to Icahn as a white knight to save Eastern Airlines, as the machinists had done earlier at TWA.[54]

At the same time that IFFA members were waging their protests against TWA, they were also showing their support for Local P-9 in the Hormel strike—flight attendants went to Austin, Minnesota, and P-9 workers marched with flight attendants in Kansas City. IFFA publicized the paperworkers' strike against IP in Pennsylvania, Maine, Wisconsin, and Alabama.[55] IFFA helped the National Football League Players Association (NFLPA) who were striking the owners in an attempt to procure real free agency. Flight attendants joined the picket lines of football players from California to New York, and rallied against NFL owners and their use of replacement players.[56]

One of the ways that IFFA publicized the Boycott of Conscience was through purchased highway billboards to alert the public: MAD AS HELL

AND *NOT* GIVING UP, Join the Boycott, Support IFFA's Labor Dispute! TWA managed to get the billboard companies in Chicago and Columbus, Ohio to whitewash the billboards. Reportedly, IFFA was sent the bill![57] The chance of that bill being paid was about as great as the chance that Susan B. Anthony would have paid the $100 fine for voting in a national election!

MS. MAGAZINE

Ms. Magazine selected Vicki Frankovich as one of their ten Women of the Year for 1986, "For her idealistic fight to show the country, in this year of corporate takeovers that workers are more than passive assets and that flight attendants are proud professionals."[58] Christine Doudna, authored the profile piece, and interviewed Icahn. She commented, "Icahn may be an easy mark for feminists."[59] In her interview, Icahn suggested that she speak to the husband of a crossover flight attendant "to get the other side of the story," rather than to speak to the flight attendant herself. Doudna pointed out Icahn's denial of sexism, "That's a lot of nonsense," flanked by so many examples throughout the dispute to the contrary. Included in her examples was Icahn comparing Frankovich to a "spoiled farmer's daughter who throws a temper tantrum because her father is spending money to mend a leaky roof instead of spending it on her." Seemingly, Icahn missed the denigration of father to child reference, the implication that their actions were unreasonable and without cause, and their demands were frivolous in comparison to the needs of the father.

Doudna quoted Icahn, "I think my side of this should be told," Icahn said. "I met Gloria Steinem once; she seems intelligent. Maybe I'll call her—do you mind? I really think it does the women's lib movement no good hiding behind sexism and all that. It doesn't do working women a lot of good to use power like a Frankovich—to mislead and fabricate."

In her most recent book, Gloria Steinem recounted a chance meeting she had with Icahn. "When I met him quite accidentally, I discovered he was furious about the *Ms.* article supporting Frankovich. He told me he didn't discriminate again women. As proof, he said that if he needed one of this top male executives on a national holiday—and that executive spent the holiday with his family instead—he would fire him, too."[60]

Steinem has a long history of support for flight attendants, and was an active contributor to the Stewardesses for Women's Rights (SFWR) founded in the 1970s. She helped them with organizing early meetings, spoke at their national conferences, and in 1973, *Ms.* published an article by Lindsy Van Gelder that acquainted a larger audience with the SFWR and altered the stereotypic way that flight attendants were portrayed.[61]

THE PAPAL VISIT

Pope John Paul II, now canonized as St. John Paul II, made his second trip to the United States in September 1987. Known for his support of Lech Walesa, leader of the Solidarity Movement in the Pope's home country of Poland, the Pope was a potential ally to labor struggles going on in the United States. In 1981, he had written the Encyclical, "Laborem Exercens" (On Human Work), affirming the rights of labor over capital. In it, he referred to unions as "an indispensable element of social life," and the legitimate use of strikes by workers.[62] "There is a need for ever new movements of solidarity of the workers and with the workers. . . . The Church is firmly committed to this cause, for it considers it to be its mission, its service, a proof of its fidelity to Christ."[63]

Early on, IFFA had requested that the Pope's visit honor their Boycott of Conscience and not fly on TWA. But, in January 1987, the U.S. Conference of Catholic Bishops announced that they had accepted TWA's bid to be the U.S. carrier for the papal ten-day visit in September. The Bishops' decision was based on the low bid by TWA, their route structure which coordinated best with the nine city tour, and the fact that TWA had been the papal airline in both 1979 and earlier in 1965.[64] Immediately, IFFA protested and argued that their decision violated the social teachings of the Catholic Church on labor. Perhaps even more importantly than the position of the Pope was the fact that the U.S. Conference of Catholic Bishops had been vocal supporters of labor. Most noteworthy of the time was their support of Cesar Chavez and the UFW and the Solidarity Movement in Poland. Monsignor Daniel Hoye, Secretary General of the U.S. Conference of Catholic Bishops, responded to the flight attendants' objection to their January decision by saying that he had not known "the depth of dispute" at TWA. Frankovich, never one to mince words, rejected this as an explanation and said, "We were at war and everyone knew it."[65] Monsignor Hoye did review his decision in consultation with other church and legal counsel, but in May 1987, reaffirmed his original decision to go with TWA. He used as part of his support the fact that the EEOC had denied IFFA's charges of sex and age discrimination that March. He wrote to IFFA that "I have no reason to conclude that the decision to go with TWA should not stand."[66]

IFFA did not take this May decision as final and members used everything in their arsenal to get the Catholic Church to reconsider. "We have never been able to give our side of the issue. We just feel the information they have gotten is very one-sided." In letter campaigns to the Vatican and to U.S. Bishops the membership continued to press for a reversal and ever reminded them of the contradiction they saw this decision to be in relation to the Catholic Church's stand on labor. In July, Monsignor Hoye did set up a panel, headed by Archbishop Roger Mahony of Los Angeles, allowing both IFFA and TWA to state their positions. In a letter to its members, IFFA wrote, "After two months of pressure we succeeded in persuading the Catholic Conference of Bishops to hear our case."[67] Though hopeful, the letter expressed concern that many of the questions asked by the panel "seemed to have been prompted by information provided by TWA." To help persuade the panel, IFFA launched a postcard campaign to show support, "Our efforts paid off in getting the meeting—let's do it again!"[68]

Bolstering the side of TWA, IAM and ALPA urged the Bishops to remain with TWA for the papal visit. Even though they did not have inter-union support on the property, they did have other labor supporters: "In a demonstration of labor union support for our cause, vice presidents from the United Auto Workers, United Farm Workers, Transport Workers Union, Communications Workers of America, the Teamsters and the President of the United Black Coalition of Trade Unions attended the meeting to protest the immorality of Carl Icahn/TWA's treatment of us and to request that the travel plans be changed to another airline."[69]

Even before the panel decision was rendered, the expectation was that there would be no change. In fact, Monsignor Hoye said, "If we reversed our decision now, it would look as if we're taking sides for [the flight attendants' union] and against TWA." He added, "We don't intend to take a position one way or the other." As one flight attendant noted, by the decision that they originally made, they had already taken a position.[70] In the end, the panel ruled in favor of TWA. Excerpts from a letter to the editor by one of the full-term strikers relayed her disappointment with what felt like a dismissal of their struggle:

> One of the greatest honors that I can imagine is to be able to personally meet the Holy Father . . . a thought shared by many and yet realistic to few.
>
> Knowing the disparity of concession demands and IFFA's on going struggle with TWA, the U.S. Catholic Conference refers to our crisis as "some labor dissatisfaction" and our loss of jobs and livelihoods as "some outstanding issues in contention which need to be settled through either the courts or negotiations."
>
> Those individuals who were hired as replacements, as well as those who crossed our picket lines for their own behalf, stand in direct contradiction of the Pope's personal advocacy on union solidarity and the right to strike. Ironically, the Flight Attendants who will be privileged to meet and serve the Holy Father will consist of those who took our jobs while we struggled for equitable standards for all.[71]

Pope John Paul II did have a record of support for labor, but his traditional stance on women's issues was already receiving criticism from women's groups in the United States: his stance against women as priests, his reaffirmation of the Church's ban on contraception, and his opposition to abortion. His encyclical on work supported the rights of labor over capital, but he also viewed the role of women in social labor as misdirected and focused his writings on women in terms of their role within the family.[72]

For their part, the Alitalia flight attendants tried to intercede with a letter handed to the Pope on the flight from Rome to Miami, asking him to bring some "comfort" to the U.S. flight attendants and their struggle. IFFA translated the letter and shared it with its members:

> Your Holiness,
>
> It is with humility and devotion that we make an appeal to you in favor of our U.S. Flight attendant colleagues at TWA, approximately 4,500 who for more than one year have suffered the discomfort and humiliation of unemployment.
>
> We Italian Flight Attendants are moved by that spirit of solidarity that unites the working world at all levels.
>
> Today, our U.S. colleagues, less fortunate than us, need a word of comfort, a gesture that gives them and their families the hope of being able to regain the dignity of employment.
>
> Many of us, Italian Flight Attendants, have the privilege and the joy of accompanying you during your pilgrimages around the world and we know the goodness of your works and your sensitivity of the problems of labor that you take with you everywhere.
>
> We beseech you to grant them an ear and comfort them.
>
> We ask for your holy apostolic blessing.[73]

Despite the final verdict by the U.S. Bishops, flight attendants continued their protest, and as one of the flight attendants said "Until he steps on the [TWA] plane, we still have hope that can be changed."[74] Beginning in Miami, there were multiple groups protesting during the papal visit. IFFA members rallied both prior to his visit, and in the cities he visited.[75] A large rally was held at New York City's St. Patrick's Cathedral, with "Don't Fly TWA" and "U.S.A. Solidarity" balloons.[76] IFFA marched in New York City with the support of other unions; recalled flight attendants marched as well, wearing masks to disguise their participation.[77] Phoenix had its own "IFFA-Popemobile" that went everywhere the Pope went.[78] At the St. Louis Cathedral flight attendants tried to get parishioners to honor their boycott, and carried signs "TWA Flight Attendants Appeal to Pope John Paul II—Please Don't Fly TWA."[79] Standing outside the Cathedral on Sundays, they tried to get parishioners to write the pope to urge him not to fly TWA. One son of a flight attendant carried a sign, "T.W.A. took away the means for my Catholic Education. *Why* is the Pope Flying TWA????"[80]

The contradiction apparent between the support of labor, on the one hand, and the rejection of the flight attendant labor conflict, became all the more difficult to understand when U.S. Catholic Bishops rallied behind permanent replacement legislation in the early 1990s, linking their support to their historical position on the side of labor. In his March 1991 testimony in support of Senate Bill 55, Bishop Frank Rodimer announced the Catholic Conference's Committee on Domestic Social Policy January vote in support of a ban on permanent replacements. He said that it was "especially appropriate" at this time because it marked the 100th anniversary of the first papal encyclical by Pope Leo XII in 1891. This encyclical, "On the Conditions of Workers," was reaffirmed by Pope John Paul II 1991 encyclical "On Human Work." "The role of unions in promoting the dignity of work and of workers is very important in Catholic Teachings."

Bishop Rodimer referred not only to the long standing papal support of labor but the U.S. Catholic Bishops' 1986 pastoral letter, "Economic Justice for All." In that letter, penned the same year as the flight attendants' strike, they emphasized "the benefits to workers and society of strong and effective labor unions and opposes efforts to break existing unions and prevent workers from organizing." In his Senate testimony in support of S. 55, Bishop Rodimer rendered an eloquent argument about the importance of the strike and how permanent replacement weakens that right. "When employers are allowed to offer permanent jobs to strikebreakers, strikers lose their jobs. It's that simple. If workers lose their jobs, what does it mean to have the right to strike? If there is no effective right to strike, what does it mean to have the right to organize?"[81]

Nine months earlier, in the first of the Senate hearings on banning permanent replacements, Norma Adams, an IFFA member with twenty-four years' experience with TWA at the time of the strike, was one of three workers to start the hearings off with descriptions of the personal and financial difficulties they and their fellow strikers endured in strikes where permanent replacements were used.[82]

THE SLOW RETURN

The return of the first full-term strikers was an important and difficult time for individual flight attendants and the union. The first 198 came back to jobs substantially changed and to a climate that was overwhelmingly hostile to them. IFFA no longer had representatives on the property much less offices, and reported being bodily thrown off if they tried to come on the property if they were not part of the 198 recalls. The 198 were processed and returned to employment on May 29. Local full-term strikers not recalled came out in support and IFFA gave yellow carnations to each recallee to wear as they returned to TWA.[83] In a congratulatory hotline devoted to this first group, Frankovich said:

> Although the honor may seem small, it is important that we begin to return our loyal members to the payroll. The responsibility you bear is great, but your experience, perseverance and determination make you the perfect people for the task.
>
> You must bear the initial shock of returning to a workplace that is not as "friendly" as when you left. You must deal with scabs who will ask you to absolve the guilt they feel for betraying our fight and actively working against you. You must deal with a Company management feels it can take liberties against an unprotected workforce.
>
> As you have for so many years, we know you will maintain your dignity, poise and control to prevail in the near future as you have so admirably in the past. You need not succumb to management, absolve the guilty nor tutor the untrained.[84]

They walked onto airplanes with multiple sets of workers who had taken their jobs. So greatly were these first 198 overwhelmed by "scabs and crawlies" that some of the recalled flight attendants requested that the union issue ID cards and new pins "so that the IFFA union members can be forevermore distinguishable."[85] As more recallees entered the line over the years, this issue of identification was a constant concern for the full-term strikers.

The new hires were easily visible because of their age and were known as scabbettes, hostess twinkies, and 18-day wonders, among other names. IFFA flight attendants had tried to dissuade them with their visits to recruitment meetings and the training center, and there had been multiple skirmishes between the two groups.

Less visible were three other groups of flight attendants that were on board: Clipped Wings, Remos, and crossovers. Clipped Wings was the official retirement group for TWA flight attendants made up of former TWA flight attendants who had retired either out of choice or through earlier imposed status barriers (age, marital status, pregnancy). Both TWA and IFFA made appeals to them, but when members of Clipped Wings responded to the call of TWA to return to work, it so angered full-term strikers that they formed a new retirement group with a far more positive name, Silver Wings International. Some Remos, a set of returning mothers who had won a court battle to regain seniority for years lost, also came to work for TWA. Of the three groups, the most difficult group to face was their own members that had crossed. It was this group, 1,280, that the sense of betrayal was the greatest and the feelings the strongest. "Once you are a scab, you are a scab for the rest of your life."[86]

The recallees went from the collective struggle where they were in unison over the strike, to being 198 in the midst of thousands of flight attendants whose chosen course of action had secured jobs for themselves and assisted Icahn and TWA to redefine the job at much reduced wages and working conditions. For the first 198, it was a pretty good guess that just about everyone, if not everyone, they were flying with had crossed the picket lines. And for over a year, these are the sole returnees to the line. As the years go on, and more and more flight attendants were returned to the line, it became increasingly difficult to know who was a full-term striker and who was not. And, there were instances of scabs misrepresenting their role in the strike and their status. For the full-term strikers, it was imperative to them to know who they were flying with, who they felt they could trust. To solve this issue, flight attendants, ostensibly without the knowledge or assistance of IFFA, published a *Little Black Book.* And, it was a little black book. The cost was $5 and it listed the flight attendant numbers of all full-term strikers. When full-term strikers went on flights and were unsure of the people they were flying with, they could secretly check their black book to identify the person and their status.

The label "FTS" for full-term striker developed meaning and identity over time. As the struggle wore on, another way that flight attendants kept in contact was through an informal newsletter, *The F.T.S. News & Muse.* Self-defined as a "rowdy underground publication which has absolutely no connection to IFFA other than the fact that we support our union and its goals with steadfast loyalty, pride and dignity. Well, maybe not always with dignity. But certainly with loyalty and pride."[87] With a heavy overlay of humor, this 6–10 page pamphlet kept full-term strikers connected through shared conceptions of the goings on about the airline. It was a place to vent, to laugh at the hubris of Uncle Ca Ca (Icahn), the Hoar, and the folly of TWA. They relayed comical stories about those that had betrayed them, aimed mostly at scabs (crossovers) and scabbettes (permanent replacements). Even though they acknowledged that not all pilots were bad and relayed positive examples, they directed their derision to the group for actively working against them in their dealings with Icahn.

As this first group of full-term strikers was processed and brought on line, the confrontational relationship between TWA and IFFA continued. The 198 wanted the full-term strikers to come out in support of them as they were processed for recall, in part because they knew it bothered the active flight attendants. TWA made the process uncomfortable by their overall treatment of the 198, such as holding them outside in the heat, unwelcome reception and endless paperwork for the most minor of issues.

GRIEVANCE PROCEDURES

As unpleasant as these endless hurdles of recall were, other actions by TWA were more aggressive and much more threatening to IFFA and its membership. According to TWA, the agreement between TWA/IFFA at the end of March 6, 1986 expired. Although they would later lose this argument in a

Supreme Court decision on union security, one of the first things that TWA did was to institute a new grievance procedure. The procedure that was designed was only open to "active" employees. What this meant was any full-term striker that was terminated for alleged strike misconduct was barred from recourse. They could submit a grievance against termination on an IFFA grievance form. If they did, however, TWA failed to recognize its legitimacy claiming that there were no grievance procedures in which IFFA had a role because there was no contract between TWA/IFFA. If they filed a grievance on the new TWA grievance form, it would be denied because the grievance procedure was only open to active employees and not full-term strikers who had yet to be returned to work. An in flight manager's letter of response to a flight attendant who had filled out *both* forms to contest his termination for strike misconduct illustrated the predicament:

> As to the complaint submitted on a TWA Grievance Report form, TWA records show that you were on strike and not in TWA's active service at the time of the events on which your termination was based, and on the date you were terminated. Accordingly, you are not covered by the grievance procedures established by TWA for working Flight Attendants.
>
> As to your complaint submitted on an IFFA grievance form, TWA's obligation to deal with such matters in the manner prescribed by the former TWA-IFFA agreement which expired at midnight March 6, 1986. There is not contractual or statutory "status quo" obligation to consider your complaint as to your termination under the grievance and arbitration procedure of the expired agreement.[88]

Similar responses were given to IFFA staff when they made complaints, for example, about "being denied access to the reprocessing of Rehired Flight Attendants."[89] Any IFFA representative that had not been recalled was not on "active" status and, according to TWA, had no legal rights of representation because the agreement had expired. When one full-term striker was terminated for charges that she had in June 1986 "harassed, intimidated, and assaulted flight attendants in the service of Trans World Airlines," she followed up her first set of grievance forms which had been denied with a Step II Appeal. The in-flight manager's letter was short and summarized the full-term striker's grievance rights, "I am returning to you the Step II Appeal which you filed with this office on July 23, 1986. There is no grievance process available to you."[90]

UNION DUES

The struggle over having access to a grievance procedure was just one of many obstacles that flight attendants had to face once they began the very slow process to return. One of the biggest and most persistent battles was over finances, and specifically the issue of union dues. The union security case brought by TWA was based on "whether working flight attendants are required to pay dues to IFFA in the absence of a currently effective collective bargaining agreement."[91] Borden expressed TWA's view in a letter to working flight attendants who, with the exception of the 198, were composed of crossovers and replacements:

> As I have previously told you, TWA strongly believes you should not have any legal obligation to financially support IFFA and will continue to vigorously pursue this issue in the courts. In the meantime, however, it is *imperative* that you timely comply with Article 24 of the 1983 TWA-IFFA Agreement, either through direct payment to IFFA or by dues check-off authorization, so as not to jeopardize your job.

Borden goes on to offer an interest free loan, especially geared to the permanent replacements, to help them pay their dues amount. For replacements their money could be put in an escrow account until the court determined the legal point raised by TWA.[92] Crossovers were to pay directly to IFFA; their money was not to be held in escrow, but "someone" gave them the idea of how to lodge a protest about paying IFFA dues. Appearing in flight attendant mailboxes was a sample letter of protest that could be sent to IFFA by crossovers when they sent in their dues payment. The letter covered two different bases: in the event that the courts found that the TWA/IFFA agreement had indeed expired, they wanted all their money back with interest and, therefore, requested that all their money be placed in an escrow account which would be a parallel position to the replacements' account. In the event that the contract had not expired, they were prepared to pay "an agency shop fee to cover proper expenditures," which were defined as expenditures made to enforce and administer the contract but not "objectional expenditures" such as "costs associated with organizing other employee groups, political and lobbying activities, social events, publicity relating to any of these areas."[93]

The union dues issue was a problem for everyone. By law, all full-term strikers also had to pay union dues. Even flight attendants who had walked off the job prior to their first flight and joined the strike had to pay. And, as time stretched over years, this accrued to a fairly high amount. IFFA had to enforce the union dues requirement, however, uniformly or risk even further entanglements. This proved to be a real hardship for the flight attendants who were out the longest.

THE GREAT PLANE ROBBERY

TWA's treatment of individual full-term strikers sometimes bordered on incredulity, but unfortunately with serious personal consequences. One such incident became the subject of a *60 Minutes* newscast in Spring 1988.[94] The story revolved around the termination of Liz Rich, a twenty-four and a half year veteran flight attendant and full-term striker, for "theft." After a ten-hour flight from New York to Paris, the flight arrived at 6:30 AM. As the flight attendants were cleaning up the plane, there were four and a half pints of milk and a used travel kit from the Ambassador Class that they were throwing away. Another flight attendant mentioned not throwing the leftover cartons of milk away, and Rich thought about it and decided, based on not having had time to eat on the flight and the fact that it was garbage, she would take the milk and fix her broken fingernail with the travel kit. When they got off the plane they were met by a supervisor who conducted a "crew kit search" of their baggage. ("I don't think I even know anyone who has had one."). They took her garbage as "evidence," and she was removed from the flight and sent home: first class where she was given two travel kits! Rich admitted that she was wrong to take the milk, but as theft, she "didn't think that it meant garbage."

"They say the question was that I took the four cups of milk which I did indeed take. I say the question is why didn't I have time to eat. I wouldn't have taken the milk if I had had time to eat. To lose 24 years of seniority, my retirement, and all my benefits, for a quart of milk is *les miserable* I think. It is a very harsh punishment."[95] As the story unfolded, it was a micro representation of the post-strike relations at TWA. The search was not random but initiated by information supplied from a crossover co-worker. Rich interpreted TWA's actions as retaliation for her participation in the strike. She had been active in the strike, organizing a "lie down" in front of the TWA headquarters in New York; and, she had been openly critical of Icahn's cost-cutting the airline. To that point, the flight itself had been understaffed. Rich reported that "she and other senior flight attendants who have been recalled to duty since the strike ended have been 'harassed' and 'spied on' by management personnel intent on replacing them." Frankovich in IFFA's support of Rich saw this as part of an overall strategy of TWA and other corporations "to find a way to rid themselves of the more senior and more costly work force."[96]

TWA insisted that it was theft, and in doing so, overreached what would have been normally the sanction—minor, such as being talked to—to termination. TWA agreed to allow Rich to retire but only if she gave up her right to any backpay from the strike court cases that were now weaving their way through the judicial system, something she was unwilling to do. "No, I will put in a grievance, accept being fired, and I will figure it out." Not an easy decision for someone fifty-three years old, a perfect record up to this incident, and someone who articulated what many of the full-term strikers articulated, their love of the job.

By April 1988, almost two years after the strike, only 1,400 flight attendants had been recalled, leaving approximately 3,800 still on the recall list.

Rich saw herself as fighting for herself and every one of them. "The majority have not committed themselves to another career. They want to go back to flying."[97] Despite TWA's position that this was standard treatment of worker wrongdoing, they went the extra distance to further oppose her right to receive unemployment. The Department of Labor ruled in her favor on the right to unemployment insurance, finding that "picking up discards . . . at most an error of judgement but no misconduct."[98]

The tenor of the *60 Minutes* investigation was clearly on the side of the flight attendant and highlighted the absurdity of TWA's position. TWA's management personnel who were interviewed to explain the company predictably did not come off looking well. IFFA reported that TWA reservation phone agents logged numerous complaints from listeners. The calls were "mostly male who also mentioned that they are frequent flyers," and the most common comment was, "will never fly TWA again until employee is reinstated." It was easy to see how a listener could legitimately want to criticize the treatment of Rich; and, it was also easy to appreciate the fact that flight attendants are spread across the United States and creative in getting their message across, any and all ways.[99]

There was a discussion of this *60 Minutes* segment at one of the recall meetings—meetings put on by IFFA to share information about the formal and informal aspects of the recall process. As it was relayed, Icahn called Rich after the airing and told her she should have called him, clearly with the implication that the whole matter could have been resolved amicably. Similar to his Saturday morning coffee klatch strolls to talk with the picketers outside his home, such a phone call was discordant with the overall treatment by Icahn and TWA. Even in this situation, that was true. Some months past this incident, TWA instituted a program for its employees, Asset Protection Program, known as C.A.R.E. As they described this new program in the company *TWA Skyliner*:

> Recognizing the importance of protecting corporate assets, the Company recently announced a program to reward the vast majority of employees who are honest and dedicated.
>
> To combat this problem [stealing], the Company recently established a hot line which employees may call anonymously to report acts of theft or other wrong doing. Any employee may simply call (800) TWA-CARE to report such acts as stealing company property, white collar fraud being perpetrated against the company, or any other unethical act. Employees need not identify themselves and they will be assigned a confidential code number.
>
> If the information proves correct, and depending on the seriousness of the matter, the employee may be paid up to $5000.[100]

C.A.R.E. became another layer of surveillance in an environment that already felt menacing. With the acronym "care" feeling like anything but, the flight attendants responded with derisive humor and suggestions of what constituted an appropriate topic for a call. In a *News and Muse*, the editors shared a set of instructions that TWA gave to flight attendants in an in-flight weekly. The TWA missive prompted a cynical rejoinder:

> The only aircraft that you will need an oven rake for are two of our 1011's that still have Bowmar ovens. However, the oven rake is *not* a no-go item so please do not incur a delay waiting for one!" The very next article states that "The Bowmar ovens operate at a much higher temperature and cook much faster." That means your personal flesh will cook much faster too when it comes into contact with the hot trays that are stuck in the back and can't be retrieved, without the rake that wasn't boarded because it's not a no-go item. TWA-CARE?[101]

THE CHICAGO CASE

Throughout the strike and its aftermath, TWA battled the flight attendants by obstructing their ability to operate as a union as well as their ability to earn a living. From declaring the entire contract as void to countless sanctions of individual workers, TWA created obstacles that hampered the livelihoods of the flight attendants. Initiated by flight attendants Kaphy Long et al., what came to be known as the Chicago Case involved the operation of the Airline Deregulation Act (ADA) of 1978. In anticipation of the impact of deregulation on employee disruptions, furloughs, and layoffs, Congress had included the Employee Protection Program in the ADA. Before implementation, however, Congress failed to approve appropriations that would supply subsidies to employees that were hurt by deregulation. The only protection that remained operational was a provision for the preferential hiring of workers who had been in the industry for at least four years, and had lost their jobs due to deregulation.

The ADA's hiring preference gave a right of first hire to eligible employees who had been "furloughed or otherwise terminated. . . . Subject to certain exceptions, an employee armed with this right can demand that another airline hire him or her over other new applicants."[102] Employers were to issue "designated rights letters" to affected workers. The Chicago case claimed that TWA had violated the ADA by refusing to give eligible flight attendants "designated rights" letters at the conclusion of their strike. The plaintiffs sought wage and benefit compensation. Based on less than 200 jobs available to full-term strikers, and the seniority of the labor force, fully 3,000 flight attendants were affected by TWA's decision. U.S. District Judge Ilana D. Rovner, N.D. Illinois, ruled in favor of the flight attendants, January 26, 1989:

> the Court concludes that replaced strikers are entitled to first hire rights under the Employee Protection Program. On May 17, 1986, when plaintiffs unconditionally offered to return to work, they ceased being voluntary strikers and were effectively terminated by TWA. TWA therefore became obligated at that time to deliver designated rights letters to plaintiffs.

The court continued in a footnote:

> It may be noted that this conclusion does not result in any unfair surprise to TWA. . . . TWA knew since at least March, 1984, that there was at least a substantial possibility that it was required to deliver designated employee notices to plaintiffs. Furthermore, delivering such notices would not have been burdensome for TWA. The court can only conclude that TWA deliberately chose not to deliver the notices, accepting the risk that they would someday be found liable, in an attempt to punish plaintiffs for exercising their right to strike.[103]

TWA appealed the decision and lost at the 7th Circuit Court of Appeals, September 21, 1990. In addition to affirming the district court's decision, the appellate court clarified the connection between the strike and deregulation,

> TWA contends that protection of economic strikers would be inconsistent with the Employee Protection Program's provisions, which TWA interprets as only assisting employees in the event of a work force reduction. TWA reads the statute too narrowly. Congressional concerns over deregulation's impact on front-line air industry employees promoted the passage of the Employee Protection Program. In this case, the industry's economic climate after deregulation forced TWA to ask the IFFA to agree to concessions at the bargaining table. Just because the union tried to protect its interests through a labor strike does not mean that the hardships suffered by individual unions members were any less the result of airline deregulation. . . . In this case, the plaintiffs lost their airline jobs amid economic upheaval in the industry.[104]

All of these struggles hit at the core of the union and its viability. Without financing coming in, their entire union was in jeopardy. Without the ability to represent flight attendants who had supported the strike as well as those who were working, the strength of the union as a legitimate representative was in jeopardy. These are attacks made directly on IFFA and it is clear that when Icahn said they would never be back, these actions were meant to bring action to those words. IFFA had to continually fight to establish its right to be the "exclusive representative of all TWA Flight Attendants."

The 198 would weather the cost of the strike from the inside. Many media and news analysts believed, like Icahn had stated in the final hours before the strike that they would never return.[105] Echoed as well by Hoar who reportedly remarked, there was "no reasonable expectancy of a return to work" for the strikers. It would take them over three years—July 14, 1989, the two hundredth anniversary of Bastille Day—to reclaim their jobs. Return would come exceedingly slow at the beginning, but in increments, all full-term strikers would be offered their jobs back. The first 198 were the only ones to return in 1986, and by the end of 1987, less than 1,000 had returned. Over the next year and a half, they came back—60 in March 1988, 516 in April, 149 in May—slowly returning to the line. In St. Louis in mid-July 1989, after thirty-eight months, Frankovich handed over her Missing in Action bracelet to the very last returnee, Kit Furness.

These last returning flight attendants had never flown—recruited in 1986, they refused to cross the picket line before ever flying. And, in the midst of essentially everyone they were training with crossing, their commitment was extraordinary. The more senior full-term strikers felt protective of them, and in an unofficial publication, listed their names, supplementing the original *Little Black Book.* Based on the flight attendant occupation where the mix of flight attendants can vary over flights, coupled with the fact that they were young similar to the majority of permanent replacements, it was important for full-term strikers already back on line to be able to identify which side they were on. This last group showed their solidarity in a number of ways, as the following story, reported by the *News and Muse,* described:

> After an International layover, an '86 FTS climbs on board the bus en route to the airport and seats herself in the front. The captain happens to be one of those 2 or 3 jerks that has always floated around the TWA system and who has deluded himself into thinking that he's the Great White Father of the Crew Bus as well as the Aircraft, and when he boards, he says she has to move. "I always sit in the front of the bus" is his irrefutable reasoning. The '86er moves to another seat, digs out her In Flight Service Procedures manual and proceeds to study it diligently. Sometime later, she marches to the front of the bus and proceeds with a well-thought-out harangue along the order of "You know, I've just looked everywhere in this manual and I can't seem to find where it says that the captain must sit in the front of the bus. Maybe I'm looking in the wrong place. Can you help me find it? I'd really like to know." And she went on and on and on! In short, she just let him have it. It was undoubtedly the most uncomfortable bus ride he has ever taken![106]

Flight attendants had fought for separate ground transportation precisely due to situations like this where they were treated as second class citizens. Having lost separate international ground transportation in the unilateral implementation of changes in 1986, it must have been gratifying to other full-term strikers back on line to see their younger sisters develop creative, informal, strategies for asserting their equality.

NOTES

1. "TWA Attendants End Strike," *New York Times*, May 23, 1986; TWA's Flight Attendants Reject Contract Proposal," *Wall Street Journal*, May 23, 1986.
2. "TWA and Union Clash on Rehiring," *Honolulu Star-Bulletin*, May 21, 1986.
3. TWA is Apparent Victor," *Kansas City Times*, May 20, 1986.
4. IFFA, *Hotline,* May 20, 1986.
5. "TWA Strike is over, but the Dispute isn't," *Los Angeles Times*, May 20, 1986.
6. IFFA, *Hotline*, May 24 86.
7. IFFA, *Hotline*, 900, May 25, 1986.
8. TWA, *TWA Skyliner*, May 26 1986. "The company has reminded IFFA that, with nearly 2,800 new hires and more than 1,300 crossovers now at work, there is a very limited number of positions available for those who might now wish to return."
9. IFFA, *Hotline*, 900, May 28, 1986.
10. "Union to Vote on TWA Pact," *Kansas City Times*, May 19, 1986.
11. "Attendants Say Battle against TWA isn't Over," *Kansas City Times*, May 23, 1986,
12. "Union to Vote on TWA Pact," *Kansas City Times*, May 19, 1986.
13. *Grounded*, produced by IFFA, 1987. IFFA puts the number at 5400.
14. IFFA, *Hotline*, 900, May 29, 1986.
15. IFFA, *Hotline*, May 18, 1986.
16. Ibid.
17. "Union Rejecting TWA Pact," *Kansas City Times*, May 22, 1986.
18. IFFA, *Off the Line: The Newsletter of Un-Flight Services*, Summer 1986.
19. Ibid.
20. Associated Press, "Vote on T.W.A. Contract Set," *New York Times*, May 19, 1986.
21. "Union Rejecting TWA Pact," *Kansas City Times*, May 22, 1986.
22. IFFA, *Hotline*, 900, May 22, 1986; "Union Rejecting TWA Pact," *Kansas City Times*, May 22, 1986.
23. "IFFA/TWA Conflict Not Over," *Labor Beacon*, May 30, 1986.
24. IFFA, *Off the Line: The Newsletter of Un-Flight Services*, Summer 1986.
25. "TWA Flight Attendants Reject Contract Proposal," *Aviation Daily*, May 23, 1986.
26. Ibid.
27. IFFA, *Hotline*, 900, June 5, 1986.
28. IFFA, *The 630 News: The Official Publication*, Summer 1987.
29. "Union to Vote on TWA Pact," *Kansas City Times*, May 19, 1986.
30. IFFA, *Hotline*, June 18, 1986.
31. Jill Lawrence, "TWA Boycott Urged by Women's Groups, Seven House Members," *Associated Press*, June 18, 1986.
32. "IFFA Calls for a National Boycott of TWA," *PR Newswire*, June 18, 1986.
33. Jill Lawrence, "TWA Boycott Urged by Women's Groups, Seven House Members," *Associated Press*, June 18, 1986.
34. IFFA, *Off the Line: The Newsletter of Un-Flight Services*, no date, est., May/June, 1986.

35. Ibid.

36. Wilma Pearl Mankiller, ed., *The Reader's Companion to U.S. Women's History* (Boston: Houghton Mifflin, 1998).

37. TWA, *TWA Skyliner*, March 15, 1987; "U.S. Equal Employment Opportunity Commission Dismisses Charges," *PR Newswire*, March 15, 1987.

38. IFFA, *Hotline*, 900, July 3, 1986.

39. IFFA, "IFFA Supports other Union Action," *Boycotts and Rallies*, 1988.

40. Barry Hudock, "America," *National Catholic Review*, August 27, 2012; "Cesar's Choice: How America's Farm Workers Got Organized," *El Malcriado*, April 1, 1969.

41. Renate Robey, "Airline Reserves Phone Work for Young Prisoners," *Los Angeles Times*, January 13, 1986; "California Wards of State used by TWA to Fill in For Strikers," *Las Vegas Review Journal*, March 14, 1986.

42. "California Wards of State used by TWA to Fill in For Strikers," *Las Vegas Review Journal*, March 14, 1986.

43. Renate Robey, "Strikers Angry, Airline's Use of CYA Labor," *Los Angeles Times*, March 14, 1986.

44. IFFA Documents: Samples of Support from Organized Labor; Endorser List; and, Samples of City and State Resolutions.

45. *Corporatecampaign.org*, ret., May 11, 2007.

46. IFFA Documents, Letter to IFFA, National Spokesperson, Solidarity Movement, Poland.

47. IFFA, *Off the Line: The Newsletter of Un-Flight Services*, December 1987.

48. Studs Terkel, *The Great Divide: Second Thoughts on the American Dream* (New York: Pantheon Books, 1988).

49. "UFW Broadens Grape Boycott," *Food and Justice*, December 1986.

50. Arthur B. Shostak and David Skocik, *The Air Controllers' Controversy: Lessons from the Patco Strike* (New York: Human Sciences Press, 1981).

51. August 16, 1981, advertisement in *the New York Times*.

52. "Labor Chief Recalls Futile Effort to Support Controller Strike," *New York Times*, October 5, 1981.

53. IFFA, *The 630 News: The Official Publication*, Summer 1987, "An Anniversary Remembered."

54. "Union Had Prepared Strategy to Counter Bankruptcy Filing," *Los Angeles Times*, March 10, 1989; *Workers Vanguard*, March 17, 1989.

55. IFFA, "IFFA Supports other Union Action," *Boycotts and Rallies*, 1988.

56. IFFA, *Off the Line: The Newsletter of Un-Flight Services*, 1987.

57. *National Boycott News*, Spring/Summer 1989, 68.

58. *Ms*, January 1987.

59. Ibid., 99.

60. Gloria Steinem, *My Life on the Road* (New York: Random House, 2015), 93.

61. Kathleen M. Barry, *Femininity in Flight: A History of Flight Attendants* (Durham: Duke University, 2007), 192–93; Lindsy Van Gelder, "Coffee, Tea Or Fly Me," *Ms.*, January 1973.

62. "Laborem Exercens, Summary," *Catholic-pages.com*, ret. October 1, 2013.

63. "What Does Catholic Church Teach About Labor Unions,"*BustedHalo.com*, ret., June 6, 2015.

64. Laura Sessions Stepp, "Papal Flight Plans Anger Ex-Attendants," *Washington Post*, July 14, 1987.

65. Ibid.

66. Robert Furlow, "Bishops Choose TWA for Pope's Visit, Despite Union's Objections," *Associated Press*, May 15, 1987.

67. IFFA, *Letter*, July 8, 1987; *Los Angeles Times*, "Papal Visit Update," July 25, 1987.

68. IFFA *Letter*, July 8, 1987.

69. Ibid.

70. Laura Sessions Stepp, "Papal Flight Plans Anger Ex-Attendants," *Washington Post*, July 14, 1987.

71. IFFA, *Off the Line: The Newsletter of Un-Flight Services*, October 1987.

72. Monica Rhor, "Protests, Rallies during Papal Visit Will Range in Focus," *Sun Sentinel* (Miami), August 21, 1987.

73. IFFA, *Off the Line: The Newsletter of Un-Flight Services*, October 1987.

74. Monica Rhor, "Protests, Rallies during Papal Visit Will Range in Focus," *Sun Sentinel* (Miami), August 21, 1987.

75. Ibid.; Associated Press, "Protesters Plan to Stay Busy during Pope's Visit," *Tampa Bay Times*, August 22, 1987.

76. IFFA, *Off the Line: The Newsletter of Un-Flight Services*, December, 1987, 18.

77. Ibid., October 1987, 12.

78. Ibid., December, 1987, 18.

79. Ibid.

80. Ibid., October, 1987, 13.

81. *Prohibiting Discrimination against Economic Strikers: Hearings on S. 55 Before the Subcommittee on Labor of the Committee on Labor and Human Resources, March 12*, 102d Cong., First (1991).

82. *Preventing Replacement of Economic Strikers: Hearings on S. 2112 Before the Subcommittee on Labor of the Committee on Labor and Human Resources, June 6*, 101st Cong., second (1990).

83. IFFA, *Hotline*, 900, May 30, 1986.

84. IFFA, *Hotline*, May 31, 1986.

85. IFFA, *Hotline*, June 10, 1986; 900, May 28, 1986.

86. *Grounded*, produced by IFFA, 1987.

87. *The F.T.S. News & Muse*, September 1989, 3.

88. IFFA v. TWA (W. D. Missouri, Bad Faith Bargaining 1988), Exhibits, 421.

89. Ibid., Exhibit 425.

90. Ibid., Exhibit 415.

91. Ibid., Exhibit 464.

92. Ibid., Exhibit 453.

93. Ibid.

94. *60 Minutes*, "The Great Plane Robbery," CBS, March 20, 1988, produced by Joseph Wershba.

95. Ibid.

96. Beverly Beyette, "The Case of the Missing Milk Cartons: It Was Only a Minor Theft but Airline and Attendant Agree It's Now a Major Case," *Los Angeles Times*, April 10, 1988.

97. Ibid.

98. *60 Minutes*, "The Great Plane Robbery," CBS, March 20, 1988, produced by Joseph Wershba.

99. IFFA, *Off the Line: The Newsletter*, n.d. est. May 1988, 16.

100. TWA, *TWA Skyliner*, December 15, 1988, 1.

101. *The F.T.S. News & Muse*, November-December 1990, 5.

102. Kaphy Long v. TWA (7th Cir. 1990).

103. Kaphy Long v. TWA (U.S. District Court, N.D. Illinois, E.D. 1989).

104. Kaphy Long v. TWA (7th Cir. 1990).

105. Carolyn Friday, "A Fatal Flight Takes its Toll," *Newsweek*, September 8, 1986, 38–40.

106. *The F.T.S. News & Muse*, October 1989.

Chapter 8

Legal Challenges and the Development of Labor Law

The legal dimensions of the conflict between IFFA and TWA spanned the District to Supreme Court level, and in the determinations of the cases, labor law would be changed, and major debates over the rights of labor and the viability of the strike would be carried out on a national level. One of the outcomes of changing labor relations and deregulation in the airline industry has been the elongation of labor disputes through judicial filings. Both parties file suits and counter suits that weave their way through the court system resolving sometimes years after the initial labor dispute.

The legal side of this labor dispute was broad in the total number of cases filed, long in the time it took to resolution and the sheer amount of court time, and significant in its reach to the Supreme Court and its impact on the labor movement. Though the number of court cases was seemingly infinite, there were three legal contests that occupied much of the energy and attention of both parties: bad faith bargaining; status quo/union security; and, the case that stands at the core of this dispute and the one that has reverberated throughout the labor movement, the crossover case. The status quo/union security case was initiated by TWA. For its part, IFFA fought the battle on two different fronts, arguing in a bad faith bargaining case that the workers were unfair labor practice strikers eligible for reinstatement and back pay; and failing that, IFFA argued that the workers were economic strikers illegally displaced by new hires, trainees, and crossovers.

BAD FAITH BARGAINING CASE

IFFA's bad faith bargaining case actually began in the final days of the cooling off period with a request for a temporary restraining order against TWA implementing their wage and work rule reductions in the event that the two parties entered the self-help stage. The court denied the injunction and urged the two parties, unsuccessfully, to try to come to agreement. IFFA struck and TWA implemented wage and work rule reductions.[1]

Shortly after the strike, IFFA filed suit in July 1986 and argued that the strike was caused by TWA's failure to bargain in good faith and because of that, strikers should be defined and treated as *unfair labor practice strikers* eligible for reinstatement and back pay. Hearings began in November 1986 in Kansas City and occupied thirty-one days of actual court time and spanned four and a half months—reported at the time as the longest court case in the history of the U.S. District Court for the Western District of Missouri. It was also the first bad faith bargaining case ever tried under the RLA. IFFA's lead counsel was William Jolley from the offices of Jolley, Walsh, Hager, and Gordon from Kansas City, Missouri; and, Murray Gartner and Paul E. Donnelly from Proskauer; Rose, Goetz & Mendelsohn, LLP, New York City represented TWA. Compiling over 7,000 pages of court transcripts, Gartner and Donnelly requested a dismissal of the complaint after IFFA presented its position. On March 3, 1988—almost two years to the date of the beginning of the strike—Judge Howard E. Sachs dismissed the case, and the Eighth Circuit Court of Appeals refused to hear it on appeal. In its refusal to hear the case, the Court of Appeals provided a succinct description of the main points in the case:

> In broad terms, IFFA's theory in the district court was that TWA bargained in bad faith. IFFA claimed TWA consequently failed to carry out its obligation under the Railway Labor Act "to exert every reasonable effort to make and maintain agreements concerning rates of pay, rules, and working conditions, and to settle all disputes." . . . IFFA made a number of specific allegations of TWA's bad-faith bargaining, including: failing to provide requested information concerning bargaining proposals; dealing with a union other than the flight attendants' authorized bargaining representative; making impermissible agreements with flight attendant trainees before the strike; bargaining to impasse on a nonmandatory subject of bargaining; adopting a negotiating posture that showed bad faith, intent not to reach agreement, and sexual discrimination; and maintaining that negotiating posture in a manner that prolonged the strike.[2]

In dismissing the case at the district level, Judge Sachs rendered the decision that, even though many of the arguments that IFFA made against TWA had validity and he favored IFFA witnesses for their credibility over TWA (and specifically Icahn), he concluded that the strike occurred because the two parties were too far apart in the final hours. Judge Sachs in his seventy-seven page decision, wrote, "It plainly appears from the record that the sole cause of the impasse was the wide divergence between the demands of TWA

(Icahn) and the more modest concessions proposed by IFFA."[3] Further, Judge Sachs believed that the demands of TWA met the wide latitude test of reasonableness, and that TWA was not guilty of prolonging the strike by its actions.

One of the most difficult issues for the flight attendants was what they perceived, and argued in court, as the sex discrimination imbedded in the dispute. On its most general level, this played out as differential treatment of the primarily male labor forces, ALPA and specifically the more comparable IAM, and the primarily IFFA female labor force of flight attendants. As IFFA explained, an 85 percent female labor force was asked to concede $100 million among its 6,000 members, but the primarily male IAM labor force was asked to concede $50 million spread over 10,000 members.[4]

Compounded by the higher demands made of the flight attendants, was the manner in which both TWA/Icahn and the male unions operated in their relationships with IFFA. On the one hand, IFFA was part of the coalition of the three unions that came together early on to find an alternative buyer to Icahn, but once Lorenzo entered the picture, the males unions quickly moved toward negotiations with Icahn. From the beginning of these negotiations, it appeared that Frankovich and the flight attendants were relegated to the periphery. When the male unions made a deal with Icahn, and what seemed to IFFA that they had also made the deal *for* IFFA and at a much harsher rate, it raised the specter that *male* unions collaborated with *male* employers to the detriment of a *female* union.

IFFA directed their primary charges of sex discrimination at Icahn and his dealings with the flight attendants. The most infamous comments came from the August 1985 meeting where Icahn reportedly explained why he was demanding more from the flight attendants than the machinists. Icahn explained that IAM members, even ones with less skills than other IAM workers, were "breadwinners."[5] Other comments he made in the course of the conflict, e.g., flight attendants were second incomes, they should have married a rich husband, perpetuated the stereotype of women workers.

Sex discrimination falls under Title VII of the Civil Rights Act of 1964, and Judge Sachs noted that a case under the RLA had every right to make a judgment on a case of sex discrimination as well. Judge Sachs did not dispute that Icahn made such statements. And, if Icahn dealt with the flight attendants differently because he did not believe they were breadwinners, then TWA/Icahn would be guilty of sex discrimination and a violation of Title VII of the Civil Rights Act.[6] In dismissing IFFA's case, however, Judge Sachs interpreted Icahn's statements as "mere" rationalizations for what was really his economic motivation. Icahn believed he could get other workers to do the job of flight attendants at less pay, and ultimately, the flight attendants lacked the power on their own to shut down the airline. As Icahn had said to Frankovich, "what are you going to do, blow up the airline?"

Perhaps the most surprising explanation offered by Judge Sachs to support his opinion that Icahn's "'breadwinner' statement was a foolish and offensive rationalization, having no probable relationship with Icahn's true rationale for demanding disproportionate concessions from IFFA," came from his interpretation of Marx:

> IFFA's theory, that the breadwinner reference reveals Icahn's motivation, would signify that he is a devotee of the Marxist or utopian distribution system, "to each according to his needs." While even normally doctrinaire capitalists may be influenced by such motivations occasionally in setting wages for persons in their immediate entourage, it is entirely implausible that a hard-boiled "corporate raider" (to use the label of the Court of Appeals) would subscribe to that method of setting wages for middle income personnel. When Icahn ultimately acknowledged that some flight attendants really did need the old wage-rates, he said they must 'accept the realities here.' Tr. 4023. That statement reflects probable thought processes, and I believe it to be the key to this controversy. There has been no persuasive showing that sex stereotyping governed or influenced Icahn's economic demands—only his rationalizations."[7]

IFFA tried to counter the interpretation of flight attendant skill in its brief to the U.S. Court of Appeals, but it was a complicated issue to try to explain. They argued that the very perception of flight attendants as less skilled than machinists arose out of a sex stereotype. In its appeal, IFFA counsel footnoted the following:

> Even the "greater skill" and "greater power" allegedly possessed by the IAM are sex-biased considerations. Icahn's skill/marketplace assessments of F/As are inherently tainted by the "second income" perception: the "greater economic power" attributed to the IAM clearly has its roots in a male-female stereotype."

And in the body of the appeal:

> Icahn negotiated for one month, and settled terms, with the men (ALPA and IAM); he afforded IFFA (the girls) a single, undefined day to accept agreement on terms the men had established. . . . Icahn insisted on far greater concessions from IFFA than any other segment of the workforce. Icahn provided a snap-back to both the IAM and ALPA, . . . but denied it to IFFA. This is not power or marketplace; it is "second income" versus "breadwinner."[8]

Judge Sachs' dismissal was an important victory for TWA and a devastating loss for IFFA. As Jolley commented, "to say Judge Sachs' decision was a disappointment is an understatement." Conversely, TWA counsel explained, "Of all the cases they've brought, this is probably the most significant and all-encompassing." Icahn was quoted in the *TWA Skyliner*, "we're very grateful that the judicial system has worked by vindicating us."[9]

The U.S. Court of Appeals for the Eighth Circuit affirmed Judge Sachs' decision on June 28, 1989, and denied rehearing on August 16, 1989. In a letter to flight attendants, IFFA acknowledged their disappointment in the decision but also acknowledged what they had been able to accomplish:

> We cannot minimize the impact of this decision, but we should not blow it out of proportion. The Bad Faith lawsuit had three objectives—full reinstatement of all strikers, back pay, and restitution of pre-strike work rules and benefits. Of these, the most important was the full reinstatement of strikers—and through our perseverance and previous court victories full reinstatement has become a reality. Some 200 full term strikers still await recall, and their return is imminent.[10]

On January 16, 1990, The Supreme Court refused to hear the case, and as Jolley concluded, "The wage reductions and more onerous working conditions imposed by TWA (in 1986) are now set in stone."[11]

STATUS QUO/UNION SECURITY CASE

Under the RLA, no contract ever expires, it is only amendable. Those parts of the contract that are not on the table for discussion in the negotiations remain intact. The idea is that there is an ongoing relationship that is not severed with each contract. As the United States Court of Appeals, Eighth Circuit explained negotiations under the RLA:

> [t]hese collective bargaining agreements are the product of years of struggle and negotiation; they represent the rules governing the community of striking employees and the carrier. That community is not destroyed by the strike, as the strike represents only an interruption in the continuity of the relation. Were a strike to be the occasion for a carrier to tear up and annul, so to speak, the entire collective bargaining agreement, labor-management relations would revert to the jungle.[12]

TWA challenged this basic assumption of labor relations under the RLA about six weeks into the strike—April 17, 1986—"seeking declaration that the collective bargaining agreement had expired and that TWA therefore was not obligated to observe the union security or related provisions, whether subject to negotiations or not."[13] TWA's position was that once both parties were released to self-help the contract in its entirety had expired. They were free to implement not only the wage and work rule changes that had been the basis of negotiations under the watchful eye of the NMB, but they could make any changes, essentially do anything, because the agreement no longer existed. Although TWA would lose at the District, Appellate, and Supreme Court, in the two years that it took to judgment, TWA acted as if the contract had expired and circumvented seniority, instituted new policies, and obstructed IFFA's ability to operate.

The specific focus of the TWA suit was on the union security clause. From the very beginning TWA vacillated between arguing that the case was only about the union security clause and acknowledging the broader implications of their suit. This clause, Article 24, established the obligation of union membership: the ability of IFFA to collect monthly dues from all flight attendants, as well as initiation dues from new flight attendants; the requirement of dues check-off for TWA to collect monthly dues from wages; and, the right of IFFA to initiate termination for flight attendants who did not pay. TWA argued they no longer had an obligation to dues check-off for flight attendants and ceased to do so. TWA argued that "once all statutory procedures have been exhausted, no purpose of the RLA is served by continuing the dues check-off provision in effect, as such regulation of the relationship between the union and its members is lawful only by virtue of the collective agreement."[14]

Jolley explained to the flight attendant membership the connection between TWA's union security case and the broader challenge to their negotiated agreement. Once IFFA went out on strike:

> [TWA] took the position that your contract expired. That no provision of the Red Book survived, that it wasn't bound by any restrictions that previously existed in the contract and that it could change whatever provision whenever it wanted at any time in connection with any segment of the workforce. The issue arose in the context of the union security or the dues obligation—that's because that was the first provision that TWA hadn't negotiated about that it told IFFA it was changing . . . but the impact goes way beyond the union security provision and way beyond the obligation to pay dues."[15]

On August 1, 1986, District Court Judge Sachs ruled against TWA and concluded, "The contract in question is amendable in accordance with its provisions [duration clause] and the Railway Labor Act. It does not wholly terminate, either automatically or upon service of notices of a limited number of intended changes."[16] With the union security clause in operation, Judge Sachs ordered TWA to resume dues check-off and adhere to Article 24 (union security).

On October 15, 1986, TWA appealed the decision to the United States Court of Appeals, Eighth Circuit. The three judge panel focused on the duration clause in the agreement between TWA and IFFA which outlined the effective dates of the contract (1981–1984), the provision that the contract would "renew itself without change for yearly periods" unless either or both parties issued a Section 6 notice of changes at least ninety days before the renewal date.

In a unanimous decision on January 14, 1987, the appellate court affirmed the district court decision, and concluded with:

> To read the clause as proposed by TWA frustrates the basic purpose of the RLA. An airline employer, such as TWA, may flout the entire purpose of the RLA by not filing a section 6 notice with regard to certain changes it intends to make. Under such circumstances, the carrier may hide its true intention to make certain changes so that the change is never negotiated and the NMB never has an opportunity to mediate the dispute. This leaves the carrier free to unilaterally change a condition of employment, here the extremely important condition of union security, without ever having to negotiate, mediate or arbitrate the dispute. There is simply nothing in the duration clause at issue here which leads this court to conclude that the parties intended a result so at odds with the RLA."[17]

The U.S. Supreme Court agreed to hear the case, and oral argument was held on January 12, 1988. Although the case focused specifically on the issue of union security, the broader implications of TWA's position were addressed and the discordance between TWA's position and the purpose of the RLA were highlighted. At the Supreme Court level, the tension between TWA's limited focus on union security and their unlimited view that the contract expired in its entirety and left TWA free to change anything, occupied a significant amount of the hearings. Gartner representing TWA said that the only issue before the court was the termination of the union security clause, and yet Justice Antonin Scalia noted that he spent a lot of time talking about the broader agreement:

> *Justice Scalia:* I thought you said that question was not before us here. The way you are talking now, you are expanding that proposition not just to the union security provision but to all the provisions of the contract.
>
> *Mr. Gartner:*—I agree, Justice Scalia, it is not before you. The only reason I am mentioning it is that Respondent has spent too much time trying to persuade the Court that it is before you . . .
>
> And later,
>
> *Unidentified Justice:* So it really is your view, is it not, then, that the entire contract terminated when you gave whatever the date period was after the notice?
>
> *Mr. Gartner:* That is our view, yes, Justice Stevens.
>
> And again,
>
> *Unidentified Justice:* So you really have two provisions. One, the whole contract is over, or two, even if it is not, this one [union security] is.
>
> *Mr. Gartner:* Yes.[18]

When Steven Fehr argued for IFFA, he emphasized their belief that this was a much larger case than the single issue of union security:

> *Mr. Fehr:* Thank you, Mr. Chief Justice, and may it please the Court: I would like to start by attempting to clarify some things in the record. First, the notion that this case was tried upon a narrow ground related to the sole change of union security is untrue. TWA filed this case as a declaratory judgment asking the Court to declare, among other things, that the contract expired.[19]

In a 4–4 tie vote (Justice Anthony Kennedy had joined the court after oral arguments), the Supreme Court decision left in place the appellate opinion. This was a major victory for IFFA, and as Frankovich said, "This decision ensures the continued survival of our union." And, as IFFA noted, this was an important victory for all unions under the RLA because it prevented an employer from sidestepping the negotiation process and waiting until self-help to introduce changes without negotiation.[20] As Fehr stated in oral argument to the Supreme Court justices, in explaining the effect of a system that would allow employers to make changes outside the negotiation process, "The carrier can simply hold back and wait and say during self-help I can break the union by implementing all these changes." And, that was pretty close to what happened in this case prior to the Supreme Court decision.

The Supreme Court decision came on March 2, 1988, almost two years to the date of the commencement of the strike. In that time, TWA had ignored over 20 provisions of the contract, and this decision would force compliance. In addition to union security, TWA had created a new grievance procedure that barred full-term strikers from application, prevented union representatives from entering the property to represent flight attendants, violated seniority in allocation of flight service manager jobs, and failed to terminate the employment of flight attendants who did not pay dues.[21] The case not only addressed what TWA had changed but stopped further erosion of negotiated agreements. In an occupation that has an intricate set of rules governing work, Jolley told IFFA members, "What stands between TWA and further elimination of rest, further raising the cap, lowering the salaries, lifting all restrictions from balancing, reducing crew complement, is your status quo victory. It is a case in which every flight attendant has won."[22] TWA requested a rehearing, but the request was denied by the Supreme Court on March 6, 1989.[23]

THE ECONOMIC REINSTATEMENT CASE: TRAINEES, NEW HIRES, AND CROSSOVERS.

IFFA's bad faith bargaining case was based on the argument that the flight attendants were *unfair labor strikers*. The second front upon which IFFA fought was based on the argument that the flight attendants were *economic strikers*. When President Frankovich made an unconditional offer to return to work on May 17, 1986, there were only 198 positions available to the full-term strikers, leaving approximately 5,000 flight attendants without jobs.[24] IFFA argued for reinstatement of strikers over three different classes of flight attendants: trainees, new hires, and crossovers. They would prevail in one of these: trainees.

Trainees

TWA had 463 individuals who were still in training on May 17, 1986. Decided at the district level on September 9, 1986, affirmed at the appellate on May 26, 1987, and the Supreme Court refused hearing on March 21, 1988. These trainees were not yet employees and were judged to be illegally put on the line, denying reinstatement to 463 full-term strikers and setting in motion a backpay penalty to TWA. Icahn, who had made a personal promise to all replacement workers that they would always have a job, had to make a decision to either add 463 full-term strikers in addition to keeping the 463 trainees, terminate the trainees, or find alternative employment for them. TWA elected to offer the 463 trainees other jobs within TWA.[25]

New Hires

A second part of the reinstatement case was IFFA's argument that the first set of flight attendants employed by TWA on March 7, 1986, about 1200, were not legally *permanent replacements*, but simply *new additions* to the workforce. Although IFFA recognized the right of employers to permanently replace workers under the Mackay Doctrine, they argued here that this first group of flight attendants hired by TWA were not permanent replacements because TWA planned to hire new flight attendants whether there was a strike or not. IFFA lost this argument at both the district and appellate levels, on September 9, 1986, and May 26, 1987, respectively. As District Judge Sachs concluded:

> The only reasonable understanding beginning March 7 was that the new hires were being employed for permanent jobs, with initial service that may be legalistically referred to as "strike replacement" or more commonly termed strikebreaking. This is doubtless the way IFFA described the work at the time, and the description seems accurate. In the derogatory term of the labor movement, the new hires were "scabs."[26]

Crossovers

Of all the cases, what came to be known as the "crossover case" hit labor the hardest, strengthening the rights accorded to employers. Seen as an expansion of the Mackay Doctrine, one of the most criticized Supreme Court decisions in labor law, the crossover case expanded the Mackay Doctrine and dealt a "fundamental blow" to labor.[27] To understand the significance of the crossover case, a closer examination of the Mackay Doctrine is necessary.

NLRB v. Mackay Radio & Telegraph Co. established that employers have the right to permanently replace economic strikers in order to run their businesses.[28] The right was given, and "has haunted the labor movement ever since."[29] The 1938 Supreme Court case involved a strike by the American Radio Telegraphists' Association (ARTA) against Mackay Radio. Mackay hired replacement workers. When the strike was over, Mackay rehired some of the strikers but did not rehire the most active unionists, who were also some of the most highly skilled, highly paid workers. The Supreme Court upheld the right of workers to strike and argued that Mackay had discriminated against workers who had been active unionists in the strike, a clear violation of the NLRA. The Court ordered the reinstatement of these workers.

Hidden within this victory for labor, was a remark, or dictum, by the Supreme Court justices that came out of a discussion of unfair labor practices. Mackay Radio had argued that, because they had not been charged with any unfair labor practices, the Board should not have been involved in the first place. In chronicling the events that took place, prior to the charge of discrimination in the rehiring of striking workers, the Court affirmed that Mackay Radio had not committed any unfair labor practices, and went on to say:

> it does not follow that an employer, guilty of no act denounced by the statute, has lost the right to protect and continue his business by supplying places left vacant by strikers. And he is not bound to discharge those hired to fill the places of strikers, upon the election of the latter to resume their employment, in order to create places for them. The assurance by respondent to those who accepted employment during the strike that if they so desired their places might be permanent was not an unfair labor practice nor was it such to reinstate only so many of the strikers as there were vacant places to be filled.[30]

What has come to be known as the Mackay Doctrine, the right to hire permanent replacements when workers exercise their right to strike, has had devastating effects on workers and communities. As Julius Getman wrote, a court dictum "announced with no serious discussion and no evidence" has caused enormous hardship for workers. "The harm caused by the *Mackay* doctrine over the years has been immense. Lives have been wrecked, deaths have been caused, families have been torn apart, lifelong friendships have been terminated, and communities have been destroyed."[31]

The Mackay Doctrine sat unnoticed within this case for some time. The first critique of it came three years later, but its full implications were really not addressed until the 1960s, and reflects the changing strength of the labor movement.[32] There are two interesting strains in the discussion of the Mackay Doctrine. First, why did it have such a slow beginning; and second, how do labor and management explain the growing usage of the Mackay Doctrine. To the first issue, in the past, when a strike was over, employers and employees were more likely to enter into back to work agreements that returned striking workers to the workplace, replacing temporary replacement workers. Employees wanted their workers back, and workers wanted to return to work. But as the labor force has become increasingly deskilled the need to return workers because of the value of their skills to the employers, attenuated.[33] Other reasons have been cited as well. For example, in addition to wanting your skilled workers back, the strength of unions at the time was a factor and community support for strikers made the cost of employing strikebreakers high. Employers at the time of the Mackay case had enough incentives to avoid using permanent replacements in times of conflict.

The second issue involves labor and management's differential perceptions of the use of the Mackay Doctrine over time. Management has maintained the position that there has been a steady use of permanent replacements in strike situation throughout history. Labor has been more likely to make the argument that, although the Mackay Doctrine has been on the books since the late 1930s, permanent replacements were rarely used until the 1980s. In this scenario, the watershed event was Reagan's overnight firing of some 12,000 PATCO strikers and their permanent replacement, and the blacklisting of these public employees and striking air traffic controllers. According to labor, Reagan's actions opened a floodgate of management animosity to labor and gave them free license to go after labor, knowing that they had a friend in the White House. This theme is echoed from labor leaders to analysts to politicians. Democratic Senator Howard Metzenbaum saw Reagan's actions as having "legitimized a much more aggressive, and even hostile, employer strategy during labor disputes."[34]

Both scenarios presented by labor and management are at least partially correct. It is correct that permanent replacements were not often used in the decades following the Mackay Doctrine. Labor, on the other hand, was slightly off on the date of its increase. The increase started in the mid-1970s, and there was a corresponding increase in the use of consultants to assist management in the creation of antiunion and union-avoidance strategies on the part of management.[35] The 1970s was a decade of growing strain in the labor/management relationship as increased globalization began to deteriorate the American wage—a wage that had been a trade-off for managerial decision-making power that was at the basis of the Post WWII social contract.[36]

Labor's date may have been off but their focus on the 1980s was certainly warranted based on the surge in its usage. Reagan's resolute actions against PATCO workers advanced the union busting agenda of private employers:

> It was among private sector union workers that the influence of the controllers' strike proved enduringly devastating, for PATCO's destruction marked the beginning of the end of one of organized labor's most reliable weapons: the strike. Occurring at a vulnerable moment in U.S. working-class history, the PATCO debacle catalyzed a revival of strikebreaking that helped marginalize the strike as a feature of American labor relations by the end of the twentieth century.[37]

In addition to the use of permanent replacements by TWA, there were high-profile strikes that involved permanent replacements throughout industries, for example, Phelps Dodge (1983), Hormel (1985), Iowa Beef (1986), International Paper (1987), Pittston Coal (1989), and Eastern Airlines (1989).[38] Newspapers found themselves particularly vulnerable already in the late 1970s, and the onslaught continued in the 1980s and beyond.[39] The surge of the 1980s carried into the early 1990s by employers such as Bridgestone-Firestone, Caterpillar, and Diamond Walnut Growers.[40] The 1985 United pilot strike and the 1990 lockout at Ravenswood, employing permanent and temporary replacements respectively, were noteworthy for their positive outcome.[41] The decline in labor strikes since the mid-1980s has been dramatic, and has been directly linked to the threat and use of permanent replacements, raising the serious question of the viability of labor's most powerful legal right. National legislative attempts to ban permanent replacements grew in strength until the mid-1990s, but failed to clear Senate opposition.[42]

Whereas the Mackay Doctrine set in place the employer's right to hire permanent replacements, IFFA's crossover case challenged the definition of permanent replacement. IFFA's argued that union members who either chose not to go out on strike or abandoned the strike, both defined as crossovers, should not be equated with permanent replacements and treated as such under the law. IFFA described their basic argument to their members:

> federal law affords employees protection of the right to strike; that under federal law, full term strikers are entitled to their jobs at the strikes end; that the only exception under federal law is the right of an employer to operate his business during a strike by hiring if necessary, "permanent replacements;" and that crossovers were not hired as "permanent replacements."[43]

IFFA position was that crossovers were *not* permanent replacements and any available jobs not occupied by permanent replacements should be filled by seniority and not on the basis of whether an employee exercised their right to strike or chose to exercise their right not to strike. The practical consequences of this argument would be a reshuffling of workers: all available positions not occupied by permanent replacements would be determined by seniority, bumping many junior crossovers out of jobs and onto the recall list. The largest contingent of crossovers came from the most junior workers; 95 percent of the 1986 hires, and about 50 percent of the 1985 hires, crossed. Jolley explained that all of the reinstatement cases:

> The purpose and effort of these three cases [trainees, new hires, and crossovers] is not to punish or reward based on strike activity or union activity but to enforce legal rights and obligations. Seniority systems have always given benefits to some and not to others when there are too few benefits to go around, and the purpose of these cases is to insure that non-discriminatory bases continue and not rewarding employees based on who crossed the picket line, who didn't cross the picket line, who helped the company, who exercised their right to strike.[44]

IFFA lost at the District level (September 9, 1986), won at the appellate (May 26, 1987), and, in a 6–3 decision, lost at the Supreme Court (February 28, 1989). According to Judge Sachs in District Court, there was no case precedent for deciding on crossovers, and the court relied on the Mackay Doctrine. He ruled that the logic that drives the right of an employer to hire permanent replacements can be applied equally to crossovers. Drawing on his interpretation of *NLRB v Erie Resistor Corp. (1963)*, "an employer . . . need not discharge those who work during the strike," Judge Sachs reasoned that this statement would "protect" crossovers just like new hires. In the same way that the Mackay Doctrine presumed "new" employees would need the inducement of permanence of employment, he assumed that an "inducement of similar attractiveness" would need to be offered to "old" employees to get them to refuse to strike or abandon the strike, cross picket lines, and return to work. "If *Mackay Radio* is sound . . . the same principles would seem to apply to protect crossovers."[45]

On appeal, the Eighth Circuit Court of Appeals reversed the district court's decision on crossovers, writing that "the terms of the bargaining agreement prevent the cross-overs from being considered permanent replacements." The court directed attention to the union security clause in the agreement between IFFA and TWA where union membership was a condition of employment. By definition, then, all crossovers must continue their union membership (if only to the extent that they pay union dues). Their status as union members meant that TWA cannot discriminate between them (crossovers) and other union members (full-term strikers) based on their "degree of union activity."[46]

The Appellate court based its decision on the union security clause in the collective bargaining agreement, but also their interpretation of law. Again, using *Erie Resistor*, the Supreme Court affirmed the National Labor

Relations Board's (NLRB) position that an employer could not offer permanent replacements and crossovers "superseniority" because it "unlawfully discriminated against those who engaged in union activity."[47] According to the appellate court:

> Awarding the cross-overs permanent replacement status differentiates employees on the basis of their union activity, induces employees to abandon the strike and is likely to create long-term conflict and division within the workforce of those working together under the union security clause.

The appellate courts' reversal of the district court decision was summed up, "we hold that unreinstated strikers are entitled to displace cross-over employees with lesser seniority."[48]

It was an extremely important win for IFFA and for the labor movement in general. But on February 28, 1989, the Supreme Court reversed the appellate court. In a 6–3 decision authored by Justice Sandra Day O'Connor, the court overturned the decision. IFFA had repeated its argument that crossovers are fundamentally different than permanent replacements and to treat them as the same violated the right to strike. Relying on *Erie Resistor*, IFFA argued that treating crossovers like permanent replacements created "cleavages" among workers "long after the strike." IFFA further argued that TWA's insistence that crossovers have the same rights as permanent replacements, "set up a competition among those individuals who participated in the original decision to strike, and thereby undermined the group's ability to take the collective action that is the very purpose of the [RLA] to protect."[49]

In the Supreme Court opinion, Justice Sandra Day O'Connor and the majority rejected what they viewed as IFFA's expansion of *Erie Resistor*, and interpreted TWA's actions as "lawful:"

> Because full term strikers were accorded their full seniority once they were reinstated, the Supreme Court held that the costs to workers of striking did not parallel the issue of super-seniority at issue in Erie Resistor. To the extent that there is "cleavage" among workers—crossovers and full term strikers—is "within the arsenal of economic weapons available to employers."[50]

Throughout, IFFA counsel argued that it was an error to consider flight attendants who (a) remained on the job and chose not to join the strike or (b) abandoned the strike prior to the union's unconditional offer to return to work the same as permanent replacements. To assume that someone who worked as a flight attendant, and therefore was also part of the union, was a replacement worker undermined the rights of the union to strike. An employer who gives incentives to workers to abandon a strike illegally interferes with the right of workers to organize and the corresponding right to strike. IFFA argued that

TWA's actions undermined the "statutory right that employees have to be free from employer retaliation when it engages in one of the critical aspects of union [ization]." IFFA counsel John Hurley explained the logic when answering Justice Scalia's question as to why it would be wrong to allow crossovers to stay in the jobs when, by law, new hires can stay. Hurley responded:

> the question we're arguing, where promises are made to crossovers who are members of the pre-strike working force and the striking community—those promises unlike the promise of permanence to the new hires, an outside group—those promises to the crossovers, they impact upon the striking group seeking to divide that group and to create individual competition among the striking group, to abandon the strike.

According to Hurley, further on in questioning,

> if the employer is also telling those who want to exercise fully their right to strike that they will most likely not only be replaced by permanent, new hire replacements, but also by early returning strikers because they chose to show fealty to the company at an earlier point, that they will not be allowed to keep their jobs, is blatant discrimination for engaging in union activities.[51]

Hurley then argued for a "neutral" basis for determining who of the pre-strike workforce should occupy the available jobs after an unconditional offer to return:

> the result is that neither the crossovers nor the full-time strikers are totally shut out of post-strike jobs in the active workforce. Some crossovers will be prevented from having an active job at the immediate conclusion of the strike, but so will many full-term strikers. If seniority is used, it will depend upon seniority and not how long you stayed out on strike versus how soon you came back in. [52]

Three justices—William J. Brennan, Jr., Thurgood Marshall, and Harry Blackmun—wrote dissent opinions. Justice Brennan, joined by Justice Marshall, argued that utilizing a neutral standard such as seniority, as suggested by IFFA, did not preference workers by their decision to support the strike, abandon the strike early, or refuse to strike in the first place. Under the Supreme Court ruling, i.e., treating the crossovers similar to permanent replacements, meant that workers can be divided by their individual interests in the employment. If a worker is low on seniority, under this system, they can advantage themselves by crossing over. In a system run on seniority, the decision as to who remains after the strike (assuming that not all workers will return immediately to work) will not be based on whether one crossed or not, but on seniority: some who crossed that were low on seniority may lose their positions to more senior workers; some crossovers who are high in seniority will remain.

The critical divide between the majority and the minority opinions stood at the core of the concept of organized labor: the difference between individual interests and group interests. As articulated by Brennan joined by Marshall in their dissent:

> The employer's promise to members of the bargaining unit that they will not be displaced at the end of the strike if they cross the picket lines addresses a far different incentive to the bargaining unit members than does the employer's promise of permanence to new hires. The employer's threat to hire permanent replacements from outside the existing workforce puts pressure on the strikers *as a group* to abandon the strike before their positions are filled by others. But the employer's promise to members of the striking bargaining unit that, if they abandon the strike (or refuse to join it at the outset), they will retain their jobs at strike's end in preference to more senior workers who remain on strike produces an additional dynamic: now there is also an incentive for *individual* workers to seek to save (or improve) their own positions at the expense of other members of the striking bargaining unit. We have previously observed that offers of 'individual benefits to the strikers to induce them to abandon the strike . . . could be expected to undermine the striker's mutual interest and place the entire strike effort in jeopardy."[53]

And further, in a footnote:

> The Court's argument that the crossovers should not be 'penalized' rests on its apparent belief that they should not be denied the benefit of their individual decisions not to strike . . . But '[u]nion activity, by its very nature, is group activity,' . . . and inherent in the system of exclusive bargaining representatives, which is a fundament of our labor law, is the principle of majority decision—even where such decisions may impose costs on the dissenting minority. The contrary rule, moreover, would allow the employee who abandons the collectively taken decision to strike to become a free rider, enjoying the benefit of any gains won by the strike, but without sharing in its risk . . .[54]

THE BIG BANG CASE

Although IFFA lost their argument on new hires at the District level and, more significantly, lost on crossovers at the Supreme Court, another angle resurfaced on which to attempt reinstatement of full-term strikers. What came to be known as the Big Bang case had initially been Count II of the reinstatement case in 1986 and had been spun off by Judge Sachs to be considered at a later date. When Judge Sachs ruled on that part of the reinstatement case that involved trainees, he stated that when "people are willing to pay [TWA charged trainees $2,500 for training] to cross a training school picket line, there can hardly be said to be an obvious business necessity to offer them guarantees of permanent jobs when they are in school."[55] Whereas Judge Sachs was addressing the issue of trainees, he raised the issue of economic necessity. The Mackay Doctrine was based on the assumption that employers need to hire *permanent* replacements to continue operation during a strike, which the court believed was their right. The question at the center of this case was whether TWA had to offer permanence to replacements in order to operate. The dissenting opinions in the Supreme Court crossover case in 1989 addressed this issue. Justice Blackmun tackled the issue of economic necessity most directly but Brennan and Marshall supported his reading of the Mackay Doctrine as requiring business necessity as a basis of permanent replacement.[56] "I see no need to afford the carrier the benefit of a rebuttable [or irrebuttable] presumption of business necessity even in the case of outside replacements . . . . I would require the carrier to prove the business necessity of offering permanence to replacements and crossovers on the facts of each case."[57]

Permanence was the issue, and bolstered by the dissent in the crossover case at the Supreme Court, IFFA argued that TWA had to prove that economic necessity required them to offer permanent jobs to potential workers rather than operating with other classes of workers, e.g., contingent, or more likely, temporary replacements.[58] According to IFFA, TWA had used "temporary" flight attendants before and had no economic justification to offer permanence in this strike:

> In this phase of our litigation, we seek not to overturn the Mackay decision—but to require that the employer show—as a precondition to permanent replacement—that business necessity required the hiring of permanent replacements . . . that it could not operate without *permanent* replacements (e.g., by use of other company employees, temporary replacements). *We maintain that in the absence of such a showing by TWA, permanent replacement of strikers was unlawful.*"[59]

Despite the significance of this issue, IFFA saw this argument as a "long shot." Sachs dismissed it at the District level, June 21, 1989, and the Eighth Circuit Court of Appeals dismissed as well, arguing it was premature based on other litigation in process, on September 7, 1989.

Seen in their entirety, IFFA's legal attempts were focused on returning all full-term strikers to work and preserving the rights of seniority, collective bargaining, and the union itself.[60] Results of these legal battles have found their way into the very heart of the discussion about union strength and the viability of the right to strike. Not surprisingly, since the increased use of the permanent replacements in the 1980s and early 1990s, the strike has become almost a thing of the past. In 2009, The Bureau of Labor Statistics recorded the lowest number of strikes or work stoppages since the recording of such data started in 1947.[61] The decline has been steady and significant since the beginning of the 1980s. In 2009, the lowest level, there were only five work stoppages involving 1,000 or more workers, with a total of 13,000 workers involved. Twenty years earlier, 1979, there had been 235 work stoppages affecting over one million workers.[62] The 2015 data from the Bureau of Labor Statistics continued the trend of a depressed level of work stoppages (twelve affecting 47,000).[63] When talking about the cost to labor of the Supreme Court's decision to allow crossovers to remain on the job, similar to permanent replacements, David Larson put the loss in the larger context:

> The result in *TWA [v. IFFA]*, however, allows employers to disregard the structure of the collective bargaining process and make offers to employees that can destroy collective activity from within.
>
> When an employer is allowed to undercut collective bargaining by pandering to individual self-interest, future collective attempts become much less probable and the vehicle for participation in one's own workplace quietly slips away. The majority in *TWA* is deeply concerned that prohibiting TWA's offer will unjustly penalize individual strikers. Yet the Court ignores what all employees, including junior strikers, lose when the Court impairs the potential for collective action.[64]

Even though we often think of the concept of the right to strike as confined to the labor-management relationship, Josiah Lambert makes a compelling argument that historically the strike was not only a commercial right but seen as a right of citizenship.[65] The cost of what some now refer to as the extinction of the strike in the United States is a major one.

NOTES

1. IFFA v. TWA (W. D. Missouri, Bad Faith Bargaining 1988).
2. IFFA v. TWA (8th Cir. 1989).
3. IFFA v. TWA (W. D. Missouri, Bad Faith Bargaining 1988), Revised Opinion.
4. Vicki Frankovich, "Independent Federation of Flight Attendant Strike against TWA" (speech, Fourth Annual State of Kansas NOW Conference, Lawrence, KS, September 6, 1986). As a point of comparison in 1983, the average salary and benefits for IFFA flight attendant was $39,000 compared to IAM at $44,000; ALPA in salary alone was 2 to 3 times higher than IAM. One of the issues that plagued IFFA was that their salary improvement had come late and quick, making it look like they had far outstripped IAM in percent change.

5. Both Frankovich and Icahn retold the events of this meeting in their depositions. Judge Sachs, in his disposition of the case, believed that Frankovich's telling of events was clearer and more credible than Icahn's. Icahn seemed less able to remember the specifics of the meeting and his comment on breadwinners.

6. IFFA v. TWA (W. D. Missouri, Bad Faith Bargaining 1988), Revised Opinion.

7. Ibid.

8. IFFA v. TWA (8th Cir. 1989).

9. *Teleconference*, produced by IFFA, 1988; Alison Frankel, "Bar Talk," *American Lawyer*, April 16, 1988, 16; TWA, *TWA Skyliner*, March 15, 1988.

10. IFFA, *Letter to Fellow Flight Attendants, June 28, 1989.*

11. William H. Freivogel, "Court Rejects Flight Attendants' Appeal," *St. Louis Post-Dispatch*, January 17, 1990.

12. TWA v. IFFA (8th Cir., Union Security 1987), quoting from another case.

13. TWA v. IFFA (8th Cir., Union Security 1987).

14. TWA v. IFFA (U.S. District Court, W.D. Missouri, Union Security 1986).

15. *Teleconference*, produced by IFFA, 1989.

16. TWA v. IFFA (U.S. District Court, W.D. Missouri, Union Security 1986).

17. TWA v. IFFA (8th Cir., Union Security 1987).

18. TWA v. IFFA (U.S. Supreme Court (U.S.), Union Security 1988).

19. Ibid.

20. IFFA, *The 630 News: The Official Publication,* 1988.

21. William H. Freivogel, "Attendants Prevail in Case against TWA," *St. Louis Post-Dispatch*, March 7, 1989.

22. *Teleconference*, produced by IFFA, 1989.

23. William H. Freivogel, "Attendants Prevail in Case against TWA," *St. Louis Post-Dispatch*, March 7, 1989.

24. IFFA v. TWA (U.S. District Court, W.D. Missouri, Economic Reinstatement Case 1986). TWA also argued, in the case under discussion, that IFFA did not make an "unconditional" offer to return to work but rather a "conditional" offer and therefore, TWA was not obligated to enter into any agreement with IFFA about returning workers under the RLA. Judge Sachs denied TWA's charge and affirmed that IFFA's offer was unconditional.

25. Robert W. Kaps, *Air Transport Labor Relations* (Carbondale, IL: Southern Illinois University Press, 1997).

26. IFFA v. TWA (U.S. District Court, W.D. Missouri, Economic Reinstatement Case 1986).

27. David Allen Larson, "Trans World Airlines, Inc. v. Independent Federation of Flight Attendants: A Fundamental Blow to Collective Bargaining," *Missouri Labor Review* 54 (1989).

28. Thomas C. Kohler and Julius Getman, "The Story of NLRB v. Mackay Radio & Telegraph Co.: The High Cost of Solidarity," *Boston College Law School, Legal Studies Research Paper Series* 103 (August 1, 2006).

29. Gerald E. Berendt, David Moberg, and Stephen Franklin, "The Labor Strike: Is It Still a Useful Economic Weapon for Unions?" *John Marshall Law Review* 35 (2001–2002): 258.

30. Thomas C. Kohler and Julius Getman, "The Story of NLRB v. Mackay Radio & Telegraph Co.: The High Cost of Solidarity," *Boston College Law School, Legal Studies Research Paper Series* 103 (August 1, 2006), 43.

31. Julius Getman, "Of Labor Law and Birdsong," *Connecticut Law Review* 30 (1997–1998): 1349–50.

32. Thomas C. Kohler and Julius Getman, "The Story of NLRB v. Mackay Radio & Telegraph Co.: The High Cost of Solidarity," *Boston College Law School, Legal Studies Research Paper Series* 103 (August 1, 2006).

33. Harry Braverman, *Labor and Monopoly Capital: The Degradation of Work in the Twentieth Century* (New York: Monthly Review Press, 1974).

34. Peter K. 1990, "Replacement Workers: Management's Big Gun," *New York Times*, March 13, 1990; IFFA, *The 630 News: The Official Publication*, Special Edition: State of the Union, Legal Updates, 1988; Peter T. Kilborn, "Replacement Workers: Management's Big Gun," *New York Times*, March 13, 1990.

35. Michael H. LeRoy, "The Changing Character of Strikes Involving Permanent Striker Replacements, 1935–1990," *Journal of Labor Research* XVI, no. 4 (1995).

36. Rick Fantasia and Kim Voss, *Hard Work: Remaking the American Labor Movement* (Berkeley: University of California Press, 2004).

37. Joseph A. McCartin, *Collision Course: Ronald Reagan, the Air Traffic Controllers, and the Strike that Changed America* (New York: Oxford University Press, 2011), 342–43.

38. Aaron Bernstein, *Grounded: Frank Lorenzo and the Destruction of Eastern Airlines* (New York: Simon and Schuster, 1990); Jack E. Robinson, *Free Fall: The Needless Destruction of Eastern Airlines and the Valiant Struggle to Save It* (New York: Harper Business, 1992); Jonathan D. Rosenblum, *Copper Crucible: How the Arizona Miners' Strike of 1983 Recast Labor-Management Relations in America* (Ithaca: ILR Press, 1995); Peter Rachleff, *Hard-Pressed in the Heartland: The Hormel Strike and the Future of the Labor Movement* (Boston: South End Press, 1993); Hardy Green, *On Strike at Hormel: The Struggle for a Democratic Labor Movement* (Philadelphia: Temple University Press, 1990); Julius Getman, *The Betrayal of Local 14* (Ithaca: ILR Press, 1998); Timothy Minchin, "'It tears the heart right out of you': Memories of Striker Replacement at International Paper Company in De Pere, Wisconsin, 1987–88," *Oral History Review* Summer-Fall (2004); Richard A. Brisbin Jr., *A Strike Like No Other: Law & Resistance during the Pittston Coal Strike of 1989–1990* (Baltimore: Johns Hopkins University Press, 2002).

39. Thomas J. Keil, *On Strike! Capital Cities and the Wilkes-Barre Newspaper Unions* (Tuscaloosa: University of Alabama, 1988); Chris Rhomberg, *The Broken Table* (New York: Russel Sage Foundation, 2012); *New York Daily News Strike and Permanent Replacements*, 101st, 2d 1–74 (1990).

40. Stephen Franklin, *Three Strikes: Labor's Heartland Losses and What They Mean for Working Americans* (New York: Guilford Press, 2001); *Collective Bargaining and the Hiring of Permanent Strike Replacements: Hearings Before the Government Operations*, 102d Cong., 2d Sess. 1–105 (1992).

41. David J. Walsh, *On Different Planes: An Organizational Analysis of Cooperation and Conflict Among Airline Unions* (Ithaca: ILR Press, 1994), 59–60; Tom

Juravich and Kate Bronfenbrenner, *Ravenswood: The Steelworkers' Victory and the Revival of American Labor* (Ithaca: ILR Press, 1999).

42. With the increased use of permanent replacements, and the chilling effect that even the threat of permanent replacement had on labor's ability to strike and to organize workplaces, labor prioritized a legislative solution. The first proposals came in the late 1980s, but the real push came in the early to mid-1990s. The U.S. House passed a ban on the use of permanent replacements for the first time in 1991, a measure that President George H. W. Bush promised to veto.

In his 1992 election campaign, Bill Clinton pledged support for legislation that would ban permanent replacements. The House again passed the measure in 1993, now called the Cesar Chavez Workplace Fairness Act, and twice it went before the Senate, both gaining a majority but not enough to stop a promised filibuster by Republican opposition led by Orrin Hatch. There was never a more positive chance of the bill passing than in 1994 when Democrats were in the majority in both houses, and President Clinton promised to sign the ban. The last Senate vote was 7 short of what would have been needed for cloture, and essentially marked the end of legislative attempts. President Clinton issued an Executive Order in March 1995 banning the hiring of permanent replacements in federal contracts, but in March 1996 in *Chamber of Commerce v Reich*, the appellate court struck down Clinton's executive order. After a request for a full hearing was denied, the administration chose not to pursue it further.

43. IFFA, *The 630 News: The Official Publication*, Special Edition: State of the Union, Legal Updates, 1988.

44. *Teleconference*, produced by IFFA, 1989.

45. IFFA v. TWA (U.S. District Court, W.D. Missouri, Economic Reinstatement Case 1986).

46. IFFA v. TWA (8th Cir., Economic Reinstatement Case 1987).

47. Ibid.

48. Ibid.

49. IFFA v. TWA (U.S. Supreme Court (U.S.), Economic Reinstatement Case 1989).

50. Ibid.

51. Ibid.

52. Ibid.

53. Ibid.

54. Ibid.

55. IFFA v. TWA (U.S. District Court, W.D. Missouri, Economic Reinstatement Case 1986).

56. IFFA, *The 630 News: The Official Publication*, Special Edition: State of the Union, Legal Updates, 1988.

57. IFFA v. TWA (U.S. Supreme Court (U.S.), Economic Reinstatement Case 1989).

58. IFFA, *The 630 News: The Official Publication*, Special Edition: State of the Union, Legal Updates, 1988.

59. Ibid.

60. This chapter has focused on what were the most significant court battles between TWA and IFFA. There were many more, to see the full list, see IFFA, *The 630 News: The Official Publication*, Special Edition: State of the Union, Legal Updates, 1988, 1990.

61. Bureau of Labor Statistics, Work Stoppages Summary, Rep. (2010).

62. Bureau of Labor Statistics, Work Stoppages Summary, Rep. (2010); Mike Elk, "Sad, Startling Stats: Number of Union Elections, Strikes Continue Steady Decline," *In These Times*, July 7, 2010; Matt Phillips, "American Labor-union Strikes are Almost Completely Extinct," *Quartz (cz.com)*, February 11, 2015.

63. Bureau of Labor Statistics, Economic News Release: Work Stoppages in 2015, Rep. (2015).

64. David Allen Larson, "Trans World Airlines, Inc. v. Independent Federation of Flight Attendants: A Fundamental Blow to Collective Bargaining," *Missouri Labor Review* 54 (1989).

65. Josiah Bartlett Lambert, *"If the Workers Took a Notion": The Right to Strike and American Political Development.* (Ithaca: ILR Press, 2005).

Conclusion

Returning all full-term strikers to the line was a singularly driven goal of IFFA and represented a tremendous accomplishment. Despite TWA's public assurances that they would never be back, and Icahn's position that he had no choice but to "break the union," IFFA and the full-term strikers had fought every step of the way to get every last worker back to work and to survive as a union. And, they earned the respect of unions and labor advocates throughout the country. Ted Kheel, well-known labor negotiator, was a major supporter of IFFA. "In June 1988, IFFA accepted my offer of assistance in obtaining a respectable agreement, through collective bargaining, from Carl Icahn's TWA. I made that offer because, as an observer, I was struck by the Flight Attendant courage and convinced of the justice in IFFA's stand."[1]

In their 1989 Teleconference, Kheel spoke,

> And when the full story is written and its placed against the panorama of labor's history with all the great battles that took place in the past—what little IFFA has done to uphold the right and dignity of working people and the importance of collective bargaining in the employer-employee relationship will hold a prominent place in the history of the labor movement and I am glad I am having a small part of it . . .

By the time that the last full-term striker was recalled, July 1989, there was still no signed agreement between IFFA and TWA. All flight attendants were working under the unilaterally implemented wage and work rule changes that had sent workers out on strike in the first place. Two things were apparent: the working conditions were as bad, or even worse, than they had believed; and, the disappointing loss of their bad faith bargaining case meant that the only avenue available for change was going to be through a negotiated contract.

A win in the bad faith bargaining case would have upheld the position that workers were unfair labor practice strikers and would have voided TWA's unilaterally imposed contract changes at the commencement of the strike, returned workers to their jobs, and awarded back pay from the beginning of the strike. The loss of the bad faith bargaining case meant that the flight attendants were considered economic strikers and struck in the normal course of failed contract negotiations.

The loss of the bad faith bargaining case determined that the severity of the wage and work rule changes were "set in stone."[2] As difficult as the wage cut was, it was the work rules that transformed the occupation. It was not only that they had a real understanding of their past and what they had fought to change to make the flight attendant job, a career, but in the day-to-day operation, the job had been reverted to a high turnover job. Speaking to the membership, Jolley summarized,

> Prior to 1970 there was no such things as a flight attendant career. Like a stint in the military service, it was two, three, four years—and out. Why? Because that's what the airlines wanted and that's what the airlines including TWA insured. Through a calculated combination of unrestricted, burdensome work rules, low pay,—sound familiar—and grossly discriminatory policies, the flight attendant job was limited to two, three years duration max. The term flight attendant didn't exist—you were "stewardesses." Posted literally and figuratively around the airlines including TWA were signs, "no men allowed," "men need not apply." Marriage was a capital offense, punishable by immediate and permanent termination. Motherhood, whether by childbirth or adoption, was a capital offense punishable by immediate and permanent termination of employment. Work rule restrictions were virtually unheard of, no retirement plan existed, and if the right hand didn't get you, the left hand did, because if you managed to escape the two-sided hatchet of the no marriage no motherhood policy and you still, despite all the conditions, wanted to work under the conditions as they existed, they got you at age thirty-two because it is age thirty-two and out. Why? It is fairly obvious. One, was to perpetuate the stereotype that the airlines including TWA had been so successful in molding in the world public consciousness, and second and just as important is economics. Younger, unmarried, unburdened employees, knowing it's two years and out are going to be willing to work for less, they are going to be willing to put up for more, and they are not interested in costly, long-term benefits like retirement, seniority, a livable salary, working condition improvements. In short, what the airlines perpetuated, and what they enjoyed, and what they designed was constant rapid turnover of short term employees. Flight attendants only—no other segment of airline employment.[3]

And what Jolley articulated, and the flight attendants knew, the changes in work rules and the low wages of TWA's implemented changes were a "return to the conditions that were outlawed by the Civil Rights Act and which previously existed, and which the airlines in their hearts never stopped wanting."[4]

By July 1989, Judge Sachs' District Court 1988 dismissal of the bad faith bargaining case had been upheld at the appellate level, and in the next six months the Supreme Court would refuse to hear it. Absent a declaration that they were unfair labor practice strikers, their only recourse for better wage and work conditions was through a negotiated contract that hopefully would ameliorate some of the harsh working conditions and raise wages.

RED BOOK TO GREY BOOK

Prior to the strike, IFFA members had worked under the 1983 contract, what was known as the Red Book. The contract negotiations opened by TWA in 1984 resulted in the 1986 strike. So much had happened since the strike—TWA's unsuccessful legal attempt to render the whole contract as dead, the influx of permanent replacements that had little knowledge of unions and enough antipathy to such extent that they crossed picket lines, a merged set of unionized flight attendants from Ozark, crossovers, and successive waves of full-term strikers—that it became important to have a comprehensive understanding of just what was, and was not, in the existing contract between TWA and IFFA. Because contracts under the RLA never expire but are only amendable, TWA flight attendants were working under an amalgamation of 1983 contract terms, superseded in places where TWA had been allowed to unilaterally change contract terms.

For TWA's part, they did not provide permanent replacement workers and Ozark flight attendants with the 1983 Red Book but instead distributed a twenty-eight page pamphlet, leaving out the bulk of the agreed upon contract. With the Supreme Court win on status quo, all flight attendants were required to pay dues and all parts of the contract not changed by TWA during formal negotiations prior to March 7, 1986 remained intact. IFFA set about the arduous task of editing the Red Book to take into account the implemented changes—what became the Grey Book—showing workers not only what wage and work rule changes had been implemented on the day of strike, but equally if not more importantly, what had not. The 358-page Grey Book replaced TWA's twenty-eight page pamphlet, and not surprisingly, at IFFA expense when TWA refused to do so.

By designing the Grey Book, IFFA was able to dispel rumors, underscore the importance of their legal successes, and inform new members of their rights accorded in the contract. At their 1989 Teleconference, Frankovich dismissed a rumor that was going around that TWA, on March 6, 1989, was going to unilaterally implement even further changes in flight attendant wages and work conditions. "We will stop them cold." And, she explained, the reason that they could do that was "we won the status quo lawsuit." She went on to explain that the contract could only be changed through the process of negotiation under the formal procedures of the RLA. Jolley further emphasized this when he said, "What stands between TWA and further elimination of rest, further raising the cap, lowering the salaries, lifting all restrictions from balancing, reducing crew complement, is your status quo victory. It is a case in which every flight attendant has won." [5]

The Grey Book also helped inform permanent replacements of their contractual rights. Most of them, for example, did not know their right to have a union representative present at investigation meetings. In 1987, when the flight attendant labor force was 58 percent permanent replacements, they only accounted for 14 percent of the grievances filed. In 1988, as more and more full-term strikers returned to the line, new hires represented 27 percent of the flight attendant force but filed 35 percent of the grievances. IFFA believed that this increase in grievances lodged by permanent replacements at least partially reflected a greater understanding on their part of avenues available to them for expression of their rights and the role of a union to represent all of its members.[6]

IFFA put together the Grey Book to better inform their membership of the existing contract. They were also working for a new agreement with TWA, focusing on a wage snap-back, improved work rules, and the protection of benefits. Having garnered some legal successes and with an end in sight to the return of all their workers, they were cautiously optimistic that they would make some headway on a contract in 1989. TWA's profit in 1987 and 1988 also made a better negotiated contract seem more attainable. In their March 1989 Teleconference sent to all members, IFFA thought it was possible that an agreement would be reached even before the videocassettes of the teleconference reached each member's home. But 1989 proved to be a bad year to negotiate a contract. After only two years of profit, TWA descended into a serious financial trouble.[7]

TWA IN TROUBLE

The last flight attendant did not come back to the same TWA that they had left. Not only in terms of the implemented rules and wage concessions, the divisions within the flight attendants, but the alliance between Icahn and the male unions was fraying rapidly. There had always been a contradiction of beliefs about Icahn's intentions with the purchase of TWA in 1985/1986. Purchasing an airline gave him the opportunity to try out his beliefs about how to manage, prove his point about the survival of the unfittest when it came to traditional management, and assert his own effectiveness in running a company. Conversely, purchasing an airline gave him the opportunity to do what had earned him his reputation, profiting by selling a company either in whole or in pieces. TWA represented for Icahn the possibility of reinvention:

> Icahn commenced his TWA tenure with a great burst of enthusiasm. Here was an opportunity for the fearsome raider—loathed by the corporate establishment as a parasite of the capitalist system—to reinvent himself, undergoing a dramatic metamorphosis from takeover arbitrageur to captain of industry. Increasingly sensitive to the public hue and cry over the payment of greenmail, Icahn had already begun to disavow this form of blood money that had built the base of his fortune and funded his takeover war chest. Always concerned with the worst-case scenario, he worried about becoming an object of scorn. He yearned for the respectability of the true entrepreneurs—the likes of Andrew Carnegie, Bill Paley, Tom Watson, Ross Perot—who had built enormous businesses and had become deeply engrained (*sic*) in the American folklore.[8]

Icahn also seemed to enjoy the role he saw himself in as "savior" to the airline. He often commented that he saved TWA, not only from Lorenzo but from the historical mismanagement of the airline. The pilots, and machinists, forged coalition with Icahn was predicated on that belief and that he would use their concessions to revitalize the airline, investing in much needed new aircraft, enhancing the domestic operation, and sustaining TWA's position in international travel.

The pilots and machinists initially felt that they had made a good decision in working with Icahn, and the 1987 profit picture along with the purchase of Ozark, confirmed that position. Believing that privatization would strengthen Icahn's commitment to them and the airline, the pilots in their original agreement had given Icahn the right to take the airline private."[9] Icahn withdrew his first attempt to take TWA private because of the 1987 stock market downturn, but returned to his goal in 1988 and took TWA private in a way that completely destroyed the relationship between Icahn and the pilots and machinists. An outraged ALPA joined IFFA in their petition to the DOT for a fitness hearing, arguing that the privatization was not in the best interests of TWA.[10] "In effect, Carl arbitraged the union concessions for his own equity purchase."[11] With the help of Drexel Burnham Lambert and junk bond funding, Icahn took out his original investment plus profit ($469), increased his equity to 90 percent, and strapped TWA with $540 million in debt. During this time, Icahn used TWA money to purchase stock in Texaco, stepping up purchasing during the 1987 stock market crash. When he took TWA private, he had TWA sell their Texaco stock (about 20 million shares) to his USX Company at market price. He sold it less than a year later for a gain of $175 million pre-tax profits. In addition, he made $291.4 million on "the stock he had bought through TWA for quick resale to other Icahn companies. His total estimated profit on the TWA-Texaco deals: $466.2 million."[12] Further:

> By the end of 1989, Carl Icahn had used TWA to finance his raids on USX and Texaco. And he had taken out all of his money while using the airline to make still more in personal gains.
>
> How much did he take out of TWA? Almost $1 billion, including:
>
> - $469 million he took as a repayment for his initial investment in the airline.
> - $466.2 million in gains on the Texaco shares purchased through TWA.
> - $51.2 million in stock dividends he earned as the new owner of the airline.
>
> For its part, TWA got almost nothing except more debt, which doubled to $2.67 billion. Interest payment on those debts were enough to cause $293.5 million in losses last year [1989], enough to assure continued losses into the next decade. And enough for Icahn to ring in 1990 by threatening to liquidate the airline.[13]

Icahn's privatization loaded immense debt on TWA and the next years saw a spiral downward that ended any profit for the airline and eventual bankruptcy. TWA lost so much money in 1989 that it voided an agreement made between the pilots and Icahn when he took over the airline in 1986. That agreement stipulated that Icahn could not sale the airline or parts of it, as long as the profit margin hit a specific amount. In February 1990, TWA informed the pilots that the fourth quarter of 1989 brought the annual figure of loss over that amount, allowing Icahn to sell TWA assets.[14] In anticipation of this announcement, TWA's ALPA Chair, Kent Scott had stated, "Unfortunately, we'll have to concede Icahn the right to seek concessions or sell all or part of the airline . . . we will not repeat that mistake again of granting concessions for Carl Icahn."[15]

The picture that began to form was that the only two years of profit, 1987 ($240 million) and 1988 ($260 million) mirrored the concessions given by labor itself.[16] The financial losses of 1989 ($298.5 million) after Icahn's privatization and heavy debt load then activated his right to sell off parts or all of the airline.

Amid the growing losses, Icahn demanded $80 million in further concessions from ALPA per year for five years, stating that he needed concessions first from the pilots in order to, then, go to the machinists and flight attendants for more. He dangled the carrot and stick: he would spend money to invest in the airline, most importantly in new aircraft, if he got concessions; and, if he did not get concessions he would shrink the airline. A running theme with Icahn, never materialized, was that if labor conceded wages he would buy airplanes; by this time, TWA had the oldest fleet in the industry. Additionally, by this time, the labor costs at TWA were well below other major airlines, and came in only slightly above Lorenzo's Continental Airlines. As Icahn is famously known for saying, "How can one airline pay one guy $120,000 a year when the guy at the other airline is flying the same plane for $30,000 or $40,000? It makes no sense."[17] The coalition between Icahn and the pilots and machinists was over.

The pilots and machinists realized that they had been had. It was now clear to them that he had no intention, and they now believed he never had, of investing in the airline. And, he did just what he had threatened so many times—he sold TWA off in bits and pieces, rendering the chances of survival doubtful if not impossible. In 1990 Icahn began what the unions saw as the systematic dismantling of TWA: most disheartening was his sale of the London routes to American. Over strong union protests to the DOT, Icahn gained approval to sell the Chicago to London international routes in 1990, and in 1991, again gained approval from the DOT to sell London routes from New York, Boston, and Los Angeles to American. Then Secretary of Transportation, Samuel Skinner, frustrated both IFFA and ALPA in their attempt to stop the route sales that they believed "would spell the end for long-term survival of the carrier."[18] In an IFFA publication:

> On Wednesday, February 7, 1991, IFFA President, Vicki Frankovich testified before the U.S. House of Representatives Subcommittee on Aviation addressing the financial condition of the airline industry and the adequacy of competition. In her testimony she strongly stated that problem in the airline industry today is *leverage not labor*. It is the oppressive debt load which was placed on TWA as a result of the Icahn privatization which prevents competition and not the cost of the employee salaries. She confirmed TWA employee belief that TWA can survive but not if the Department of Transportation continues to approve the sale of the most profitable routes which will soon reduce the airline below critical mass. She questioned if the DOT had made any effort to comply with the Congressional mandate to consider the viability of each carrier in a route sale, concluding that TWA was essentially cannibalizing its most valuable assets to pay off tremendous junk bond debt."[19]

Not only did Icahn's selling of route structures diminish the future prospects of TWA as a viable airline, it also thwarted the unions in their attempt to find a new owner. The pilots, unwilling to agree to further concessions to Icahn, sought out investor Kirk Kerkorian and Tracinda Corporation to purchase the airline. The pilots, flight attendants, and machinists came to agreement with Kerkorian to buy the airline, but he was only interested if they could get Secretary Skinner's tentative approval of the sale of TWA routes to American reversed, something they were unable to do. In April 1991, DOT gave final approval for the sale and effectively ended discussions with Kerkorian.[20]

HOW TO NEGOTIATE IN FINANCIAL DISASTER

Based on the mounting financial losses at TWA and the demands by Icahn for further concessions from the unions, IFFA's negotiating team revised its retrospectively optimistic 1989 strategy, and moved away from a comprehensive negotiating position to attempting to make improvements on a smaller scale. As the negotiating team explained:

> With Carl Icahn threatening ALPA to get "voluntary" give-backs—threatening to dump the Domestic operation—selling off aircraft and the like—do we go for it? There may well be a time for this all-out effort, but is now the time? Or do we wait—biding our time . . . determining, and helping to shape, ultimate airline ownership all the while chipping away, little by little, securing improvements at every opportunity?[21]

The losses of 1990 were a staggering $478.6 million, reduced to $237.6 million by one time asset sales.[22] In January 1992, Icahn took the airline into bankruptcy to decrease the debt in exchange for a decrease in his ownership. There was a sticking point—the pension funds were underfunded and because Icahn owned 90% of the airline he and his companies were responsible for that deficit. And, the Pension Benefit Guaranty Corporation (PBGC), federal guarantor of these pensions, was in no mood to let him out of that.[23]

Icahn had been unwilling to entertain the possibility of employee ownership of the airline, but had reversed his position after the crash of flight 843. On July 30, 1992, Flight 843 from JFK New York to San Francisco crashed. In an aborted takeoff, the plane burst into flames, but the crew safely evacuated all 273 passengers. Employees thought this event swayed Icahn:

> the unions were trying to talk Icahn into selling the company to the employees. He refused to even talk to the unions. Had there been one death on Flight 843—TWA would have been out of business the very next day. But that was not the case. On July 30, 1992, TWA was once again in the news. Merits of the crew, and the textbook perfect evacuation circled the world. Icahn called the unions on July 31 and said; "let's talk". August 20, 1992—Icahn and the employees came to agreement.[24]

The unions agreed to a 15 percent cut and for the flight attendants this came from a combination of wage and work rule concessions. Pressured by bankruptcy, IFFA and TWA signed their first agreement since 1983. Rather than ameliorating the damage of the unilaterally imposed contract changes of March 1986, the September 1992 agreement only exacerbated it. The 15 percent wage and work rule reduction was especially difficult because they were still working under the 22 percent imposed wage cut of 1986, having never received a snap-back as IAM had, and ALPA's partial snap-back.[25]

Even though the membership voted for the agreement, no one was happy about it. In 1993, IFFA put out a video and detailed pamphlet, "The Plane Truths," to try to address the dissatisfaction of the membership. IFFA tried to walk through the decision making process that ended with the concessions they made. It was a hard sell, and they acknowledged that not only the increased wage and benefit reductions were difficult, but they were compounded by asking the membership to make a turn-about in what had now been years of animosity between the flight attendants and TWA management. In much the same way that they had felt they had no choice but to strike, now they felt that they were facing either a 15 percent wage reduction or a $100 percent wage reduction.[26] Hoffman, now vice president of IFFA, conveyed the reason:

> The years since 1986 have brought startling developments, abrupt changes, and a full range of emotion. Unilateral changes in our salaries and work rules, our strike, the sale of valuable assets, and the downsizing of our international route structure. Most startling of all has been the filing for chapter 11 bankruptcy protection, the revelation of the stark realities of the airline's financial position and a new IFFA-TWA collective bargaining agreement.
>
> An agreement that has failed to meet the hopes and expectations of a nearly 7 year wait. IFFA's officers, representatives, and negotiating committee, are all painfully aware that our new agreement is not what anyone wanted, and is not what so many of us fought so hard for since 1986.
>
> The bottom line reason is that the TWA left behind by Carl Icahn is not the TWA that any one of us would have wished for."

Hoffman, who was also a member of the negotiating committee, addressed directly the position that they saw themselves in:

> [L]et's deal with the question of why the flight attendants had to give anything, why should we have had to give anything at all, or why couldn't we have given less?
>
> The harsh reality is that Carl Icahn left the company bankrupt. His legacy was a debt load that simply could not be supported. The Creditor's Committee had to play the hand that was dealt. That hand included a level of salaries and benefits that were in place at the time of the bankruptcy for every employee group. We did not have the luxury of protracted negotiations with the Creditor's Committee. Time was of the essence in avoiding and averting liquidation.[27]

As Frankovich explained, "For eight long years we fought to be rid of Icahn. At last it is really done. We have suffered much to bring about this transition, and now we have achieved it." She also recognized the cost:

> While the cuts were worse than painful for us, we achieved what would prove to be a very significant step in the restructuring of the airline and a trend setter in the industry: positions on the Board of Directors and 45 percent stock ownership. Although that seemed woefully insufficient, we have begun to see the rewards in the differences on the line and with the attitudes of the management

> and supervision and what we hope will be an ongoing ability to have someone listen to and address our problems. We are now entering the mostly unchartered water of participative management."[28]

As both employee-owners and creditors, IFFA leadership was in the difficult position of trying to turn the years of animosity against TWA into collaboration. As celebratory as it was, it might not be enough that Icahn was out for flight attendants to turn their animosity to support. "No one can give, however, what he or she does not have. Enthusiasm, to be shared, must first be had by the flight attendants."[29] Karen Nussbaum, Director of the Women's Bureau, was invited to "the first joint labor-management conference of the new TWA." In a letter to Safety Director Miller, she wrote, "As you know, the new Administration under President Clinton and under Labor Secretary Reich is seeking the very employee involvement and labor-management cooperation that TWA is attempting to develop."[30]

Icahn would officially end his ownership of TWA in early 1993 and later that year, twenty-one months after it entered bankruptcy—TWA emerged from its first bankruptcy. In addition to worker concessions, the bankruptcy accomplished debt reduction. TWA would become 55 percent owned by creditors, and 45 percent by unions. At the time, TWA owed IFFA about $100 million in backpay from litigation from the 1986 strike, and the flight attendants would become a creditor, accepting a reduced amount of money owed, as well as employee-owners. Icahn, who had succeeded in resolving his pension obligation with the PBGC, gave up all control and all stock, and joined the list of creditors by agreeing to finance TWA with $190 million to weather the bankruptcy.[31]

The period of transition out of Icahn's ownership to creditor/employee–owned was a sliver of hope of survival in a challenging environment. Eight years of struggle and forced to give even more, everyone was depleted. In April 1993, Frankovich wrote an open letter to all flight attendants, explaining her own mental and physical exhaustion. It was easy to see from the letter itself, that she was utterly depleted from what appeared as constant work, constant pressure, and constant stress. Her husband had moved away from the home and she was in the process of losing that home because her own reduced salary made refinancing impossible. It was just a matter of time before she would lose her home, and her marriage would end in divorce. She took medical leave and returned gradually to work over the next months. Her explanation of her exhaustion had close similarities to the almost decade earlier resignation of IFFA's first president, Teolis. An excerpt from her letter sent to members:

> With every day the demands became greater and greater. The role on the Creditors' Committee engulfed the office (and me) in paper work. I had to read and understand every document. Mounds of paper covered my desk and filled my

> briefcase. I grew more and more driven, more and more tired, more and more overwhelmed. Reading the *New York Times, Wall Street Journal, Aviation Daily*, daily financial reports from the Creditors' Committee and bankruptcy accountants, weekly court pleadings, position papers and simultaneously continuing all regular and routine IFFA tasks. Writing membership mailings, *Info Rep* mailings, thinking about strategies for solving policy issues for Flight Attendant problems. Negotiating settlements of work rules issues, defending the organization to our own members as we continued to work harder and harder. No time for breaks—too much work to be done.

The very length of the struggle had exhausted everyone. Finally, signing a contract that was an unsatisfactory conclusion to what seemed like an endless fight, left a critical mass of complaint against IFFA leadership. Frankovich tried to put what they had been able to accomplish into the equation. And, she tried to readjust her own way of thinking, trying to put the job into some kind of perspective, so that criticism did not feel so personal, and so demoralizing.[32]

BANKRUPTCY REVISITED

The changes afforded TWA in the 1993 bankruptcy were not sufficient. TWA attempted to further reorganize and reduce their debt load outside of court in 1994, and, for a second time in two years, the union agreed to further concessions. TWA, however, ended up having to resort to chapter 11 bankruptcy in 1995 to restructure the airline, going in and out of bankruptcy between July 1, 1995 and August 23, 1995. TWA came out 70 percent creditor-owned and 30 percent employee-owned, and a further reduction in its debt load. There was much optimism about this bankruptcy placing TWA in a better competitive position with multiple voices from investors to industry analysts lauding the positives of the new restructuring. Within TWA, President Jeffrey Erikson commented, "All of us at TWA take pride in the fact that TWA emerges from its reorganization as a serious contender in the airline industry."[33]

The positive outlook for the second bankruptcy was tempered by TWA's loan obligation to Icahn from the first bankruptcy. To resolve the $190 million owed to Icahn, TWA entered into what proved to be a disastrous agreement. Known as the Karabu agreement, TWA agreed to sell an unlimited number of tickets to Icahn at 45 percent reduction of fare price, an agreement that would prove extremely costly to TWA. The agreement was to last until 2003 and all but insured TWA's eventual demise. Utilizing the emerging internet, Icahn set up lowestfares.com and drew what has been estimated as $100–150 million a year from the already struggling TWA.[34] The Karabu agreement pulled much needed revenue from TWA, but at the time, TWA did not have the money to repay Icahn and he wanted out.

The overall optimism, even with the Karabu drain, was warranted. On July 17, 1996, TWA announced strong financial results and future investments in hiring, aircraft, and technology.[35] A day that had begun with the best news TWA had had in years, a day that started with TWA claiming economic recovery, would end in tragedy: TWA Flight 800, New York to Paris, would explode shortly after takeoff, killing all 229 people on board. After a four-year investigation, the National Transportation Board (NTSB) ruled the accident was caused by an explosion in the central wing fuel tank. The tragedy itself, followed by one of the largest NTSB investigations in its history, and the persistent conspiracy theories that the plane had been downed by a land missile, made TWA's financial recovery all the more difficult.[36]

TWA went on to report losses of $259 million in 1996, was the only major airline to report losses in 1997, and "While other major airlines were posting banner years, TWA again lost money ($121 million) for the tenth straight year in 1998."[37]

THE IFFA PRESIDENCY

The two bankruptcies meant two rounds of concessions for workers, and there was increasing dissension among flight attendants. In August 1995, Frankovich lost the presidency of IFFA. Sherry Cooper, a full-term striker who had been recognized by IFFA in the years following the strike for her commitment to strike activities, had never held office before.[38] Her criticism of Frankovich's leadership in agreeing to yet another wave of concessions in the second bankruptcy resonated with the membership. In a post-election interview, Frankovich explained, "I saw no alternative . . . .But I can't say I don't understand the vote. I regret the decision, but I understand it. Our people have been severely traumatized by 1986 strike and the painful concessions. The losses foisted on us by Icahn, the 1992 concession in the first bankruptcy, the 1994 concessions—it's more than the members can tolerate."[39]

Cooper's win started in motion what would be the end of IFFA, and by some analyses, the eventual elimination of all TWA flight attendant jobs. When Cooper became President of IFFA, early on she started working with IAM to replace IFFA. Unknown and in violation of IFFA's operating rules, Cooper divulged these meetings only after the fact and presented IFFA's Executive Committee her goal to merge the flight attendants with IAM. To further her plan, Cooper had provided IAM the names and contact information of all TWA flight attendants. IAM contacted the NMB to set up a representation election.[40]

Cooper believed that the strength of IAM would better serve the interests of the TWA flight attendants, obviating the problems of being a smaller independent union by attachment to a powerful union. IAM promised that the flight attendants would be able to make decisions on their own but under the strong umbrella of IAM.

IAM had long wanted the flight attendants to join them, and had articulated that during their 1986 strike. The flight attendants' experiences of poor representation by male unions had made them historically reluctant to join another male organization, but the challenge from IAM gained strength among the fragmented groups under IFFA.

In opposition to what they viewed as the hostile takeover attempt by IAM, IFFA leadership moved to affiliate with the Association of Flight Attendants (AFA). The advantage expressed for going with AFA was that it was a union devoted solely to flight attendant issues. A further advantage was that there would be no conflict of interest issues on the TWA property. IAM, representing the machinists, had by then a checkered history of support for the flight attendants, and would potentially not serve well the interests of flight attendants if they differed or adversely affected the interests of the machinists.

By 1995, the TWA flight attendant population was a collection of different groups: permanent replacements, crossovers, full-term strikers, and new hires—flight attendants hired since the last full-term striker was recalled. The allegiance of new hires was split: being young gave their leaning to permanent replacements, but full-term strikers recruited their support as well. One new hire came up with an idea, acted upon, to distribute "baby" dinosaur pins to signal support for full-term strikers who had expropriated the "extinct" dinosaur image as their own. With memories of the strike, and the continued concessionary bleeding of the workforce in two bankruptcies, the once unified voice of IFFA was fractured.

In a low turnout election, the membership voted against affiliating with AFA by eighteen votes. Because the NMB had already confirmed IAM's request for a representation vote, this loss only changed the major parties to the election. Rather than AFA/IFFA versus IAM, the January 22, 1997 vote was IFFA and IAM, with a small write-in vote for AFA. With over 90 percent of the membership voting, IAM won picking up 62 percent of the vote, and ending the Independent Federation of Flight Attendants—an independent union that had taken on a corporate raider and fought until they successfully returned every striker to their jobs.

Even though there was a solid win by IAM, the dissension in the ranks of TWA flight attendants boiled over fairly quickly. IAM had made promises to all its members and presented strong resistance to TWA management in contract negotiations in 1999, but in the summer, pulled back their position and pushed for membership support of an agreement that felt like yet another betrayal to the flight attendants. A number of flight attendants believed that the clout that IAM was to bring to the TWA flight attendants had not materialized. In the Fall 1999, a faction of dissatisfied flight attendants sought to decertify IAM and replace it with a new independent union, the Coalition of Professional Flight Attendants. The flight attendants argued that IAM had failed to deliver on promises—higher wage increases to preference a population who had been hurt worse than any other group since the Icahn era, work rule changes, and greater protection of flight attendants in grievances with TWA. The anger directed at IAM was not only from the flight attendants; aircraft mechanics initiated a decertification campaign as well.[41]

Cooper, who by then was the general chairman of IAM, remained steadfast in her support of IAM and its representation of the flight attendants and underscored the connections between the dissidents and the former IFFA. As true as that was, the dissident ranks also included officers from Local 1997, the TWA flight attendant local of IAM. Barbara Steffen, President of Local 1997, resigned and joined the decertification campaign, as did six other flight attendant representatives. She spelled out her disaffection with IAM:

> Steffen, a 32-year TWA employee, voted in favor of the switch to the IAM nearly three years ago. She said she relied on promises that the flight attendants would be given the autonomy to run their own organization, negotiate their own contracts and nominate and elect their own officers. "I can clearly state that the IAM has not lived up to its commitments," she said.
>
> Nor have the flight attendants gained the clout that it thought would come from joining a bigger, strong union, Steffen said.
>
> "Our work rules have been decimated, and our pay increases fell far short of the industry standard we were promised," she said.[42]

Within 48 hours, the dissidents had attained over 25 percent of the needed signatures to request a decertification election. By mid-March 2000, "they had gathered signatures from 'well more' than half of TWA's 4,200 flight attendants," exceeding the requirement of 50 percent for a decertification election. As one flight attendant noted, "The IAM failed in every way possible to provide the union representation they promised."[43]

The NMB election was held in June 2000 but the dissident group failed to unseat IAM. With 88 percent of the flight attendants voting, IAM won 57 percent of the vote. As IAM's Edward Manhart stated, "A lot of people voted on emotion and did not know the real truth . . . but the (election) numbers speak for themselves." From the original decision to move to representation with IAM, flight attendant support had attenuated, and the Coalition of Professional Flight Attendants claimed their 41 percent a victory as well. "We have focused flight attendants' attention on where it needs to be . . . We want more democracy in TWA, and hopefully, flight attendants will put more pressure on IAM for that and do a better job on their behalf."[44]

The Summer 1999 contract that galvanized flight attendant dissent, was to be of short duration, eighteen months. By the time of new negotiations, however, TWA was in a totally new situation. For the flight attendants, it will call into question on an even larger scale their decision to fall under the umbrella of a larger union.

THE END OF TWA: WHERE HAVE ALL THE TWA FLIGHT ATTENDANTS GONE?

As difficult as the 1990s were for TWA, there were signs of improvement in the new decade. TWA improved its public relations by improving its on-time performance, and started purchasing new planes, advertising "a plane every ten days."[45] There was, particularly among the ranks of TWA, the belief that if TWA could manage to survive the financial drain of Icahn's Karabu agreement, which was to expire in 2003, they could continue to operate and even profit.

The acquisition then of TWA by American Airlines in 2001, though not completely surprising, was not a foregone conclusion. "Depending on whom you ask, the American purchase was either inevitable or borderline criminal. Compton, the pilot-turned-executive who orchestrated the sale and claimed it was TWA's only option, is described variously as a good-hearted savior, a bumbling naif and a turncoat who sold out the employees for personal profit."[46]

On January 8, 2001, American presented an offer to buy TWA and as part of this offer, and at the behest of American, TWA filed for bankruptcy on January 10, 2001—their third bankruptcy. In the purchase, American rid itself of the Karabu agreement over Icahn's objections and threats to sue. Not one to be overlooked when it came to TWA property, Icahn and his "TWA Acquisition Group" made a last minute attempt to enter into the bidding for TWA. Bankruptcy Judge Peter Walsh dismissed their attempt and "refused to hear any testimony about the proposal, calling the brief term sheet submitted by TWA Acquisition so late in the process 'almost a joke.'"[47] Icahn may have been playing the spoiler to American, especially because of the loss of his Karabu agreement. He had repeatedly said that TWA was "the worst investment I ever made," countering the accusations that his wealth had skyrocketed due to his misuse of TWA and its workers.[48]

The merger was completed in April 2001 with American purchasing most of TWA—equipment, routes, employees—and assured Congress and the DOT that they would treat TWA employees "fairly and equitably." In the beginning, TWA LLC flew as a separate entity within American. TWA employees, and their congressional supporters, argued that American benefited from the acquisition of TWA assets, but both American management and labor proffered themselves as saviors to TWA. They each argued that if it were not for American, TWA would have liquidated and the employees would be on the street. It is hard to predict what would have happened to TWA had American not purchased it. TWA had teetered on the brink of dissolution many times, and had survived. And yet, this could have been the finale. TWA was unable to pay its bills and had gone in search of a buyer.

As a condition of entering into an asset purchase of TWA, American required TWA to file for bankruptcy, in large part, to rid the airline of the toxic Karabu agreement with Icahn. American also made it clear that the unions would have to abrogate their provisions for labor protections in the event of a merger. Known as the Allegheny Mohawk provision, this was part of the TWA labor agreements that was inserted into collective bargaining agreements when deregulation eliminated the CAB and put the airline industry under the DOT. This provision guaranteed seniority protection to TWA employees when labor forces were merged, giving them the right of "date of hire" from their original airline. American unions did not have an Allegheny Mohawk provision, and TWA unions were reluctant to give up something that would then put them in a vulnerable position vis-à-vis the new labor forces. In its bid for TWA, American assured TWA employees in congressional hearings and public statements that they would be treated fairly and equitably.[49] American brought in TWA workers with their pay and benefits and aligned them with American workers. American President Don Carty sold the plan to TWA employees as a win-win for TWA and its employees, arguing that they would be in even better shape than they were at TWA.

For the flight attendants, this could not have been further from the truth. IAM as their representative at first refused to withdraw their scope clause detailing their seniority integration protection. TWA, led by President William Compton who was anxious to sell TWA, escalated the demands and requested from bankruptcy court the complete abrogation of the collective bargaining agreement. IAM capitulated and agreed to eliminate the flight attendant scope clause rather than face the dissolution of the entire contract by the bankruptcy court. In doing so, they failed to put anything in place that would protect the flight attendants. American Airlines had agreed to "facilitate" the process of seniority integration between the unions which meant little more than offering a facilitator to the process, and said they would accept whatever plan for integration the unions agreed upon. However, American employee relations officers and the Association of Professional Flight Attendants (APFA) who represented flight attendants at American met without IAM, and created an integration plan that stapled the entire TWA flight attendant labor force to the bottom of the seniority list. Rather than using "date of hire" to merge the two flight attendant groups, which they had done before, APFA gave TWA flight attendants date of hire as of the merger date April 10, 2001.[50] In effect, TWA flight attendants were stapled to the bottom of the list, wiping out decades of flying and positioning them as the first in line to be furloughed in an industry that relied heavily on the furlough process.

The TWA flight attendants felt betrayed, and there was plenty of blame to go around. TWA's Compton for selling TWA; American for broken promises of fair treatment; APFA for its refusal to use original date of hire to determine seniority; and, the TWA flight attendants own union, IAM, for misrepresentation.

Compton was first in line for doing the sale in the first place when the employees thought the airline was beginning to hold its own. TWA had always been a premier airline and had always struggled financially. It had been through two bankruptcies in the 1990s. Icahn had financially drained the company by taking it private, selling it off in bits and pieces, underfunding the pension system, and leaving with the poison pen Karabu agreement. As Pearson related, Icahn may not have been the whole cause of the death of TWA, "but Icahn certainly sped up the process."[51] The employees felt that the only person who benefited from the acquisition was Compton himself who left with a very nice package.

American management had failed to uphold their promise to the government that they would treat employees fairly. Their promise was shallow to begin with—they agreed to provide a facilitator to help the process of merging separate flight attendant populations. As it turned out, no facilitator was utilized to help with negotiations between IAM and APFA, and despite letters from IAM requesting meetings to discuss seniority integration, American management and APFA met without IAM representatives and developed a plan that made TWA flight attendants the furlough buffer for American flight attendants. Not only did the TWA flight attendants, stapled to the bottom, mean they would be the first to go in a furlough, but APFA was able to use fuloughees as a bargaining chip in negotiations. By removing severance pay, which had been afforded fuloughees in the past, APFA was able to use that pay concession as part of the concessionary package American was demanding from APFA.[52] IAM and the TWA flight attendants they represented sued American and APFA for their actions, but the court raised the issue of who was actually at fault, the parties at American or IAM's representation of the flight attendants.

The issue of who was at fault in the seniority integration was thrown into sharp relief as the integration played out for the pilots. A similar, though somewhat less dramatic stapling of TWA pilots occurred. Some of the pilots received original date of hire seniority, but about 40 percent found themselves stapled to the bottom of the list. The local TWA ALPA sued as well, but the court threw out their claims against American Airlines and the Allied Pilots

Association (APA, pilots' union at American) but let stand their case against their national ALPA. By the court's determination, it was their own national union's mishandling of their seniority protection. The pilots won that case, and were accorded $53 million in back pay.[53]

Rather than suing their union, the flight attendants and IAM sued American, APFA, and TWA LC. When Judge Deborah Gershon dismissed their case on November 23, 2004, it was too late to consider suing IAM because they no longer were the legal representative of the former TWA flight attendants.[54] The parallels between the pilot and flight attendant integration processes raised the point that IAM had failed to represent the flight attendants adequately. In their dealings with American, IAM agreed to the elimination of the scope clause in the TWA flight attendant agreement. Clearly this was done under the duress of the even greater threat by TWA that, if they did not comply, TWA would move to have the whole union contract nullified by the bankruptcy court. IAM, however, left the flight attendants completely unprotected. IAM voluntarily agreed to withdraw the Allegheny Mohawk provisions without requiring binding arbitration in the event that an acceptable agreement between the two unions was not possible. They eventually wrote a letter of request for binding arbitration in early December 2001, but by that time it was too late. American's response to this letter was to inform IAM that they had been meeting with APFA, without IAM representation, and an agreement had already been reached—stapled to the bottom, flight attendants with decades of experience were given seniority rights below people who had been hired less than a year ago.[55]

The machinists represented by IAM fared better. American's TWU agreed to arbitration with IAM for seniority integration. Individual members of IAM had been very supportive of the flight attendants strike, but the national had not given such support and had sent mixed messages of support contingent on flight attendants organizing under them. IFFA leadership believed that had they been affiliated with IAM at the time of the strike, they would not have waged the struggle to get all the workers back to work as IFFA had done.[56] IFFA had fought fiercely to return all its workers to the line; if past actions are in anyway predictive, they would have fought equally hard in a seniority integration battle. The decision of Cooper to undermine IFFA to ally with IAM in 1996 may have contributed to the outcome at American and the devastating loss that Cooper and other flight attendants fought over seniority in the following years.

Whatever plans were foreseen for American and TWA, and the airline industry as a whole, were instantly upended on September 11, 2001. Two of the four planes that hit that day were American Airlines, the first plane that hit the North Tower of the World Trade Center, and the third plane that struck the Pentagon.[57] In the aftermath of the 9/11 terror attacks, American Airlines was particularly hard hit. Very quickly, flight travel declined, and furloughs began. Because American and TWA LLC were still separate as of 9/11, the first flight attendant furloughs were drawn from both sets of flight attendants. American made the decision to close its base at JFK which was flown by TWA, and flight attendants could either choose to commute to St. Louis, the main hub of TWA, or be furloughed.

With the ongoing crisis in the airline industry, the next furlough occurred after American and APFA's December 17, 2001 agreement that stapled TWA flight attendants to the bottom of the list. The only flight attendants that maintained their date of hire seniority were TWA flight attendants at St. Louis who fell under an agreement that allowed them to retain seniority in St. Louis. This agreement was abandoned fairly quickly. The next furlough by American was drawn solely from TWA flight attendants. By 2003, all TWA flight attendants were out with no severance pay, and the ninety days of medical reduced to thirty days.

The fate of TWA was of particular importance to Missouri because of the St. Louis hub. To that end, US Senators Kit Bond and Jim Talent conducted hearings in the summer of 2003 on the issue of seniority integration and its impact on TWA employees, grilling American management to understand how this was ever defined as "fair and equitable" treatment. As Bond relayed in his opening remarks on the hearing on this topic:

> All of us on this committee and indeed, all of us in the Senate, certainly understand how tough times are right now for our Nation's airlines. We understand how cutbacks in personnel as well as cutbacks in other expenses have been needed in order to keep the airlines in the air. There is no question that this is a difficult time, and we sympathize with all in the airline business.
>
> Unfortunately, we have seen in Missouri that when it came time to cut at American airlines, the blade fell almost exclusively on former TWA workers, including pilots, flight attendants, and to some extent, baggage handlers and ground crews.

And later,

> However, as poorly as the pilots were treated, it has been worse for TWA's flight attendants. As of July 2, 2003, 100 percent of all former TWA flight attendants will have been furloughed by American Airlines—nearly 4,200 employees. Let me repeat that—100 percent furloughed, 4,200 employees. Best efforts indeed.[58]

Bond and supporters attempted to get a bill passed, the Airline Workers' Fairness Act to insure "fair and equitable" seniority integration. Although this bill failed, U.S. Senator Claire McCaskill joined forces and in 2007 the McCaskill Bond Act passed. Seen as an outgrowth of the treatment of TWA workers, this act protects workers' seniority, requiring fair integration in mergers. The original impetus of the bill was the treatment of TWA employees, specifically the flight attendants. By the time that the act passes, their fate had already been determined. Any attempts to rectify the situation, for example, by revisiting the bill and retroactively including the TWA employees, failed.

In 2013, when American Airlines and US Airways merged, it opened up an opportunity to revisit the seniority integration debacle a decade earlier. By then, there were less than a 1,000 former TWA flight attendants at American, who had returned from furlough beginning in 2011. With the merger with US Airways, American offered a $40,000 buyout to flight attendants. As it turned out, American could have given TWA flight attendants their original date of hire, slotted them in, and because of the attrition from flight attendants taking the early buyout, no one would have lost any position. Despite the fact that APFA had admitted that it was a mistake to staple TWA flight attendants at the bottom of the seniority list, they were unwilling to revisit this decision. Integrating the two flight attendant populations of American and US Airways, in accordance with the labor protections now in place through the McCaskill Bond Act, further diluted the seniority standing of TWA flight attendants.

The former TWA flight attendants sued and argued that their unfair treatment in the seniority integration at American was the very prompt for the McCaskill Bond Act and that the decision should be revisited and overturned in light of the seniority integration of American with US Airways. In February 2016, the U.S. District Court in Brooklyn dismissed the TWA flight attendant case, and a year later, February 17, 2016, the appellate affirmed the dismissal. In November 2015, American Airlines christened another in its series "heritage airplanes" to pay tribute to TWA as part of its blended family of merged former airlines.[59]

PRIDE AND DIGNITY

Set within the context of deregulation, corporate raiding, and government and employer opposition to labor, IFFA struck when they saw no other choice. With less than 200 jobs available at the end of the strike, they waged a long and sustained battle to regain their jobs. And, they were successful against all odds. They set as their goal the return of all full-term strikers, and they did not give up. Their activism reached across the country and was supported by countless unions, organizations, and individuals.

At one of IFFA's recall meetings after the strike, labor negotiator and supporter Ted Kheel spoke about how the conflict unfolded was largely due to the Icahn/TWA's decision to use permanent replacements.[60] The congressional argument for a ban on permanent replacements spoke to this point:

> When employers permanently replace striking workers, the strike is converted from a limited dispute about working conditions to a broader confrontation about retention of jobs and the right of workers to union representation. Unions understandably insisted on the reinstatement of strikers as a precondition to settling the strike. This issue is often far more difficult to resolve than the original economic dispute separating the parties.[61]

Where permanent replacements are utilized, strikes are significantly longer, and unions are significantly less likely to survive than where employers have used temporary replacements or no replacements.[62] The mere threat of permanent replacement topples attempts to organize workplaces and leads unions to back down from exercising their right to strike. Workers' very own legal rights to organize and strike have become avenues for employers to extinguish them. "The temptation of employers to cause or prolong strikes is further fueled by the fact that permanently replacing strikers is a weapon far disproportionate to any economic weapon available to employees."[63]

With the failure of a congressional ban on replacements, and the Supreme Court's decision to expand the definition of replacements to include crossovers in a strike, the imbalance in power is further diminished.[64] Frankovich, in 1991 testimony supporting a ban on permanent replacements put their strike within the broader context of contemporary labor relations:

> Our courts have made a mockery of federal statutes regulating and promoting collective bargaining. Congress has specifically *protected* the right to strike and has specifically prohibited employee discrimination based upon *the exercise* of that right. It is unlawful, Congress has said, for an employer to discharge or otherwise discriminate against an employee because that employee exercised the right to strike. As illustrated by the IFFA-TWA post-strike litigation, the federal courts have, under the guise of interpretation, effectively repealed these statutes. The courts have in effect said: "We read that Congress has prohibited an employer from discharging or otherwise discriminating against an employee who exercised the right to strike, but we will allow that employer to 'permanently replace' any employee who exercises that right." With all due respect, this is a distinction without a difference; permanent replacement *is,* by any definition, tantamount to discharge and is clear discrimination on the basis of who did, and who did not, work during a strike. Similarly, employees who are union members, who participate in the collective decision to exercise the right to strike, who commence that strike—but who thereafter cross a picket line and return to work—may be rewarded by an employer by being retained in preference to those employees (including more senior employees) who stayed on strike for its duration. Again, and with all due respect, this is judicial approval of the notion that benefits including jobs can be doled out on the basis of the extent of protected union activity. Such discrimination is contrary to federal labor policy.

> We suffered greatly for exercising our right to strike . . . A union member risks enough by exercising the legal right to strike without also facing permanent replacement. Give us a level playing field.[65]

A balanced system of labor-management relations, a level playing field, is not possible as long as employers have the right of permanent replacement. Workers strike to save their livelihoods, not to lose them. In addition to the costs of replacement, without an effective strike, U.S. workers have seen a decline in their wages and benefits, while working harder at less secure jobs.[66] Having failed at a legislative ban, and seeing the direction of the Supreme Court to further entrench the practice, the elimination of permanent replacement seems more difficult but no less necessary. A return to policies supporting full employment could move the scales, creating an opening through increased labor strength, and in turn, impede employers' use of permanent replacements.

As difficult as the story is about permanent replacements, it would be a serious mistake to let it overshadow the extraordinary stories of solidarity among workers fighting for fair treatment. IFFA members fought for "Pride and Dignity," and achieved through collective determination and persistence the return of every full-term striker. Their activism and that of workers throughout the United States who faced the assault on labor in the 1980s is a reminder of the essential qualities of the labor movement. David Moberg, in a discussion of the Local P-9 battle at Hormel, expressed it for all workers:

> Yet in the end the labor movement relies on a continued reinvigoration of emotional commitment. Its roots lie in the belief of average workers that they deserve just treatment and a voice in their lives at work. Its ultimate strength rests on concrete expressions of solidarity among workers. Without that fiery spirit, the life and strength drain out of the labor movement, and it becomes a bureaucratic house of cards, easy to topple. Even the highest labor official in Washington ultimately depends on that raw emotion, commitment, and willingness to challenge the status quo.[67]

NOTES

1. IFFA, *Off the Line: The Newsletter of Un-Flight Services*, Fall 1989, 5.
2. William H. Freivogel, "Court Rejects Flight Attendants' Appeal," *St. Louis Post-Dispatch*, January 17, 1990.
3. *Teleconference*, produced by IFFA, 1989.
4. Ibid.
5. Ibid.
6. Ibid. As recallees returned, new hires also moved down on the seniority list for bidding flights and their lowered position would have affected grievances as well.
7. *Teleconference*, produced by IFFA, 1989.

8. Mark Stevens, *King Icahn: The Biography of a Renegade Capitalist* (NY: Dutton, Penguin Books, 1993), 202.
9. Ibid., 223.
10. James T. McKenna, "ALPA Prepares for Possible Sale of All or Part of TWA," *Aviation Week and Space Technology*, November 20, 1989.
11. Mark Stevens, *King Icahn: The Biography of a Renegade Capitalist* (NY: Dutton, Penguin Books, 1993), 224.
12. Christopher Carey and Phil Linsalata, "Advanced Icahnomics: The Airline Takes on Debt, The Raider Takes out Cash," *St. Louis Post-Dispatch*, May 21, 1990.
13. Ibid.
14. *Aviation Daily*, February 5, 1990.
15. James T. McKenna, "ALPA Prepares for Possible Sale of All or Part of TWA," *Aviation Week and Space Technology*, November 20, 1989.
16. "Carl Icahn's Crippled Airline," *The Financial Post*, April 5, 1991.
17. Moira Johnston, *Takeover: The New Wall Street Warriors* (New York: Arbor House, 1986), 317.
18. Unions Accuse Carl Icahn of Plan to Liquidate TWA," *Aviation Daily*, January 24, 1991; IFFA, *The 630 News: The Official Publication*, February 15, 1991.
19. IFFA, *The 630 News: The Official Publication*, February 15, 1991.
20. Agis Salpukas, "Kerkorian, T.W.A. Unions Agree on Bid for the Carrier," *New York Times*, March 30, 1991; Agis Salpukas, "U.S. Backs Route Sale by T.W.A.," *New York Times*, April 26, 1991.
21. IFFA, *The 630 News: The Official Publication*, Summer 1990, 14.
22. Reuters, "T.W.A. Suitor is Described by Icahn as 'a Spoiler' in Bid," *New York Times*, April 2, 1992.
23. Mark Stevens, *King Icahn: The Biography of a Renegade Capitalist* (NY: Dutton, Penguin Books, 1993).
24. "Archives of History, Carl Icahn," *Twaflight843.com*, ret., July 26, 2010.
25. IFFA, *The 630 News: The Official Publication,* "The Plane Truths, pamphlet and video," March 1993.
26. Ibid.
27. Ibid.
28. IFFA, "Rumor vs. Reality, Phase 7," *IFFA*, August 23, 1993.
29. IFFA, *The 630 News: The Official Publication,* "The Plane Truths, pamphlet and video," March 1993.
30. Karen Nussbaum to Mary Ellen Miller, September 29, 1993.
31. "Icahn Officially Ends Stint as the Chairman of TWA," *New York Times*, January 11, 1993.
32. Vicki Frankovich to IFFA Members, April 26, 1993.
33. Christopher Carey, "TWA on Feet after Bankruptcy," *St. Louis Post-Dispatch*, August 25, 1995.
34. Elaine X. Grant, "TWA—Death of a Legend," *St. Louis*, July 28, 2006.
35. Lizette Alvarez, "Rising Hopes Turn Hollow for Company on Rebound," *New York Times*, July 18, 1996.
36. NTSB Will Not Reopen TWA Flight 800 Investigation," twa800.sites.usa.gov, accessed April 10, 2016.

37. "Trans World Airlines, Inc.," Encyclopedia.com, last modified 2001, accessed June 3, 2014.

38. Fred Faust, "Flight Attendants Elect New Leader," *St. Louis Post-Dispatch*, September 8, 1995.

39. Ibid.

40. Christopher Carey, "Union vs. Union at TWA," *St. Louis Post-Dispatch*, October 31, 1996; IFFA v. Sherry Cooper, 58 F.3d (Apr. 14, 1998).

41. "TWA Flight Attendants Seek Independence," *St. Louis Post-Dispatch*, October 26, 1999.

42. "TWA Flight Attendants Seek Independence—Local Union 3 Defects," *St. Louis Post-Dispatch*, October 26, 1999; "TWA Flight Attendants Vote on New Leaders," *St. Louis Post-Dispatch*, December 10, 1999.

43. "TWA Flight Attendants Seek Own Union," *St. Louis Post-Dispatch*, March 16, 2000; "TWA Flight Attendants Will Vote this Week on Changing Union Representation," *Knight Ridder*, June 6, 2000.

44. "Flight Attendants at TWA will Stay with Machinists," *St. Louis Post-Dispatch*, June 10, 2000.

45. Elaine X. Grant, "TWA—Death of a Legend," *St. Louis*, July 28, 2006.

46. Ibid.

47. Laurence Zuckerman and Maureen Milford, "T.W.A. Judge Dismisses Icahn Group Bid," *New York Times*, March 12, 2001.

48. Paul Tharp, "Icahn's Not Beat Yet after Losing TWA," *New York Post*, March 18, 2001; Elaine X. Grant, "TWA—Death of a Legend," *St. Louis*, July 28, 2006.

49. *TWA/American Airline Workforce Integration: Hearings before the Committee on Health, Education, Labor, and Pensions, June 12*, 108th Cong., First (2003).

50. Sherry Cooper, IAM, et.al. V. TWA LLC, American, APFA (U.S. District. E.D., New York Nov. 23, 2004).

51. Adam Wilmouth, "Former Executives Recall Icahn Takeovers," *The Oklahoman newok.com*, June 3, 2012.

52. Cynthia Wilson, "Ex-TWA Workers are Hit Hard by Concessions," *St. Louis Post-Dispatch*, April 4, 2003.

53. Terry Maxon, "Ex-TWA Pilots Agree to $53 Million Settlement in American Airlines Seniority Dispute," *The Dallas Morning News*, January 23, 2014.

54. Sherry Cooper, IAM, et.al. v. TWA LLC, American, APFA (U.S. District. E.D., New York Nov. 23, 2004).

55. *TWA/American Airline Workforce Integration: Hearings before the Committee on Health, Education, Labor, and Pensions, June 12*, 108th Cong., First (2003).

56. Mary Ellen Miller, interview, Kansas City, MO, 1988.

57. Eric Benson, "The Encyclopedia of 9/11: The Planes," *New York*, August 27, 2011

58. *TWA/American Airline Workforce Integration: Hearings before the Committee on Health, Education, Labor, and Pensions, June 12*, 108th Cong., First (2003).

59. Ted Reed, "As American Rolls Out TWA Heritage Airplane, TWA Flight Attendants Still Bear a Burden," *Forbes.com*, November 21, 2015.

60. IFFA, *Recall Meetings, 1986–1989.*

61. *Workplace Fairness Act: Hearings on S. 55 Before the Committee on Labor and Human Resources, July 27*, 103d Cong., First (1993), 21–22.

62. Cynthia Gramm, "Employers' Decisions to Operate During Strikes: Consequences and Policy Implications," in *Employee Rights in a Changing Economy: The Issue of Replacement Workers*, by Economic Policy Institute (Washington, DC: EPI, 1991).

63. *Workplace Fairness Act: Hearings on S. 55 Before the Committee on Labor and Human Resources, July 27*, 103d Cong., First (1993), 23.

64. Julius G. Getman, *The Supreme Court on Unions: Why Labor Law is Failing American Workers* (Ithaca: ILR Press, 2016), 57–65.

65. *Prohibiting Permanent Replacement of Striking Workers: Hearings on H.R. 5 Before the Subcommittee on Aviation of the Committee on Public Works and Transportation, April 10*, 102d Cong., First (1991), 114–15.

66. Joe Burns, *Reviving the Strike: How Working People Can Regain Power and Transform America* (Brooklyn, NY: IG Publishing, 2011), 19.

67. Hardy Green, *On Strike at Hormel: The Struggle for a Democratic Labor Movement* (Philadelphia: Temple University Press, 1990), xv.

Bibliography

Ackerman, Frank. *Hazardous to Our Wealth: Economic Policies in the 1980s*. Boston: South End Press, 1984.

ALPA. *MEC Special Meeting: Notes, March 5*. New York: ALPA/TWA, 1986.

Alvarez, Lizette. "Rising Hopes Turn Hollow for Company on Rebound." *New York Times*, July 18, 1996.

Asbury Park Press. "Union Critical of TWA Hijack Heroine." May 14, 1986.

Associated Press. "Arbitrator Rules that TWA Mechanics Cannot Honor Attendants' Picket Line." *News Archives*, April 7, 1986.

———. "Icahn Acquires Rest of T.W.A." *New York Times*, September 27, 1985.

———. "Protesters Plan to Stay Busy during Pope's Visit." *Tampa Bay Times*, August 22, 1987.

———. "Vote on T.W.A. Contract Set." *New York Times*, May 19, 1986.

Aviation Daily, February 5, 1990.

Aviation Daily. "TWA Flight Attendants Reject Contract Proposal." May 23, 1986.

Aviation Daily. "Unions Accuse Carl Icahn of Plan to Liquidate TWA." January 24, 1991.

Barry, Kathleen M. *Femininity in Flight: A History of Flight Attendants*. Durham: Duke University, 2007.

Baskett, Bruce. "Hijack Heroine Now a 'Scab.' "*Telegraph*, May 16, 1986.

BBC News. "Nut Strike Cracks after 13 Years." *BBC News* (United Kingdom), March 3, 2005. http://news.bbc.co.uk/go/pr/fr/-/2/hi/business/4374657.stm.

Benson, Eric. "The Encyclopedia of 9/11: The Planes." *New York*, August 27, 2011.

Berendt, Gerald E., David Moberg, and Stephen Franklin. "The Labor Strike: Is It Still a Useful Economic Weapon for Unions?" *John Marshall Law Review* 35 (2001–2002): 255–86.

Bernstein, Aaron. *Grounded: Frank Lorenzo and the Destruction of Eastern Airlines*. New York: Simon and Schuster, 1990.

Bernstein, Aaron, and Chuck Hawkins. "Icahn Ponders Dismembering His Airline." *Business Week*, March 17, 1986, 57–58.

Beyette, Beverly. "The Case of the Missing Milk Cartons: It Was Only a Minor Theft but Airline and Attendant Agree It's Now a Major Case." *Los Angeles Times*, April 10, 1988.

Bleakley, Fred R. "T.W.A.'s Brief, Futile Battle." *New York Times*, June 24, 1985.

Bluestone, Barry, and Bennett Harrison. *The Deindustrialization of America: Plant Closings, Community Abandonment, and the Dismantling of Basic Industry*. New York: Basic Books, 1982.

Braverman, Harry. *Labor and Monopoly Capital: The Degradation of Work in the Twentieth Century*. New York: Monthly Review Press, 1974.

Brisbin Jr., Richard A. *A Strike Like No Other: Law & Resistance during the Pittston Coal Strike of 1989–1990*. Baltimore: Johns Hopkins University Press, 2002.

Bruck, Connie. "Kamikaze: How Texas Air's Frank Lorenzo Wrecked His Own Chance to Acquire TWA—and Carl Icahn Picked up the Pieces." *American Lawyer*, December 1985.

———. *The Predators' Ball: The Junk-Bond Raiders and the Man Who Staked Them*. New York: Simon and Schuster, 1988.

Bureau of Labor Statistics, Economic News Release: Work Stoppages in 2015, Rep. (2015).

Bureau of Labor Statistics, Work Stoppages Summary, Rep. (2010).

Burns, Joe. *Reviving the Strike: How Working People Can Regain Power and Transform America*. Brooklyn, NY: IG Publishing, 2011.

Burrough, Bryan. "Union Officials Question Icahn Pact on TWA." *Wall Street Journal*, July 5, 1985.

BustedHalo.com. "What Does Catholic Church Teach About Labor Unions." June 6, 2015.

Carey, Christopher. "TWA on Feet after Bankruptcy." *St. Louis Post-Dispatch*, August 25, 1995.

———. "Union vs. Union at TWA." *St. Louis Post-Dispatch*, October 31, 1996.

Carey, Christopher, and Phil Linsalata. "Advanced Icahnomics: The Airline Takes on Debt, The Raider Takes out Cash." *St. Louis Post-Dispatch*, May 21, 1990.

"Carl Icahn would Oust TWA President if Takeover Successful." *Aviation Daily*, May 30, 1985.

Catholic-pages.com. "Laborem Exercens, Summary." October 1, 2013.

Close, John Weir. *A Giant Cow-Tipping by Savages: The Boom, Bust, and Boom Culture of M&A*. New York: Palgrave Macmillan, 2013.

Collective Bargaining and the Hiring of Permanent Strike Replacements: Hearings Before the Government Operations, 102d Cong., 2d Sess. 1–105 (1992).

Crudele, John. "23-a-Share T.W.A. Bid is Reported." *New York Times*, June 14, 1985.

———. "Support for Strike Could Hurt T.W.A. Seriously." *New York Times*, March 9, 1986.

Cuff, Daniel F. "President is Out at T.W.A." *New York Times*, June 12, 1986.

Dallos, Robert. "Former TWA President Named Chief at Continental." *Los Angeles Times*, December 7, 1988.

Davis, Jim, and John T. Dauner. "TWA Machinists Report for Duty." *Kansas City Times*, March 12, 1986.

DeMott, John S., Lee Griggs, and Frederick Ungeheuer. "The High Price of Freedom." *Time*, March 18, 1985.

DeMott, John S., Madeleine J. Nash, and Adam Zagorin. "Three Who Watch, Wait and Strike." *Time*, March 4, 1985.

Dempsey, Paul Stephen, and Andrew R. Goetz. *Airline Deregulation and Laissez-Faire Mythology*. Westport, CT: Quorum Books, 1992.

De Young, Karen. "Blast on TWA Jet Kills 4." *Washington Post*, April 3, 1986.

———. "Turmoil Hid Loss of Passengers." *Washington Post*, April 4, 1986.

Draw the Line. Narrated by Vicki Frankovich. By IFFA. Audiocassette. Recorded Spring 1985.

Ehrman, John. *The Eighties: America in the Age of Reagan*. New Haven: Yale University Press, 2005.

Elk, Mike. "Sad, Startling Stats: Number of Union Elections, Strikes Continue Steady Decline." *In These Times*, July 7, 2010.

El Malcriado. "Cesar's Choice: How America's Farm Workers Got Organized." April 1, 1969.

Fantasia, Rick. *Cultures of Solidarity: Consciousness, Action, and Contemporary American Workers*. Berkeley: University of California, 1988.

Fantasia, Rick, and Kim Voss. *Hard Work: Remaking the American Labor Movement*. Berkeley: University of California Press, 2004.

Faust, Fred. "Flight Attendants Elect New Leader." *St. Louis Post-Dispatch*, September 8, 1995.

The Financial Post. "Carl Icahn's Crippled Airline." April 5, 1991.

Frankel, Alison. "Bar Talk." *American Lawyer*, April 16, 1988.

Franklin, Stephen. *Three Strikes: Labor's Heartland Losses and What They Mean for Working Americans*. New York: Guilford Press, 2001.

Frankovich, Vicki. "IFFA Strike 1986." Speech, National Organization for Women Convention, Lawrence, KS, Spring 1987.

———. Interview. St. Louis, MO. July 1989.

———. Vicki Frankovich to IFFA Members, April 26, 1993.

Freivogel, William H. "Attendants Prevail in Case Against TWA." *St. Louis Post-Dispatch*, March 7, 1989.

———. "Court Rejects Flight Attendants' Appeal." *St. Louis Post-Dispatch*, January 17, 1990.

Friday, Carolyn. "A Fatal Flight Takes its Toll." *Newsweek*, September 8, 1986. *The F.T.S. News & Muse*.

Furlow, Robert. "Bishops Choose TWA for Pope's Visit, Despite Union's Objections." *Associated Press*, May 15, 1987.

Gartner, Murray. *Defendant TWA's Suggestions in Support of Its Motion to Dismiss*. NY: n.p., 1987.

Getman, Julius G. *The Betrayal of Local 14*. Ithaca: ILR Press, 1998.

———. "Of Labor Law and Birdsong." *Connecticut Law Review* 30 (1997–1998): 1345–51.

———. *The Supreme Court on Unions: Why Labor Law is Failing American Workers*. Ithaca: ILR Press, 2016.

Gramm, Cynthia. “Employers’ Decisions to Operate During Strikes: Consequences and Policy Implications.” In *Employee Rights in a Changing Economy: The Issue of Replacement Workers* by Economic Policy Institute, 33–49. Washington, DC: EPI, 1991.

Grant, Elaine X. “TWA—Death of a Legend.” *St. Louis*, July 28, 2006.

Green, Hardy. *On Strike at Hormel: The Struggle for a Democratic Labor Movement.* Philadelphia: Temple University Press, 1990.

Grounded. Produced by IFFA. 1987.

Harrison, Bennett, and Barry Bluestone. *The Great U-Turn: Corporate Restructuring and the Polarizing of America.* New York: Basic Books, 1988.

———. *The Great U-Turn: Corporate Restructuring and the Polarizing of America.* NY: Basic Books, 1988.

Hicks, Jonathan. “Texas Air Halts Pact with T.W.A.” *New York Times*, September 14, 1985.

Honolulu Star-Bulletin. “TWA and Union Clash on Rehiring.” May 21, 1986.

Hudock, Barry. “America.” *National Catholic Review*, August 27, 2012.

IFFA. *Hotline.*

———. *IFFAgrams to Flight Attendants.*

———. “IFFA Supports other Union Action.” *Boycotts and Rallies*, 1988.

———. IFFA to TWA Flight Attendant Recruits, January 24, 1986.

———. *Information Representative Cards.*

———. *Letter to Fellow Flight Attendants, June 28, 1989.*

———. *Off the Line: The Newsletter of Un-Flight Services.*

———. *Recall Meetings, 1986–1989.*

———. “Rumor vs. Reality, Phase 7.” *IFFA*, August 23, 1993.

———. *The 630 News: The Official Publication of the Independent Federation of Flight Attendants.*

IFFA v. Sherry Cooper, 58 F.3d (Apr. 14, 1998).

IFFA v. TWA (U.S. District Court, W.D. Missouri, Economic Reinstatement Case 1986).

IFFA v. TWA (8th Cir., Economic Reinstatement Case 1987).

IFFA v. TWA (U.S. Supreme Court (U.S.), Economic Reinstatement Case 1989).

IFFA v. TWA (U.S. District Court, W. D. Missouri, Bad Faith Bargaining 1988).

IFFA v. TWA (8th Cir., Bad Faith Bargaining 1989).

International Directory of Company Histories. “Trans World Airlines, Inc.” Encyclopedia.com. Last modified 2001. Accessed June 3, 2014.

Johnston, Moira. *Takeover: The New Wall Street Warriors.* New York: Arbor House, 1986.

Jolley, William A. *Plaintiff IFFA’s Suggestions in Opposition to Defendent TWA’s Motion to Dismiss.* Kansas City, MO: n.p., 1986.

Juravich, Tom, and Kate Bronfenbrenner. *Ravenswood: The Steelworkers’ Victory and the Revival of American Labor.* Ithaca: ILR Press, 1999.

Kansas City Times. “Attendants Say Battle against TWA isn’t Over.” May 23, 1986.

Kansas City Times. “Letters to the Editor.” April 16, 1986.

Kansas City Times. “TWA Flight Attendants Resume Contract Talks.” April 25, 1986.

Kansas City Times. "TWA is Apparent Victor." May 20, 1986.

Kansas City Times. "TWA Says It's Quit Hiring Attendants." April 29, 1986.

Kansas City Times. "Union Rejecting TWA Pact." May 22, 1986.

Kansas City Times. "Union to Vote on TWA Pact." May 19, 1986.

Kaphy Long v. TWA (U.S. District Court, N.D. Illinois, E.D. 1989).

Kaphy Long v. TWA (7th Cir. 1990).

Kaps, Robert W. *Air Transport Labor Relations*. Carbondale, IL: Southern Illinois University Press, 1997.

Kaul, Donald. "They're Stewing, and with Reason." *Philly.com*, March 12, 1986.

Kaye, Tony, and Miriam Rozen. "Icahn's Words Come Back to Haunt Him." *American Lawyer*, March 1988.

Keil, Thomas J. *On Strike! Capital Cities and the Wilkes-Barre Newspaper Unions*. Tuscaloosa: University of Alabama, 1988.

Kilborn, Peter T. "California Strike Becomes a Battle Over Permanent Job Replacements." *New York Times*, April 17, 1994.

———. "Reagan Plan to Privatize Government is Gaining Support from Democrats." *New York Times*, February 15, 1988.

———. "Replacement Workers: Management's Big Gun." *New York Times*, March 13, 1990.

Knight Ridder. "TWA Flight Attendants Will Vote this Week on Changing Union Representation." June 6, 2000.

Kohler, Thomas C., and Julius Getman. "The Story of NLRB v. Mackay Radio & Telegraph Co.: The High Cost of Solidarity." *Boston College Law School, Legal Studies Research Paper Series* 103 (August 1, 2006).

Labor Beacon. "IFFA/TWA Conflict Not Over." May 30, 1986.

Lambert, Josiah Bartlett. *"If the Workers Took a Notion": The Right to Strike and American Political Development*. Ithaca: ILR Press, 2005.

Larson, David Allen. "Trans World Airlines, Inc. v. Independent Federation of Flight Attendants: A Fundamental Blow to Collective Bargaining." *Missouri Labor Review* 54 (1989).

Las Vegas Review Journal. "California Wards of State used by TWA to Fill in For Strikers." March 14, 1986.

Lawrence, Jill. "TWA Boycott Urged by Women's Groups, Seven House Members." *Associated Press*, June 18, 1986.

Leinster, Colin. "Carl Icahn's Calculated Bets." *Fortune*, March 18, 1985.

LeRoy, Michael H. "The Changing Character of Strikes Involving Permanent Striker Replacements, 1935–1990." *Journal of Labor Research* XVI, no. 4 (1995): 423–37.

———. "Regulating Employer Use of Permanent Striker Replacements: Empirical Analysis of NLRA and RLA Strikes 1935–1991." *Berkeley Journal of Employment & Labor Law* 16, no. 1 (1995): 169–208.

Loomis, Carol. "The Comeuppance of Carl Icahn." *Fortune*, February 1986.

Los Angeles Times. "The Nation." April 25, 1986.

Los Angeles Times. "TWA Strike Is Over, but the Dispute Isn't." May 20, 1986.

Los Angeles Times. "Union Had Prepared Strategy to Counter Bankruptcy Filing." March 10, 1989.

Mankiller, Wilma Pearl, ed. *The Reader's Companion to U.S. Women's History.* Boston: Houghton Mifflin, 1998.

Maxon, Terry. "Ex-TWA Pilots Agree to $53 Million Settlement in American Airlines Seniority Dispute." *The Dallas Morning News*, January 23, 2014.

McCartin, Joseph A. *Collision Course: Ronald Reagan, the Air Traffic Controllers, and the Strike that Changed America.* New York: Oxford University Press, 2011.

———. "Remembering the Day the Strike Died." *Chicago Tribune*, August 10, 2005.

McKelvey, Jean T., ed. *Cleared for Takeoff: Airline Labor Relations since Deregulation.* Ithaca: ILR Press, 1988.

McKenna, James T. "ALPA Prepares for Possible Sale of All or Part of TWA." *Aviation Week and Space Technology*, November 20, 1989.

Message to IFFA Membership. By Arthur Teolis. 1984, audiocassette.

Miller, Mary Ellen. "Follow-up on Supporters." E-mail message. August 20, 2016.

———. Interview. Kansas City, MO. 1988.

———. Interview. Kansas City, MO. 2009.

Minchin, Timothy. "'It Tears the Heart Right Out of You': Memories of Striker Replacement at International Paper Company in De Pere, Wisconsin, 1987–88." *Oral History Review* Summer- Fall (2004): 1–27.

Morrison, Steven A., and Clifford Winston. *The Evolution of the Airline Industry.* Washington, DC: Brookings Institution, 1995.

Ms, January 1987.

National Boycott News, Spring/Summer 1989.

National Transportation Board. "NTSB Will Not Reopen TWA Flight 800 Investigation." twa800.sites.usa.gov. Accessed April 10, 2016.

Newsday. "Union Offers TWA Deal." April 25, 1986.

New York Daily News Strike and Permanent Replacements, 101st, 2d 1–74 (1990).

New York Post. "Strikers Hassle TWA Hijack Heroine." May 13, 1986.

New York Times. "Executive Changes." September 24, 1985.

New York Times. "Icahn Officially Ends Stint as the Chairman of TWA." January 11, 1993.

New York Times. "Labor Chief Recalls Futile Effort to Support Controller Strike." October 5, 1981.

New York Times. "Proposal to T.W.A." December 10, 1985.

New York Times. "Spinoff Approved at Trans World." December 29, 1983, Financial Desk.

New York Times. "TWA Attendants End Strike." May 23, 1986.

New York Times. "T.W.A. Deal: Losses Shaped Tactics." January 6, 1986.

New York Times. "T.W.A. Has Loss; UAL Posts Profit." July 22, 1986.

New York Times. "T.W.A. Purser Is Hailed as Courageous." July 1, 1985.

New York Times. "T.W.A. Studies New Icahn Bid." December 18, 1985.

New York Times. "2 T.W.A. Appointments." September 25, 1992.

Nielsen, Georgia Panter. *From Sky Girl to Flight Attendant: Women and the Making of a Union.* Ithaca, NY: ILR Press, 1982.

Norman, Michael. "T.W.A. Cancels Half of its Flights as Attendants Strike over Wages." *New York Times*, March 8, 1986.

Nussbaum, Karen. Karen Nussbaum to Mary Ellen Miller, September 29, 1993.

Orenic, Liesl Miller. *On the Ground: Labor Struggle in the American Airline Industry*. Urbana, IL: University of Illinois Press, 2009.

Palley, Thomas. "Reviving Full Employment Policy: Challenging the Wall Street Paradigm." *EPI Briefing Paper* 191 (June 22, 2007): 1–4.

Petzinger, Jr, Thomas. *Hard Landing: The Epic Contest for Power and Profits that Plunged the Airlines into Chaos*. Armonk, NY: M.E. Sharp, 1995.

Phillips, Matt. "American Labor-union Strikes are Almost Completely Extinct." *Quartz (cz.com)*, February 11, 2015.

Potts, Mark. "Texas Air to Acquire TWA Inc." *Washington Post*, June 14, 1985.

Preventing Replacement of Economic Strikers: Hearings on S. 2112 Before the Subcommittee on Labor of the Committee on Labor and Human Resources, June 6, 101st Cong., second (1990).

PR Newswire. "IFFA Calls for a National Boycott of TWA." June 18, 1986.

PR Newswire. "U.S. Equal Employment Opportunity Commission Dismisses Charges." March 15, 1987.

Prohibiting Discrimination against Economic Strikers: Hearings on S. 55 Before the Subcommittee on Labor of the Committee on Labor and Human Resources, March 12, 102d Cong., First (1991).

Prohibiting Permanent Replacement of Striking Workers: Hearings on H.R. 5 Before the Subcommittee on Aviation of the Committee on Public Works and Transportation, April 10, 102d Cong., First (1991).

Rachleff, Peter. *Hard-Pressed in the Heartland: The Hormel Strike and the Future of the LaborMovement*. Boston: South End Press, 1993.

———. "They Say Give Back, We Say Fight Back." *Dollars & Sense*, August/September 2000.

"The Raiding Game." *Dollars and Sense*, March 1987.

Reed, Ted. "As American Rolls Out TWA Heritage Airplane, TWA Flight Attendants Still Bear a Burden." *Forbes.com*, November 21, 2015.

Reuters. "T.W.A. Suitor Is Described by Icahn as 'a Spoiler' in Bid." *New York Times*, April 2, 1992.

Rhomberg, Chris. *The Broken Table*. New York: Russel Sage Foundation, 2012.

Rhor, Monica. "Protests, Rallies During Papal Visit Will Range in Focus." *Sun Sentinel* (Miami), August 21, 1987.

Robey, Renate. "Airline Reserves Phone Work for Young Prisoners." *Los Angeles Times*, January 13, 1986.

———. "Strikers Angry, Airline's Use of CYA Labor." *Los Angeles Times*, March 14, 1986.

Robinson, Jack E. *Free Fall: The Needless Destruction of Eastern Airlines and the Valiant Struggle to Save It*. New York: Harper Business, 1992.

Rosenblum, Jonathan D. *Copper Crucible: How the Arizona Miners' Strike of 1983 Recast Labor- Management Relations in America*. 2nd ed. Ithaca: ILR Press, 1998.

Rossinow, Doug. *The Reagan Era: A History of the 1980s*. New York: Columbia University Press, 2015.

Salpukas, Agis. "Icahn Back in T.W.A. Bidding." *New York Times*, August 6, 1985.

———. "Icahn Closes in on Control of T.W.A." *New York Times*, August 8, 1985.

———. "Icahn Gets Control of T.W.A." *New York Times*, January 4, 1986.

———. "Icahn Is Closing in on T.W.A." *New York Times*, January 3, 1986.
———. "Icahn Raises T.W.A. Stake to 40.6%." *New York Times*, August 7, 1985.
———. "Icahn Said to Ask for New Funds." *New York Times*, November 28, 1985.
———. "Icahn Said to Weigh Shift in Bid." *New York Times*, December 9, 1985.
———. "Icahn's T.W.A. Bid Reportedly Revised." *New York Times*, December 21, 1985.
———. "Kerkorian, T.W.A. Unions Agree on Bid for the Carrier." *New York Times*, March 30, 1991.
———. "Pilot Pact Puts Curbs on Icahn." *New York Times*, July 4, 1985.
———. "T.W.A. and Northwest Post Losses." *New York Times*, April 26, 1986.
———. "T.W.A. Deal: Losses Shaped Tactics." *New York Times*, January 6, 1986.
———. "U.S. Backs Route Sale by T.W.A." *New York Times*, April 26, 1991.
Schmidt, Eric, and Kenneth N. Gilpin. "Consultant Guided Icahn's T.W.A. Bid." *New York Times*, April 1, 1986.
Sherry Cooper, IAM, et.al. v. TWA LLC, American, APFA (U.S. District. E.D., New York Nov. 23, 2004).
Shostak, Arthur B., and David Skocik. *The Air Controllers' Controversy: Lessons from the Patco Strike*. New York: Human Sciences Press, 1981.
60 Minutes. "The Great Plane Robbery." CBS. March 20, 1988. Produced by Joseph Wershba.
Slater, Robert. *The Titans of Takeover*. Englewood Cliffs, NJ: Prentice-Hall, 1987.
Snyder, Rodney A. *Negotiating with Terrorists: TWA Flight 847*. Washington, DC: Georgetown University, 1988.
Steele, Donna. *Wings of Pride: TWA Cabin Attendants, A Pictorial History 1935–1985*. Marceline, MO: Wadsworth Publishing, 1985.
Steinem, Gloria. *My Life on the Road*. New York: Random House, 2015.
Stepp, Laura Sessions. "Papal Flight Plans Anger Ex-Attendants." *The Washington Post*, July 14, 1987.
Stevens, Mark. *King Icahn: The Biography of a Renegade Capitalist*. NY: Dutton, Penguin Books, 1993.
St. Louis Post-Dispatch. "Flight Attendants at TWA will Stay with Machinists." June 10, 2000.
St. Louis Post-Dispatch. "TWA Attendants, Icahn Still Far Apart as Strike Looms." March 4, 1986.
St. Louis Post-Dispatch. "TWA Flight Attendants Seek Independence." October 26, 1999.
St. Louis Post-Dispatch. "TWA Flight Attendants Seek Independence—Local Union 3 Defects." October 26, 1999.
St. Louis Post-Dispatch. "TWA Flight Attendants Seek Own Union." March 16, 2000.
St. Louis Post-Dispatch. "TWA Flight Attendants Vote on New Leaders." December 10, 1999.Stockton, William. "Tearing Apart Eastern Airlines." *New York Times*, November 6, 1988.
Teleconference. Produced by IFFA. 1988.
Teleconference. Produced by IFFA. 1989.
Teleconference, April 1. Produced by IFFA. 1986.
Telegraph. "TWA Deal." June 14, 1985.

Terkel, Studs. *The Great Divide: Second Thoughts on the American Dream*. New York: Pantheon Books, 1988.

Tharp, Paul. "Icahn's Not Beat Yet after Losing TWA." *New York Post*, March 18, 2001.

Thibaudeau, Chuck. "Sweat inside the Boardroom with Icahn." http://www.twaseniorsclub.org.

Thomas, Jr., Robert. "John Testrake, 68, T.W.A. Pilot Who Became Hero in Hijacking." *New York Times*, February 7, 1996.

Tran, Mark. "TWA Drifts as Icahn Dithers." *Guardian* (London), December 20, 1985.

TWA. *Petition to the Department of Transportation*. N.p.: n.p., 1985.

———. *TWA Skyliner*.

TWA/American Airline Workforce Integration: Hearings Before the Committee on Health, Education, Labor, and Pensions, June 12, 108th Cong., First (2003).

Twaflight843.com. "Archives of History, Carl Icahn." July 26, 2010.

TWA Flight Attendants' Strike on Cabin Safety: Hearings Before the Subcommittee of the committee on Government Operations, April 10, 99th Cong., Second (1986).

TWA v. IAM (W. D. Missouri Mar. 18, 1986).

TWA v. IFFA (U.S. District Court, W.D. Missouri, Union Security 1986).

TWA v. IFFA (8th Cir., Union Security 1987).

TWA v. IFFA (U.S. Supreme Court (U.S.), Union Security 1988).

"UFW Broadens Grape Boycott." *Food and Justice*, December 1986.

Urquhart, Michael A., and Marillyn A. Hewson. "Unemployment Continued to Rise in 1982 as Recession Deepened." *Monthly Labor Review*, February 1983, 3–12.

Van Gelder, Lindsy. "Coffee, Tea Or Fly Me." *Ms.*, January 1973, 86–91.

Wall Street Journal. "Flight Attendants Unions Are Losing Strength." April 8, 1986.

The Wall Street Journal. "Trans World Corp. Expected to Approve Spinoff of Airline." October 25, 1983.

Wall Street Journal. "TWA's Flight Attendants Reject Contract Proposal." May 23, 1986.

Walsh, David J. "Accounting for the Proliferation of Two-Tier Wage Settlements in the U.S. Airline Industry, 1983–1986." *Industrial and Labor Relations Review* 42, no. 1 (October 1988): 50–62.

———. *On Different Planes: An Organizational Analysis of Cooperation and Conflict Among Airline Unions*. Ithaca: ILR Press, 1994.

———. "Strikes in the U.S. Airline Industry 1919–2004." In *The Encyclopedia of Strikes in American History*, edited by Aaron Brenner, Benjamin Day, and Immanuel Ness, 577–86. Armonk, NY: M. E. Sharpe, 2009.

Washington Post. "Chronology of Hostage Crisis." June 30, 1985.

Washington Post. "Icahn, TWA Modify Takeover Deal." January 4, 1986.

Washington Post. "TWA Union Votes to Continue Strike." April 3, 1986.

Whitelegg, Drew. *Working the Skies: The Fast-Paced, Disorienting World of the Flight Attendant*. New York: New York University Press, 2007.

Wilmouth, Adam. "Former Executives Recall Icahn Takeovers." *The Oklahoman newok.com*, June 3, 2012.

Wilson, Cynthia. "Ex-TWA Workers are Hit Hard by Concessions." *St. Louis Post-Dispatch*, April 4, 2003.

Workers Vanguard, March 17, 1989.

Workplace Fairness Act: Hearings on S. 55 Before the Committe on Labor and Human Resources, 103d Cong., 1st Sess. 1–51 (1993).

Zuckerman, Laurence, and Maureen Milford. "T.W.A. Judge Dismisses Icahn Group Bid." *New York Times*, March 12, 2001.

Index

ABC Nightline, 99
Abzug, Bella, 132
Acker, Ed, 47
activism, 9, 85, 130, 145, 148
Adams, Norma, 139
adopt–a–scab program, 114
Air Line Pilots Association (ALPA), 4, 20;
agreement with Icahn, 65–68, 74–75;
Continental strike, 107;
cross picket lines, 70;
Icahn deal over flight attendant concessions, 107;
increased union identity, 70;
Lorenzo and the bidding war, 59, 82–83;
Pan Am machinists strike, 47;
support for TWA on papal visit, 137;
TWA pilot integration at American, 191–92;
United pilots strike, 86, 107
Airline Deregulation Act (ADA), 1, 10, 85, 146
Airline Stewards and Stewardesses Association (ALSSA), 3–4
Allegheny Mohawk provision, 190
ALPA. *See* Air Line Pilots Association
Amalgamated Transit Union, 134
American Airlines, 3, 4, 13, 59;
acquisition of TWA, 189–94;
comparative costs, 32, 46;
London routes, 181;
two-tier wage structure, 28
American Radio Telegraphists' Association (ARTA), 162
Americans for Democratic Action, 131
anti-Darwinian theory, 53
antiunion strategies, 6, 83–84
Association of Flight Attendants (AFA), 187
Association of Professional Flight Attendants (APFA), 190–94
Aviation Daily, 185
away from domicile scheduling policy, 24

b-scale. *See* two-tier wage structure
back to work agreements, 118, 143
bad faith bargaining case, 153–57, 161, 177
bankruptcy, 55, 182–84, 185, 189
Big Bang Case, 168–69
billboards, 134–35
Black, Leon, 75
Blackmun, Harry, 167–69
block to block in-air time, 24
Borden, William, 19, 31, 41, 104
Boston, 23, 52, 100
Boxer, Barbara, 131
Boycott of Conscience, 131–32

breadwinner comments, 72–74, 113
Brennan, William J., Jr., 167–69
Bridgestone-Firestone strike, 164
Brotherhood of Railway, Airline
 and Steamship Clerks, 134
Brown, Bob, 88, 117–19
Bryan, Charles, 134
business unionism. *See* social contract
buyout 46, 118, 194

C.A.R.E., 145–46
California Youth Authority
 (CYA), 132–33
Caterpillar strike, 164
Chavez, Cesar, 132–33, 136, 173n42
Chicago Case, 146–47
Chicago, 23, 86, 87, 100, 102, 135
Children's participation in
 strike activities, 138
Civil Aeronautics Board (CAB), 52
Civil Rights Act 1964, 3, 155, 176–77
Clipped Wings, 45, 104, 114, 140
Coalition of Flight Attendants, 134
Coalition of Labor Women, 102
Coalition of Professional Flight
 Attendants, 188
Coalition to Support Economic Equity
 for Women in the Workplace, 131
Coleander, Ralph, 86
collective versus individual
 interests, 168, 170
Columbus, Ohio, 135
Communication Workers of
 America (CWA), 102, 137
compensation systems, 26
competitive industry comparisons, 117
composition of flight attendant
 labor force 3
Compton, William, 190, 191
concessionary bargaining after
 deregulation, 31
Congressional Subcommittee on
 Government Operations
 and Transportation, 104
Conley, Tim, 64
consultants in union avoidance, 163
Continental Airlines, 11, 55,
 57, 79, 81, 180
contingent workers, 44, 114, 169
Cooper, Sherry, 186–88, 192
Corporate Campaign, Inc., 133
Corr, Joseph, 96–97n17
Cosgrove, Dick, 39
Crandall, Robert, 32, 40–41
Crossover Case, 164–68, 195
crossovers, 114, 165

Dan River, 60n18
Delta Airlines, 32
Department of Transportation (DOT),
 53–54, 179, 181, 189–90
Derickson, Uli, 57, 114
Diamond Walnut Growers strike, 8, 164
domicile system, 23, 45, 100, 130
Donahue Show, 133–34
Donnelly, Paul E., 154
Doudna, Christine, 135
Drexel Burnham Lambert, 10–11,
 52, 58–59, 65, 83
dues check-off, 29, 94, 143, 158
Duke, Patty, 133
duty period, 24, 92–93
duty rig, 24

Eastern Airlines, 55, 134, 164
economic growth post-war, 5
economic improvement in
 airline industry, 40
economic necessity and the
 Mackay Doctrine, 169
Economic Reinstatement Case 164–68
economic strikers 160–61
Employee Stock Ownership Plan
 (ESOP), 41, 55, 56, 68, 118, 183
Equal Employment Opportunity
 Commission (EEOC) 3, 131–36
Erikson, Jeffrey 185

F.T.S. News and Muse, 141, 146, 148
Federal Aviation Administration
 (FAA), 103–6, 116
Federal Reserve, 6

Fehr, Steven, 160
Ferris, Richard, 47
Figueiredo, Cynthia de, 26, 27
financial analysis, IFFA package 118–19
flexible monthly credit cap, 25, 92
Floyd, Dick, 133
Fonda, Jane, 134
Frankovich, Victoria, 5;
August meetings with Icahn, 66–70;
comparative arguments to support union position, 79;
election lost, 186;
exhaustion, 184–85;
first meeting with Icahn, 63–65;
Icahn versus Lorenzo, 57;
letter to NMB on premature request for release, 31;
MIA bracelet, 148;
Ms. Women of the Year, 135;
Pearson meetings, 42, 82–83;
presidency, 22;
reaction to Icahn deal with pilots over flight attendant concessions, 71;
request to Clipped Wings, 45;
support of IAM, 108–10;
testimony on permanent replacement ban, 195–96;
Weekend, 66–70.
See also Independent Federation of Flight Attendants
Freeman, Brian, 56, 63, 66
fundraising, 102
Furness, Kit, 148

Gartner, Murray, 154, 159
Gelder, Lindsy Van, 135
Getman, Julius 162
golden foot pin, 111
golden parachutes, 56
Great Plane Robbery, 143–45
greenmail, 11, 53, 58, 179
Grey Book, 177–78
grievance procedure, 141–42
ground transportation 26, 91–92, 148
Grounded, 132, 134

Hilton International, 58
Hoar, William:
ascendancy, 83;
demands increased in final days of strike, 129;
dissatisfaction with TWA proposal change, 41;
explanation of first comprehensive proposal, 23;
likelihood of flight attendant return, 147–48;
midterm wage negotiations, 19;
negotiations to Red Book, 18;
NMB arbitration rejected, 87;
offer off the table, 88;
proposals as requirements, 30, 81;
rejection of IFFA proposals, 30–31.
See also Trans World Airlines
Hoglander, Harry, 55, 58, 63–64, 71, 108
Hormel strike, 8, 16
hotline messages,110
House Affairs and Transportation Subcommittee, 104
House Committee on Public Works and Transportation, 54
Hoye, Msgr. Daniel, 136
Hurley, John, 167

IAM. *See* International Association of Machinists and Aerospace Workers
Icahn, Carl, 2, 11;
alliance with pilots and machinists, 58, 178–81;
bidding war with Lorenzo, 51;
Case 1 and Case 2 reasoning on final offer, 89–90;
control of the Board of Directors, 58;
control of TWA, 79;
final offer to IFFA, 87–90;
Frankovich August meetings, 66–70;
Frankovich first meeting, 63–65;
Karabu agreement, 185–86;
managerial decision making prior to formal ownership, 79;

Meyer first meeting, 52;
misinterpretation of work rules, 82;
offer to repurchase TWA, 189;
owner of TWA, 59;
pilot agreement voided, 180;
privatization of TWA, 179–80;
promise to ALPA about flight attendant concessions, 71;
rejection of IFFA proposal January 22, 1986, 87;
sale of London Routes, 181;
60 Minutes, 145;
stock purchase of TWA May 1985, 51;
Texaco, 179;
unequal treatment comments, 80;
USX, 179;
view of management, 53.
See also Trans World Airlines

IFFA. *See* Independent Federation of Flight Attendants

Immigration and Naturalization Service (INS), 106

Independent Federation of Flight Attendants (IFFA), 2;
activism, 9, 85, 130, 145, 148;
age composition, 110–11;
agreement 1992, 182–84;
comparative look at other flight attendant contracts, 46–47;
composition of members post-strike, 177;
comprehensive proposal from TWA December 1985, 80–82;
comprehensive proposal January 1985, 42;
contract negotiations 1984, 30;
drawing the line, 44;
employee ownership and creditor, 182;
final day of countdown, 87–90;
final negotiating meeting during strike, 119;
final offer of negotiating committee, 87–90;
final proposals, 90–91;
financial analysis of package, 118–19;
first contract 1978, 17–18;
handling crossovers, 113;
history of supporting other unions, 134;
history of, 4–5;
Independent Union of Flight Attendants (IUFA), 47;
Lorenzo, 59, 83;
media use, 84;
membership identification, 45–46;
membership vote to remain on strike, 118;
midterm negotiations, 19–20;
mobilization, 45, 84, 86–87, 100;
monitoring flights and load factors, 115–16;
negotiating meeting summary during strike, 120–21;
organization of work and pay, 23;
organizational structure, 45, 86, 106–7, 110;
papal travel, 136–37;
pins, 111;
Popemobile, 138;
position on bad faith bargaining, 154–55;
post-strike vote on TWA package 129–30;
presidency, 186;
Red Book negotiations, 18–19;
release request May 1985, 48;
release to thirty-day countdown, 87;
representation election loss, 187;
rumors, 120, 127;
safety obscured by stereotype, 112;
strike headquarters, 87;
strike solidarity, 99;
strike vote, 48;
strikers and labels, 114;
support, 102, 108, 131–34;
unconditional offer to return to work, 121, 127

Information Representatives Program, 45, 48, 110

International Association of Machinists and Aerospace Workers (IAM), 20;
Icahn agreement, 67, 74–75;
Lorenzo and the bidding war, 59, 82–83;
loss of arbitration, 110;
machinist integration at American, 192;
misrepresentation in American acquisition, 191–92;
mixed messages of support, 108–9;
no strike clause, 70;
ordered back to work, 109–10;
Peterpaul meeting with Icahn, 65;
president no official support, 109;
representation election win, 187;
support for TWA on papal visit, 137;
workers support of strike, 109
International Paper strike, 9
inter-union support, 107, 137
intra-union strength, 110

Jack Frye Training Center, 85, 101
Jackson, Rev. Jesse, 134
John Paul II (pope, saint), 136–38
Jolley, Walsh, Hager, and Gordon, 154
Jolley, William, 43, 69, 82–83, 154, 158–60, 176
junk bonds, 10–11, 58, 179

Kansas City, 23, 52, 100–1, 109
Karabu agreement, 185–86
Keilin, Eugene, 56, 63, 66
Kerkorian, Kirk, 181
Keynesian policies, 5
Kheel, Ted, 175, 194

LaGuardia, 52
Lantos, Tom, 104
Lantz, Karen, 119, 120
Larry King Live, 99–100
Little Black Book, 141, 148
Local 14 of the United Paperworkers International Union, 9
Local 601 of the Teamsters Union, 8
Local P-9 of the United Food and Commercial Workers, 8
Long, Kaphy, 146–47
Lorenzo, Frank, 55;
bidding war with Icahn, 57–59, 65, 82–83;
comment to flight attendant on home ownership, 112–13;
early interest in TWA, 55;
reputation with labor, 55;
sought as buyer of TWA, 56
Los Angeles, 3, 24, 87, 100, 101, 102
low-cost airlines, 32
Lyons, Jeffrey, 132

Mackay Doctrine, 2, 162–64
Mahony, Archbishop Roger, 134
management seniority, 26–27, 42–43, 94
Marshall, Thurgood, 167–69
McCaskill Bond Act, 193–94
McNeil-Lehrer Newshour, 99
Metzenbaum, Howard, 163
Meyer, Ed:
economic outlook for TWA 1984, 39;
financial presentation to IFFA, 32–33;
first meeting with Icahn, 52;
Lorenzo sought as buyer, 55;
midterm negotiations, 20;
position in corporate shake-up, 41;
resignation and new position, 58
MIA bracelet, 148
Milken, Mike, 10
Miller, Mary Ellen, 104, 107
Missouri suit against Icahn takeover, 53
Moberg, David, 196
monetary policy, 6
Morin, Tom, 104
Ms. Magazine, 135

National Federation of Business and Professional Women, 131
National Football League Players Association (NFLPA), 134
National Guard, 8

National Labor Relations Act (NLRA), 162
National Labor Relations Board (NLRB), 101
National Mediation Board, 4, 17;
arbitration proffer, 87;
decertification election, 188;
early request for mediator, 31;
move away to informal negotiations, 120;
negotiations resume 1984, 39;
recessed negotiations, 31, 41, 51, 79;
release and countdown, 86–87;
release not granted, 51;
representation election, 187;
resumption of negotiations, 117–18;
unfair advantage, 106;
United strike, 51
National Organization for Women (NOW), 102, 131
National Women's Political Caucus, 131
Natividad, Irene, 131
New Hire Case, 161
new hires, 85–86, 140
New York City, 23, 100, 102, 109, 138
New York Times, 54, 84, 134
Newspaper strikes, 164
Nichols, Jerry, 96–97n17
NLRB v Erie Resister Corp., 165–66
NLRB v Mackay Radio & Telegraph, 162
NMB. *See* National Mediation Board
no strike clause, 70
Northwest Airlines, 46, 59
Nussbaum, Karen, 184

O'Connor, Sandra Day, 166
O'Hare, 52
Off the Line: The Newsletter of Unflight Attendants, 102, 111
Oppenberg, Gale, 39
Ozark Airlines, 28, 46, 119, 129, 177, 179

Paine Webber, 58
Pan American Airlines, 18, 32, 40, 47, 107
Pearson, Richard, 40;
ALPA meeting, 108;
evaluation of Icahn's tenure, 191;
Frankovich meetings, 42, 82–83;
position in corporate shake-up, 41;
presidency, 58;
resignation, 83
People Express Airline, 32–33
permanent replacements, 1–2;
ban, 164, 42n173;
Crossover Case and, 164–68;
economic necessity, 169;
IFFA vote and, 129;
impact on labor, 195;
job loss and, 130–31;
Mackay Doctrine and, 161–64;
monitoring of, 115;
new hires definition, 161;
strikes and, 7–9;
threat of, 7, 10;
TWA use of, 84–85;
unconditional offer to return to work and, 127;
union dues and, 143;
U.S. Catholic Bishops and, 139;
work stoppages and, 169–70
Peterpaul, John, 65, 69, 74, 108–9
Phelps Dodge strike, 7–8, 164
Philadelphia, 52, 117
Phillips Petroleum, 54
Phoenix, 87, 100, 108, 138
phone trees, 106, 110
Pickens, T. Boone, 54
Piedmont Airlines, 46
Pittston Coal strike, 164
Post Falls, Idaho, 101
Pride and Dignity, 111, 141, 194, 196
Professional Air Traffic Controllers Organization (PATCO) strike, 1, 7, 134, 163–64
Project on Equal Education, 131
Proskauer, Rose, Goetz & Mendelsohn, 154

Railway Labor Act (RLA), 17, 42, 86, 154, 157, 177
Rainbow Coalition, 134
Ravenswood lockout, 164
Reagan, Ronald 6, 7, 10, 132, 134, 163
recalls, 128, 139–40, 148
Red Book, 117, 177–78
Rederer, Sanford, 52
Rich, Liz, 144–45
RLA. *See* Railway Labor Act
Rodimer, Bishop Frank, 139
Rogers, Ray, 133
Rovner, Judge Ilana D., 146–47

Sachs, Judge Howard E., 30, 74, 109, 154–56, 158, 165
St. Louis, 24, 52, 87, 100, 109, 138, 148, 193
St. Louis Post-Dispatch, 108
same calendar day balance, 25, 91, 93
San Francisco, 24, 87, 100, 111, 182
Scalia, Antonin, 159–60, 167
Scott, Kent, 180
Securities and Exchange, 52
Senate Committee on Commerce, Science and Transportation, 54
September 11, 2001, 192–94
sex discrimination, 67, 72–74, 86, 155–57
Silver Wings International (SWI), 115, 140
60 Minutes, 143–45
Skinner, Samuel, 181
Smart, Edwin, 55
Smeal, Eleanor, 131
snap-back, 65, 67–68, 118
social contract, 5–6, 163
Solidarity Movement, 133
Southwest Airlines, 32
Special Assistance Fund, 102
Status Quo Case, 157–60
Steinbeck, Anne, 131
Steinem, Gloria, 135
Stevens, John Paul, 159–60
Stewardesses for Women's Rights (SFWR), 135
Stockton, California, 8
Stop Carl Icahn buttons, 54
Strike Coordinators, 106
strike fund, 102
strike headquarters, 87, 110, 130
super seniority, 86, 166

Teamsters Union, 8, 137
temporary replacements, 115, 133, 163, 164, 195
Teolis, Arthur, 4, 5, 20–22, 33, 184
Terkel, Studs, 134
Testrake, John, 57
Texaco, 179–80
Texas Air Corporation, 11, 55
Texas International Air, 55
Thomas, Clarence, 131–32
Trainee Case, 161
Trans World Airlines, 2, 3;
  American Airlines acquisition of, 189;
  bankruptcies, 182–84, 185, 189;
  Board of Directors, 55–56, 58–59, 82–83;
  cancelled recruitment of replacements, 127;
  comprehensive proposal December 1985 final, 87;
  comprehensive proposal February 1985, 40–41;
  comprehensive proposal February 1985 withdrawn, 79;
  contract negotiations 1984, 22;
  corporate shake-up, 40;
  decision on permanent replacements, 84;
  early request for a mediator, 31;
  financial position, 117, 178–80, 186;
  Flight 184 smoke-filled aircraft, 184;
  Flight 800 explosion, 186;
  Flight 840 bomb, 105;
  Flight 847 hijacking, 40, 51, 102, 114;
  IAM arbitration, 110;
  increased demands during strike, 118;

initial response to takeover, 53–54;
international route increase, 39;
Lorenzo approached by, 55–56;
management and golden parachutes, 56;
opposition to IAM sympathy strike, 109;
Pan Am strike and, 47;
position on union security, 157;
privatization by Icahn, 179–80;
Red Book negotiations, 18;
release requested January 1986, 87;
thirty-day countdown final day, 92–95;
unprepared for takeover, 52;
up for sale, 55;
voluntary expedited negotiations 1978, 17.
See also Carl Icahn
Trans World Corporation, 21, 53, 58
Transport Workers Union (TWU), 4, 47, 107, 137, 192
travel agents, 103, 105
trip rig, 24, 91, 93
TWA. *See* Trans World Airlines
two-tier wage structure, 7, 28, 32, 41, 46

unequal treatment, 72–75, 80, 112
unfair labor practice strikers, 154, 160
union dues, 142–43, 158, 160, 165, 177
union offices, 29
union representatives, 29
union security clause, 158, 165
United Airlines, 3, 32, 46;
gains from Pan Am machinists strike, 47;
pilots' strike, 51, 86, 107, 164;
pilots support TWA flight attendants, 132–33;
United Auto Workers (UAW), 102, 137
United Black Coalition of Trade Unions, 137
United Farm Workers (UFW), 134, 136–37
United Food and Commercial Workers (UFCW), 8
United Paperworkers International Union (UPIU), 9
United States Conference of Catholic Bishops, 136–39
United States Court of Appeals, Eighth Circuit, 154, 157, 158–59, 165
United States District Court for the Southern District of New York, 53
United States District Court for the Western District of Missouri, 154
United States Supreme Court, 157, 159, 166–68
United Steelworkers, 7, 134
US Airways, 194
USX Company, 179

Walesa, Lech, 136
Wall Street Journal, 54, 185
Warren, Murray, 132
Washington Post, 84
Weaver, Fritz 132
Winpisinger, William W., 109, 134
Winters, Shelly, 132
Witt, Helen, 86, 117
work stoppages, 170

XCAP, 26, 70–71, 107

About the Author

Sandra L. Albrecht is associate professor of sociology at the University of Kansas. Her primary area of interest is the American Labor Movement and the preservation of the legal right to strike.

www.ingramcontent.com/pod-product-compliance
Lightning Source LLC
LaVergne TN
LVHW090321210926
848480LV00001B/317
9781498537728